Making War at Fort Hood

Making War at Fort Hood

LIFE AND UNCERTAINTY IN A MILITARY COMMUNITY

Kenneth T. MacLeish

PRINCETON UNIVERSITY PRESS
PRINCETON AND OXFORD

Published by Princeton University Press, 41 William Street, Princeton, New Jersey 08540
In the United Kingdom: Princeton University Press, 6 Oxford Street, Woodstock, Oxfordshire
OX20 1TW
press.princeton.edu

Jacket photograph: *Welcome Home.* © Dan Winters.

Library of Congress Cataloging-in-Publication Data

MacLeish, Kenneth T., 1979–
    Making war at Fort Hood : life and uncertainty in a military community / Kenneth T.
MacLeish.
        p. cm.
    Includes bibliographical references and index.
    ISBN 978-0-691-15274-5 (hbk.)
    1. Fort Hood (Tex.)—Social conditions. 2. Soldiers—Texas—Fort Hood. 3. United
States. Army—Military life. 4. Families of military personnel—Texas—Fort Hood—Social
conditions. 5. Iraq War, 2003–2011—Psychological aspects. 6. Iraq War, 2003–2011—
Social aspects—United States. 7. Iraq War, 2003–2011—Veterans—Mental health—
United States. I. Title.
    UA26.F663M33 2013
    956.7044′3409764287—dc23   2012030868

British Library Cataloging-in-Publication Data is available

This book has been composed in Janson Text

Printed on acid-free paper. ∞

Printed in the United States of America

10 9 8 7 6 5 4 3 2 1

For my parents

Contents

Abbreviations

ACU	Army combat uniform
AR	Army Regulation
EFP	explosively formed penetrator
FOB	forward operating base
FRG	family readiness group
IED	improvised explosive device
MOS	military occupational specialty
MRAP	mine-resistant, ambush-protected vehicle
NCO	noncommissioned officer
OEF	Operation Enduring Freedom
OIF	Operation Iraqi Freedom
PDHA	post-deployment health assessment
PT	physical training
PX	postal exchange
PTSD	posttraumatic stress disorder
ROE	rules of engagement
SAPI	small-arms protective insert
SGLI	Servicemen's Group Life Insurance
TBI	traumatic brain injury
VA	Veterans Administration
WTU	Warrior Transition Unit

Making War at Fort Hood

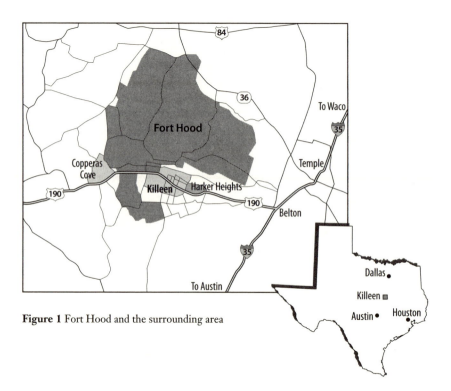

Figure 1 Fort Hood and the surrounding area

Prologue

"Don't Fuckin' Leave Any of This Shit Out"

Dime is in his mid-thirties, white, tall, and broad shouldered. In conversation he engages people with an intensity that is alternately charming and unsettling, veering back and forth between enthusiasm and vehemence. When he talks he calls you "brother," and his chalky blue eyes lock straight on to you. He had enlisted in the Army late, when his work as a freelance carpenter and musician wasn't enough to support his kids and provide them with health insurance. At age thirty-five, Dime was an E-4 only four years into his service.[1]

When we first met, he immediately began to recount stories about his most recent tour in Iraq. He was a tank driver, and spent much of the last of his two tours on patrol in the Sunni Triangle, sitting almost prone in the cramped, bathtublike cockpit of an Abrams. The Sunni Triangle insurgents, Dime told me, constructed extremely powerful roadside bombs out of explosively formed penetrators (EFPs), antitank mines, and artillery shells, frequently in quantity and combination. The whole situation seemed crazily askew from his description. His unit's mission was purely terrain denial: maintaining exclusive control over the space. The only threat came from bands of lightly armed insurgents and these tank-killing roadside bombs (or improvised explosive devices, known by the now-familiar abbreviation IED), typically detonated via wire or cell phone by paid-off but otherwise-unaffiliated civilians.[2] "Peasants and farmers were taking out tanks with the push of a button, man!"

There were no big or dangerous military targets for the tanks to engage, and when they did respond to small arms and IED attacks, the effects were wildly disproportionate and absolutely devastating. The lightest weapon on an Abrams is an M240 machine gun, which can fire a dozen or two 7.62-millimeter rounds in the length of time it takes to squeeze and release the trigger. Dime's and his fellow soldiers' rules of engagement (ROE) permitted them to respond when threatened or attacked, and they did so with everything they had. They leveled whole city blocks, he said, and it was all according to the rules. Dime had survived two catastrophic IED strikes. He was the only one to live through the second one, and was trapped inside the tank for four hours as it burned. A third time he had a near miss and watched the tank in front of him get ripped apart by an explosion that lifted all 67 tons of it into the air. The driver was his best friend, and his body was just gone.

I was introduced to Dime by a friend—a volunteer at a civilian soldier support organization at the US Army's Fort Hood in central Texas.[3] Fort Hood is one of the largest military installations in the world, and the single biggest point of deployment to for all US forces overseas, including those serving in Operation Iraqi Freedom (OIF) in Iraq and Operation Enduring Freedom (OEF) in Afghanistan (Fort Hood Public Affairs Office 2009). The base, along with its host city Killeen and the surrounding community, may contain the greatest concentration of people directly involved in the production of US military force outside of Iraq, Kuwait, and Afghanistan. During the height of the Iraq War, as many as half of the fifty-five thousand soldiers based at Fort Hood were deployed at any given time, and even in 2007 and 2008, when I lived by the base and was conducting fieldwork there, and when those wars were several years younger than they are now, many soldiers had served two or three or more tours.

For the community that inhabits, serves, and encircles Fort Hood, the making of war is a basic aspect of everyday life. War violence there is ordinary, in that it is routine, anticipated, and institutionalized, even as it remains extraordinary—intense, unpredictable, profoundly disruptive, and difficult to communicate. The length, scale, and distinct character of the Iraq War have subjected American soldiers and their families to longer and more frequent deployments, leading to unprecedented rates of posttraumatic stress disorder (PTSD) and traumatic brain injury (TBI) and the overburdening of military institutional supports. The more general fallout washes over the whole community, straining relationships with long absences, generating physical and mental health problems that are hard to diagnose and treat, and manifesting in diffuse feelings of loss, fatigue, and unease. And as all of this goes on, the civilian public seems alternately curious, naive, sympathetic, and indifferent. Dime's story is part of a whole realm of experience shared by those who make war under these conditions.

Dime's tiny apartment was in a midsize building a quarter mile off Killeen's former main drag, a neighborhood of run-down bungalows, dollar stores, lots full of trailers, and no-name gas stations. There wasn't much that you could easily (or pleasantly) walk to, but Dime was stuck without a car because his TBI made it impossible for him to drive—he could not concentrate on the road, attend to traffic, or read signs. His apartment was crowded with furniture from the much larger house he had moved out of when he returned from his first deployment to find that his now-ex-wife had left him. An armoire and box spring crowded the entrance to the tiny kitchen, and an Army combat uniform (ACU) tunic and a tangle of nylon webbing were draped over the legs of an upturned armchair.[4] Across the room, an amp and electric guitar kept company with a wall of cardboard boxes. A television fuzzed with dust faced the two chairs where we sat in the blue afternoon light talking and drinking beer—or rather, Dime talked, and I listened.

Next to the front door was a rifle with a blond wood butt stock and a slim bayonet folded under the barrel. It looked antique, but it was a new, Chinese-made copy of a Soviet SKS carbine. Because of his head injury, Dime was on a "no-weapon" profile, but he had gotten the SKS plus six hundred rounds of 7.62-millimeter ammo for $339 at a store in town.[5] That price was a great deal, he said. "I'm gonna turn a whole lot of people on to these fuckers." He handed the rifle to me and urged me to check it out, but I don't know much about guns—where to hold them and what to look at—and it felt awkward and heavier than its nine pounds in my hands. He took it from me, opening the breach and working the action to show me. He said he hadn't fired it yet, but a few weeks later he used it to shoot over the heads of two fleeing robbers who had broken into his neighbor's apartment. Living in Killeen, you need a gun, he said.

Dime walked away from each of the IED blasts and served out his full tour. Though now he had been diagnosed with and was being treated for multiple complex barotraumatic and orthopedic injuries (the result of the concussive, whiplashing force of explosions), TBI, and PTSD. Sitting on the toilet tank in his bathroom was a basket filled with dozens of prescription bottles. There were antidepressants, anticonvulsants, antipsychotics, sedatives so he could sleep, pain meds, and muscle relaxers—so many chemicals to stop his brain, body, and nervous system from doing what they were doing. "As far as medications go, man, . . . they throw so many of them at you and then hope to God one of them sticks." His doctors were still looking for a combination that worked. He was getting medically retired from the Army, but the process of diagnosis, treatment, and evaluation that was to determine his disability pension and shore up his battered body in the meantime seemed like one extended Kafkaesque convolution of appointments, briefings, treatments, and "Army red tape bullshit"—"it's like they don't wanna let you go!"

War had made him into a different person. "I mean look at me, Ken, dude, do I look normal to you? . . . After you've been through all this bullshit, everything about you changes, man! You can't go back, that's the problem." He was tired of being hassled, bullshitted, ignored, talked down to, and made a spectacle of. He was tired of people. But he was proud of what he had done. "You know what? I'm prejudiced as shit! I hate everybody that ain't me. But you know what? . . . I went and fought for every goddamn one of ya." He turned to me:

> Don't fuckin' leave any of this shit out. You tell the fuckin' truth. . . . Say, "Listen, there's some fucked up fuckin' veterans out there who did their goddamn job and did it to the best of their goddamn ability. They did what they were supposed to do.' Give 'em that. At least give 'em that much. I'm not asking for anything from anybody. Just give us . . . [*he trails off*]. Goddamn it, we did what we could. We did it so you didn't have to go over and do it.

In all this anger, resentment, and pain, Dime stalled out when he reached the point of asking for something: "Just give us . . ." what? This book begins from this blank and questioning space—the space that opens up when we realize that we don't know as much as we think we do about what the violence done by and visited on soldiers means for them or for us. As a soldier, as someone who enlisted to take care of his family, as someone wounded in combat, as an angry and injured and traumatized and "crazy" and potentially violent combat vet with a broken personal life, as someone who followed orders and protocol and likely killed civilians through the indiscriminate use of high-tech force, as someone who watched his friend die a gruesome death right in front of him, Dime is an utterly overdetermined figure. This is a condition he shares with all soldiers and all people who are close to soldiers. Every one of these features lends itself readily to a story we have heard before: the noble hero, the burned-out victim, the unrepentant killer, and the crazy, dangerous war vet who rages equally against foreign enemies, oblivious civilians, and the indifferent Army. The point, though, is not to edit Dime's story so that it fits one of these molds or proves the truth of one account over another. It is to see what happens when, as he urges, we don't leave anything out—or rather, when we leave in everything that comes with the telling of the story, no matter how oddly it may initially seem to fit. This work of recognition begins by foregoing bigger stories and grappling with the place where Dime finds himself: having done "what he could," "what he was supposed to do," and with only that to hold onto.

Introduction

When it comes to war and the people touched by it, there are always stories involved, myths to be forged, biographies to be exalted, and absences to be sutured over. These are stories that leave some killing and dying overstuffed with meaning, and neglect other killers and other dead altogether. In these stories, war's productive and destructive violence—the empowerment, construction, and shaping of the soldier, his wearing down, injury, and death, and the terrorizing, maiming, and extermination of civilians—is the exception rather than the rule. All the harm that comes with war is cast as tragedy or side effect, as something that should not have happened. The ostensible necessity of violence gets chalked up to a kind of facile metaphysics in which the roots of war are reduced to platitudes about greed, primordial aversions, hunger for power, and "human nature."

At the time of this writing, four years after I sat with Dime in his apartment, the war in Iraq is nominally over. The country continues to be rocked by sectarian violence, but the United States' massive occupying force—all of it—is on its way out. Many of these troops are being sent to Afghanistan, even though the Obama administration announced in June 2011 that all US troops would be withdrawn from there by the end of 2014. These apparent conclusions further enforce the sense that war is an exception that pops up occasionally and with discreet eventfulness before drawing neatly to a close. But things continue despite this appearance of an end: war persists in the lives, bodies, and social worlds it has touched, and the enduring structural conditions from which war necessarily arises guarantee that these most recently ravaged lives, bodies, and worlds will not be the last.

In contrast to this seeming finitude, this book begins in the middle of things, before a reassuring story can knit itself closed around an uncertain aftermath—a reassuring story of the sort that even Dime himself is aspiring and failing to tell. Indeed, the impetus for this book comes from a frustration that in spite of the surfeit of ready-made narratives, the language available to help us understand what is happening here is rather impoverished. It is no wonder that Dime runs out of words. He is not the only one grasping for them. There is no end to the unexamined things we think we already know about war: that violence is an instrument that can be directed to clear goals and precise outcomes, or that it is only chaos; that its impacts can be known, understood, measured, and communicated, or that they can never be known; that a war is definitively "about" something, or that it is "meaningless"; and that war makes heroes out of people, or that it turns them into monsters. Any one of these things may be true in one or another instance, but none of them is a good explanation for everything, or even for Dime's simple appeal. So it may be useful here to place such notions to the side. These platitudes and their all-encompassing intellectual equivalents reveal little about what is going on in the middle of things.

Soldiers are not the only people who do violence in war, or the only people to whom violence is done. In fact, it is civilians, including many children, not soldiers or other combatants, who make up the vast majority of modern war dead. In World War I they were 15 percent of the total. In World War II they were 65 percent. In the wars of the 1990s and 2000s, civilians make up as much as 90 percent of the casualties.[1] Despite this horrific disproportion, soldiers remain in many ways at the center of war—of war's production and the discourses that make sense of war. War happens to civilians by accident, or so we assume, at least. With soldiers, however, there is a certain frankness: we know that for them, violence is happening *on purpose*, and happening, whether we like it or not, in the name of upholding norms that we depend on and take for granted. Attending closely to soldiers' experiences reveals the ways that war is not at all an exceptional condition, that soldiers—and we as civilians—are always already in the middle of it and its unfinished present. Precisely because of this vexing contradiction, this present can be tough to get a purchase on.

For most of the war and at the time of this writing, Fort Hood was home to two full combat divisions, the First Cavalry and Fourth Infantry Divisions, as well as the Thirteenth Sustainment Command, Third Armored Cavalry Regiment, and numerous smaller expeditionary units.[2] Most of these units followed some version of the Army's grueling rotational schedule: twelve-month tours frequently extended to fifteen months, separated by twelve months of "dwell time" back in Texas. Portions of these respites at home were inevitably consumed with weeks of predeployment field training for the next tour.[3] With this schedule, going off to war was often less a one-time event than a repeated shuttling between home and Iraq. Even for soldiers who did not deploy or who may have ended up serving just one tour, the sense of indefinitely ongoing movement and the uncertainty that came with it loomed over everything, just as it did for military families and the entire community. I remember my surprise when a friend who was waiting impatiently to learn when her husband, a career infantry noncommissioned officer (NCO), would return from his third deployment casually mentioned that he already expected orders to deploy again a year later.

It can be difficult to even begin addressing the normalcy of this sort of situation when so many accounts of war remain bound by the conceit that war violence is something that happens by accident or as a last resort, or that it is best spoken about in terms of cruelty, pathology, moral and ethical failure, and illegality. In liberal democracies, the power to kill and expose, to cause others to die or to keep them from death, is treated as an exceptional prerogative, whether those others are foreign enemies, civilians on the battlefield, or the soldiers we send to fight. Instances in which the rules protecting life are suspended or abandoned are generally regarded as atrocities, as scenes of scandal and evil that lie safely in the past, or that represent nightmarish backslidings in the steady progress of history. In this category we might place Guantanamo Bay, Abu Ghraib, internment camps, wars of colonial dominion, police brutality and extrajudicial execution, migrant detention and deportation, slavery, torture, and the Holocaust.

But states—even liberal democracies—parcel out legitimate violence on a daily basis, making real the force of law by doing what law prohibits others from doing. This book argues that these and other forms of violence wrought or abetted by states and other sovereigns are fundamental to the exercise of power over human beings rather than regrettable exceptions to enlightened ideals.[4] Violence waged in the name of protecting innocent life—like the "war on terror," the wars in Iraq and Afghanistan, and various other US military interventions—also inevitably involves subjecting human lives to a cost-benefit analysis. Even in so-called just wars, anything is ultimately permissible in the name of necessity (Asad 1996, 2007). How many of "them" can be allowed to die in the effort to protect "us," or furnish "their" freedom and well-being? What are we willing to demand of "our" own in the name of protecting "our" security? Whether they are spoken aloud or not, these questions are being asked, and they are answered with efficacious violence.[5] As citizens of states whose "just" law is necessarily enforced by violence, we cannot shirk our own responsibility for this violence and the lives it touches.

If war entails deciding what lives are worth, not just incidentally but deliberately, this suggests a more complex story about what the soldier does for war and what war does to the soldier. It is a story in which, per Dime's appeal, even if it is impossible that nothing is left out, we must suspend our assumptions about the difference between intended goals and side effects. It is a story in which all the effects of war violence inhabit the same plane, as in this observation by journalist Evan Wright (2004, 30) of the allied invading force entering Iraq in March 2003.

> Though at the small-unit level all I see is friction among the moving parts—Marines shouting at other vehicles to get out of the way, guys jumping out to hurriedly piss by the side of the road, people taking wrong turns—the machine works. It will roll across 580 kilometers to Baghdad. It will knock down buildings, smash cars and tanks, put holes in people, shred limbs, cut children apart. There's no denying it. For certain tasks, the machine put together in this desert is a very good one.

The way Wright tells the story makes a point of not assigning different levels of intentionality or moral value to these certain tasks. There are narratives that tell us how we should understand the things that this machine—ultimately our machine—does. Some of war's effects are necessary and worthy, we think, and others are abhorrent and avoidable. In a similar fashion, we might understand Dime's service to have a straightforward value and meaning to which his pain and discontent are a mere sidebar or a mark of tragic valor. We might open the newspaper to read human-interest stories describing the "necessary sacrifice" of injured or exhausted soldiers, or anxious and suffering military families, as if such things were only secondary to war's larger purpose, whatever that may be.

But the machine that Wright so vividly portrays, the same machine that is responsible for both sustaining and endangering soldiers' lives, does not distinguish in this way in the present tense of war making: rule and exception are a backward-looking projection on a welter of indiscriminant effects. To cast any unwanted excesses of war's violence as second order, peripheral, or "collateral" to its "necessary" violence is not only to misunderstand war but also to conspire in a confusion of its means and ends. In this confusion, the instrumental destruction of life recedes from view, and the abstracted goals and principles ostensibly at stake in the conflict are all that can be seen.[6] The machine that does the injuring at the center of war cannot be "fixed" because it already works perfectly. Nor can it easily be turned off. The typical mythological narratives of war do not recognize this and embrace only the story of how things are meant to happen, either in glorious validation or tragic breakdown.

But war can be rendered without recourse to retrospective narrativization, and the people producing its violence can appear as complex and conflicted persons rather than caricatured tragic heroes or anxiety-provoking victims. In such an account, the civilian citizens of liberal democracies, though they rarely experience war violence firsthand, may find themselves entangled in an uncomfortable complicity with and responsibility for the violence done to as well as endured by soldiers, violence that serves the norms with which persons outside war are accustomed to living. It is the story that Dime suggested when he commanded me to "tell the fuckin' truth," when he enjoined, "Just give us . . . ." It is a story in which violence *makes* the social, the rules, the nations, and the people, rather than simply corrupting, undermining, or destroying these things. It is a story that helps show how Dime ended up where he is. It is a story in which war does not simply find its way from some foreign elsewhere as an exceptional and intrusive menace but instead comes at human life from all sides, destructively and productively, to color even the deepest layers of what normalcy is or could be. It is story about war sitting with you at home in your living room or bed, in the touch of a familiar person, in your bones and muscles and brain, and in your feelings and dreams.

AN EXCEPTIONAL CONDITION

This book, then, proceeds from the unique and exemplary position, the exceptional status and bodily experience, of the soldier. The human body, what Marcel Mauss (2006, 83) dubbed "man's first and most natural instrument," is perhaps the most taken-for-granted and essential piece of equipment in the day-to-day labors of war making. The body's unruly matter is war's most necessary and most necessarily expendable raw material. While many analyses of US war violence have emphasized the technologically facilitated withdrawal of American bodies from combat zones in favor of air strikes, smart bombs, remotely piloted drones, and privately contracted fighting forces (Virilio 1989; Baudrillard 1995; Singer 2003, 2009), the wars in Iraq and Afghanistan could not carry on without the physical presence of tens of thousands of such bodies. Even outside of combat, soldiering is a distinctly bodily undertaking, involving the disciplining, monitoring, and cultivating of the body, the tedious chores of mandatory exercise, or physical training (PT), marching, lifting heavy loads, being compelled to wakefulness at any hour of the day or night, and so on.

The physical depredations and mortal threat of combat cannot be separated from the system of bodily discipline that produces the soldier in the first place—his training, reflexes, skills, and capacities—and the system of maintenance and care that manages, evaluates and conserves the integrity of the soldier's body, both in the immediate wake of violence and over the long term. A soldier's lacerations, broken bones, and TBI from an IED blast are the result of more than just that bomb exploding in that time and place. They are the product of the strategy and tactics that placed the soldier in the target area and the protective gear that kept the soldier alive and in so doing subjected him to injuries that he would not otherwise have lived to endure. The significance of these injuries is shaped by how they are recognized, diagnosed, and treated; by the Army's judgment about whether the soldier can still do his job and is therefore still useful; and by a family's ability to care for and live with a loved one who is in pain, impaired, or altered. The spectacular violence of a foreign battlefield and the routinized violence of the military apparatus bleed by various, complex routes into one another and into the everyday lives of soldiers and those close to them. There is not just the violence of meeting the enemy to consider: how that violence is anticipated, accommodated, forestalled, or aggravated by the Army itself, the lives that surround that violence, the prerogatives that drive it, and the discourses that make it intelligible all determine the sum and shape of living in and with war.

The soldier is at once the agent, instrument, and object of state violence. He is simultaneously protected from and exposed to power's manifold dominion over life and death by both the circumstances of war and the institution he serves. The soldier is coerced and empowered by discipline—discipline that, as Michel Foucault (1979) writes, renders a docile body productive by subjecting it to countless minute and technical compulsions. The soldier is permitted to go outside the law—to kill—in the name of upholding the law, under conditions closely circumscribed by the law. In this respect the soldier *is* the sovereign, "he who decides on the exception" (Schmitt 1985, 5), on when life can be taken, even though he acts only as the final point of articulation for the vast armature through which this authority over life is vested.[7] At the same time, the soldier is expected to place himself in harm's way; it is acceptable for him to be injured or killed. The soldier in this respect falls into the category that Giorgio Agamben (1998, 83) deems *homo sacer*: human life that is outside the law and therefore can be killed.[8] And finally, the soldier is the subject of extensive measures to protect and maintain life, to keep him alive and able to continue working, fighting and killing effectively. Through means ranging from the armor and medical technologies that make previously fatal injuries survivable, to the psychiatric counseling, medication, and community services that are meant to ameliorate the impact of deployment and combat on soldiers' mental and emotional well-being, to the economic subsidies that provide housing, health care, and even employment and education for the soldier and his spouse and children, the soldier is a biopolitical subject not merely kept from dying but also made to live (Foucault 2003, 241).

In liberal democracies, and by extension any place where the conventionalized idea of humans as rights-bearing actors holds sway, personhood is unquestioningly rooted in the fantasy of an autonomous, self-sovereign individual who can reasonably expect to live free of coercion and injury. Of course none of us lives without others, and none of us lives immune to the world around us. But the fantasy that we could or do has profound implications, chiefly in its power to obscure the many coercions and injuries that ostensibly "free" human life endures and the way that those often highly unequal coercions are part of what empowers any such "freedom" in the first place. The soldier challenges this fantasy in an especially acute fashion, as he is perpetually subject to the will of others while exposed to bodily harm in ways that are utterly transparent, rationalized, and legitimate. The soldier's very particular condition raises broad questions about the limits of personhood. Who are these beings on whom so much inhumanity can be visited and of whom so much inhumanity may be anxiously expected? Who are we who share a nation, a world, and a sense of common humanity with them? And what are the circumstances that make it all possible and normalize it into a taken-for-granted invisibility that nevertheless seethes with feeling?

VULNERABILITY AND LIVED AFFECTS OF WAR

Soldiers' bodies are not end points for power but rather places in which it abides and transforms, "relays" through which it moves on to other bodies and still others.[9] If this ethnography has a single object, it is this: the entailments of living in and with bodies that are instruments and objects of violence. War does not simply shape, shepherd, and injure bodies, or mold and undermine psyches in a unidirectional fashion. Through countless contradictory and incomplete processes, war excites bodies, cultivates capacities, gives value to things, provokes subjective interpretations of surprising behaviors, and forms connections. As bodies "come up against" circumstances beyond their control, like war, those circumstances unleash affects in them—shared, heterogeneous responses directly related to the world in which those bodies find themselves (Butler 2009, 39).[10] Affect means many things to many people. This book treats it as a relational medium of bodily and psychic feeling that resides intertwined with structures of power and social organization as both their product and their object.[11] Affect describes what the social "feels like" in individuals and structures, senses and emotions, and desires and reasons without having to privilege any one of these things over the others.

From this perspective, the space of intense institutional subjection that soldiers occupy is not a final analysis, just as the soldier's body is not the place where power begins or ends, even if it is especially visible there—as it is with Dime in his upright posture, his high-and-tight haircut, his uniform with patches and badges that attest to his combat experience, and perhaps above all his injuries. The soldier's exceptional position is a stepping-off point for understanding the affective currents and exchanges in which soldiers are enmeshed: the *lived affects of war*. Soldiers are caught in the middle of some of the most restrictive, overdetermining, and glaringly vulgar power structures that it is possible to conceive of. But simply to describe these structures is not to describe the bodily and emotional impacts and excesses that such structures inevitably create—to describe these structures is not to describe soldiers' lives. The structure of power framing war moves by lateral and incidental routes—not just an through IED or an insurgent's bullet, but in a nightmare, a cold sweat, a doctor's suspicion, a lover's incomprehension, or a bureaucrat's obstinacy—to take shape in affects: in leaps, increments, sedimented layers, and sudden upheavals nestled among other concerns, stresses, and relations.

The soldier goes to war, and labors hard at it for months and months, perhaps in a job where he never even takes a shot at an enemy combatant. At the end of it, though things may seem to have changed strategically or politically for better or worse wherever he was, the war typically has been neither won nor lost. Indeed, even as politicians and the civilian public debate the "end" of the war, the soldier returning home may already be anticipating his return to it. Soldiers' lives in the midst of war thus resemble less a continuous forward movement of "decisions" over life and death than a messy temporality of harm and survival without a clear beginning or end, something like what Lauren Berlant (2007) calls "slow death." The forces that shape people's lives in the community surrounding Fort Hood unfold in ways that are episodic, slow, or stuck.[12] In the case of someone like Dime, who is alive but obscurely injured, on his way out of the Army but still infuriatingly subject to its discipline, forever changed both psychically and somatically, war injures or even kills slowly. Dime's labor is waiting—waiting to find out what was wrong with him, waiting for the last hangover of pharmaceutical withdrawal and side effects to wear off, and waiting for the Army to let him go.

Employing affect to ask these broad questions about what war feels like casts a wider net than one of the more familiar categories by which we understand the lingering effects of violence: *trauma*. From the Greek for "wound," the word connotes shock and injury, and in common usage describes both a distressing event and the long-term psychic disorder provoked by such distress. The idea has attained the status of common sense, and trauma so dominates the understanding of suffering as to make it essentially coterminous with the contemporary moral economy (Fassin and Rechtman 2009, 9). A vast theoretical literature explores both the possibilities and pitfalls of trauma as a category of analysis, but here I want to mention just a few limiting assumptions.[13]

Trauma posits a clear, linear, causal link between present suffering and a specific past event. It emphasizes individual psychic experience, and insists that such an experience requires verification, description, and elaboration. These features (as chapter 3 will analyze in depth) make it difficult for reified notions of trauma to address experiences that are collective, chronic, generalized, or obscure in their origins. This is especially the case when trauma is medicalized. PTSD has become a sort of catchall by which military medicine, the military as a whole, and the civilian public understand the various, contradictory entailments of living with violence. The full significance of this present range of understandings, and how they intersect with PTSD's institutional and diagnostic reification, are only just beginning to be explored.[14] But treating trauma uncritically can obscure more than it reveals.

Affects, on the other hand, present themselves as nothing more or less than self-evident feelings. They do not presume a single origin, or an orderly chain of causes and effects. They are not secreted away in repressed memories or the unconscious but rather are there in the moment, in the body, even if they are hard to name. While trauma focuses on bringing occluded subjective experiences to light, much of what preoccupies people in military communities concerns this uncertain present. In my fieldwork, I found the rubric of trauma unhelpful in attempting to grasp what war does to and for people. Dime's story, along with those of others recounted in this book, reveals that the terror and anxiety of war—along with many of the pleasures and satisfactions associated with it—do not stem solely from single, discrete events. Dime's outlook arose instead from the condition of existing for long periods of time and in various modes of exposure in harm's way.

To capture this condition, I turn not to trauma but rather to an adjacent concept: *vulnerability*. Vulnerability does not demand a before and after, or the exception of a disrupted psyche. It signals a condition that is ongoing or even permanent: the always precarious and susceptible nature of the human organism itself. Judith Butler (2004) suggests in her extensive meditation on the topic that this variable and relational bodily susceptibility is what defines human beings' relationships to power as well as their intimacies, attachments, and desires. War constitutes one extreme of that relationship. Beneath the historical, material, and political "causes" and the ideological discourses that surround any war lie the brute facts of the assault on human life. Killed and wounded bodies are the foundation on which the political and ideological aims of war are materialized (Scarry 1987). While this notion is something that those of us who experience war secondhand may struggle to remind ourselves of, it is a basic feature of military life, not just for soldiers, but for whole communities. Vulnerability points to the inescapably collective nature of bodily harm. It spreads outward from the soldier to the persons and institutions linked to him in the form a sense of risk and endangerment, as a sort of productive contamination that is less a strain on or disruption of attachment than it is the stuff of attachment itself.

Focusing on the vulnerability of soldiers and their families and communities allows us to ask what is involved in recognizing the harm done to those whose job it is to produce war on the nation's behalf. Soldiers and their families are iconic national avatars, and the losses they experience are valorized and fetishized in media representations and political discourse. At the same time, the people I met during my fieldwork frequently insisted that so much of the actual harm they experienced was rendered invisible in myriad ways—in the public agora, but also in the form of injuries undiagnosed by doctors, work insufficiently compensated for by institutions, or difficult experiences opaque to loved ones. Turning the logic of vulnerability to the exceptional spaces of routinized war making highlights the ways that war violence exists not just in the relationships between states or populations but within them as well. It shows the violence that lies within our own relationship to those who produce violence on our behalf, within our own links to each other and the structures that sustain us.

THE ARMY AND THE SITUATION OF INEQUALITY

The Army is but one of many overlapping and wide-ranging systems of ordered and ordering violence—systems that unify human beings into masses and populations, divide them into types, kinds, and specimens, and distribute worthiness, extract value, and wreak violence accordingly. These systems work through ideology, common sense, language, stories, desire and disgust, the regulation of space and bodies, and almost always with law and reason as their accomplice and infrastructure. They have names that are more or less useful depending on the circumstances, persons, and forces involved or the audience one wishes to hail: empire, capital, patriarchy, racism, heterosexism, militarism, ableism, and many others. These things shape the Army and the wider civilian world in which it is enfolded, and they are altered, challenged, and reproduced as they travel back and forth between the two. Such systems are incidentally or deliberately exploited by the Army for institutional purposes, and appear as problems that interfere with institutional imperatives. They structure people's differential exposure to the violence of war, whether as soldier or civilian, American or foreign. And by framing the status, worthiness, and very humanity of the people who are killing and being killed, they shade all deeper notions of what war means and what it is for.

This book is not about what different categories of personhood— such as gender, sexuality, race, nation, and class—do in the military in any straightforward way. But the distinct constellation of bodily and affective life that is my object only makes sense in the context of a broader situation of overlapping and intersecting inequalities—a situation that all these lines of difference are irreducibly part of. In the specificity of my focus, I do not possess the authority to speak to all of these things systematically or comprehensively. But many others have marked out and mapped aspects of this ground already, and continue to do so. Therefore, to provide a fuller frame for the chapters that follow, it is important to say a few things here about that ground.

The Army is a profoundly gendered institution that places men and women, and masculinity and femininity (to the exclusion of other configurations of gender), in compulsory intimacy with and highly structured opposition to one another. The Army, the profession of soldiering, and the making of war are all ostensibly masculine domains. They encourage and rely on connotatively manly practices, traits, and dispositions, including physical discipline, mastery over one's own sensitivity to pain and discomfort, and the suppression of care and empathy in order to be able to command and inflict violence (Buck-Morss 1992; Huggins, Haritos-Fatouros, and Zimbardo 2002; Mosse 1996). This physical and emotional hardness is one of the key features distinguishing soldiers from civilians' feminized "softness" and sentimentality (Lutz 2001, Ricks 1997), both in soldiers' own discourse and in public and political culture. In various ways, militaries also depend on and institutionalize the reproduction of largely male military labor by a vast array of female household, service, and sexual labor—often in ways strongly inflected by violence (Lutz 2001, 2009; Enloe 2000)—and the modern US Army has for almost a century served as a sort of social laboratory for state experiments in the regulation of normative heterosexuality (Canaday 2009).

Women constitute approximately 13 percent of active duty US soldiers, however.[15] Combat arms military occupational specialties (MOS) remain closed to women.[16] Yet in the current strategic environments in Afghanistan and Iraq, the distinction between combat and noncombat functions is increasingly blurred. Women soldiers—including many whom I met during my fieldwork—are routinely in the line of fire and even drawn on as a tactical resource precisely because of their gender, despite the fact that current US Department of Defense protocols make it difficult to formally recognize some of the labors performed and risks taken by military women.[17] This situation poses both analytic and terminological problems for any effort to speak of the Army as a generalizable mass. The challenge is compounded because many of the women soldiers I met were deeply invested in the masculine homosociality of Army corporate culture. They often both espoused the desire to be treated as equals by their male peers and professed the same negative stereotypes of (other) women soldiers—"females," in military argot—that I heard from many male soldiers: that they were disruptive of good order, relied on their femininity as a crutch, and were generally less capable. "I hate females so much," Dana, an engineer, told me. Although she ended up in the Army, Dana had originally wanted to join the Marines because they were even more disciplined and hard core. These disavowals and self-exceptions also complicate any effort to generalize about a sense of sorority among women soldiers, and to insist throughout this analysis on particularizing all experiences of women soldiers would be essentially to except them altogether from the masculine homosociality of soldiering—a sociality they firmly aver.[18]

The male Army spouse is in some ways an even more obscure and slippery category, for while the woman soldier can be figured (correctly or not) as a feminist trailblazer, I am unaware of any celebratory equivalent for the Army husband. On several occasions, informants in each role (soldier and spouse) and of both sexes remarked on the "emasculation" felt by men who were the husbands or boyfriends of deployed women soldiers. The infrastructure set up by the Army to support soldiers' spouses, primarily via organizations called family readiness groups (FRGs), is both connotatively and demographically feminine. So just as women can be made and make themselves masculine through their affiliation with the Army, men can make themselves and be made to feel feminized by their peripheral or proxy attachment to the institution.

In the Army, it is thus possible to observe the unmooring of masculinity from men (Halberstam 1998), see it taken on by women, and see its opposite foisted on men. It is an environment in which the aggressive reproduction of straightness (Canaday 2009)—due in no small part to its very aggressiveness—gives rise to highly visible queerings of heteronormativity (Berlant and Warner 2002; Serlin 2003). These things happen not just in the inversion posed by the woman soldier but also in the "manly" independence that military wives take on in their husbands' absence, or the increasingly "feminized" peacekeeping and caretaking roles that soldiers are asked to play in contemporary military interventions (Lutz 2001). And this is all without even engaging the highly vulnerable queerness of non-heterosexual soldiers themselves, or the twinned homophobia and homoeroticism of military culture (Belkin 2001). This simultaneous unmooring and retrenchment also happens, in a far darker and more violent form, in the fratri-sexual assaults visited on women soldiers by their male comrades, or what the Army calls "blue-on-blue" rapes (Benedict 2007, 2010; Goodman 2009; Moffeit and Herdy 2004).[19] Just as heteronormativity extends throughout and beyond the boundaries of the Army as a fraught but banal totalizing field (as described in some depth in chapter 4), so too does it spiral in on itself to make targets of those who are most vulnerable within the institution.

Some of these gendered dynamics are hinted at or addressed outright at various junctures throughout the book, particularly in chapters 3 and 4. Though there is still far more that could be said about, for instance, the ways that conventionally gendered roles and heteronormative assumptions structure access to military housing, medical and educational benefits for soldiers' partners and children, or how civilian and military narratives of rape and victimhood parallel or contradict one another, the foreign policy fortunes of the United States will continue to change the gendered image of the soldier. A range of new ethnographic work on militaries in the United States and elsewhere addresses these and many other questions about how gender and sexuality intersect with war violence, military institutions, and soldierly identity.[20]

Because the overwhelming proportion of soldiers are male, I choose not to switch evenhandedly between masculine and feminine pronouns, or resort to "he or she" and "his or her" when referring to them. Such a move might import a misplaced sense of gender equivalence into Army homosociality. A similar equanimity in referring to spouses would also be misleading. So throughout the book I use the gender-connotative but still gender-neutral terms soldier and spouse, and when invoking these terms as the names of generic figures, I use masculine pronouns for the former and feminine ones for the latter. In cases where I am speaking about specific individuals, I always refer to their actual gender. My intention with this approach is that within the makeup of my unscientifically representative assortment of anecdotes and quotations taken from an unscientifically representative sample of informants, the smattering of gendered exceptions will convey some hint of how such exceptions—exceptions that nearly always cling fast to the rule—make themselves felt in real life.

A similar paradox of difference and uniformity exists with race. The Army's role as social laboratory also includes an institutional antiracist ideology and history of racial integration that predates the civil rights movement by more than a decade (Moskos and Butler 1997). Some external assessments and testimony from soldiers themselves suggest that equality of opportunity and powerful sanctions against discrimination are significant parts of what makes the military attractive, rewarding work for many servicemembers of color (Hawkins 2005). Historically, the Army has promoted African Americans and Latinos to senior positions at significantly higher rates than the private sector. The contemporary trope of the military as a crucible that forges camaraderie out of racial, ethnic, class, and geographic diversity is at least as old as 1950s' World War II genre films. Military service is a symbolic badge of national belonging and sometimes a real pathway to residency or citizenship for both documented and undocumented immigrants.[21]

It would be a mistake, however, to regard these factors—and others, like the proportional overrepresentation of African Americans in the ranks (Office of Army Demographics 2010)—as existing apart from the structures of inequality that limit the opportunities of racial minorities in the civilian world and thereby make military work more attractive (Lutz 2001, 242). Consider the compounded alienation and marginalization to which many nonwhite soldiers have found themselves subject as they fight in the service of a state that marginalizes them. Examples range from Muhammad Ali's and Malcolm X's famous declamations of the Vietnam War, to debates between white and black radicalized Vietnam veterans about their shared but unequal experiences (Winterfilm Collective 1972), to the instances in 2011 of Asian American soldiers apparently driven to suicide while deployed in Afghanistan in the wake of racially motivated hazing.[22] Recent and not-so-recent events testify to the persistence of the dehumanizing racial avarice that elements of US military culture direct toward foreign others: from the invocation of putative "Arab sensitivities" to justify prisoner abuses at Abu Ghraib and elsewhere, to video released in January 2012 showing US Marines urinating on the corpses of Taliban fighters, to the widespread use of epithets like "haji," "raghead," and "sand nigger" to refer to Iraqis and Afghans (Hedges and Al-Arian 2009). The military's boosters would claim that these are residual exceptions to the institution's status as a sort of vanguard of racial equality and temperate multiculturalism—a vanguard that the rest of the country simply has not caught up to yet. Its critics see it as cynically exploiting the economic precarity of nonwhites while cultivating, in true imperial fashion, the hatred toward racial others at home and abroad that facilitates the taking of life and the domination of populations. For the present analysis, the most salient point may be something more fundamental that inheres in all these positions: questions of racial difference are inevitably entangled in the unequal distribution of harm, exposure, responsibility, and authority—in the Army as in so many other settings.

The Army's doctrine of color-blindness outlaws explicit expressions of prejudice and avarice, but naturally it doesn't automatically change people's minds. As Catherine Lutz (2001, 23) writes, people bring racial identities and antipathies with them when they enter the Army, and don't necessarily lose them when they get there. But just as in US liberalism more generally, Army policies make race and racism into entities that can be easily identified and policed, subsuming them into an institutional economy of good order and discipline without their content or practice ever having to be unpacked. Most striking at the ethnographic level is the manifest tension between demographic diversity and institutional antiracist ideology, on the one hand, and imported attitudes and everyday practices of racial affiliation and distinction, on the other hand, as when a white soldier assured me with complete confidence, "There is zero tolerance for racism in the Army," even as he and I sat chatting in an office with several other white soldiers while a group of exclusively black soldiers were gathered in the next room.

Race is not a single unitary factor here; instead it snaps into significance in daily life in manifold "racial situations" (Hartigan 1999). The combination of racial diversity with the compulsory proximity and intimacy to which Army life subjects soldiers and those close to them means that interracial friendships, romances, marriages, and kinlike soldierly solidarities abound. In my experience, racial epithets were bandied about in ways that could be read variously as signs of macho solidarity, an embarrassing breach of decorum, or hostility veiled thinly or not at all. I heard some white soldiers casually utter slurs or invoke stereotypes when superiors or nonwhite solders weren't around, but they clearly knew that to do so in mixed company would be a blatant provocation to animus or disciplinary sanction. Racialized notions of otherness—sometimes as debased, and at other times as exotic or redeemed—were commonly invoked by soldiers of all races and ethnicities in descriptions of Iraq and Iraqis, but frequently triangulated through self-consciously US-centric ideas of difference. As with gender and sexuality, the Army is a site where norms of racial difference are actively challenged in certain arenas and implicitly exploited or reproduced in others, almost always under the broader imperative to produce an effective fighting force.

Finally, class too operates in complex ways both structurally and at the level of everyday practice. The Army offers an escape from class disadvantages, and at the same time depends on them to make recruits available and help retain soldiers. As Erin Finley (2011, 15) points out, "Joining up may represent a choice from among limited options," for "even in an all-volunteer force, some volunteers are more voluntary than others." The highly dependent local economies spawned by military bases—historically dominated by low-wage, low-skill service sector work, high-risk, low-security contracting, and predatory lenders and retailers—reproduce or even exacerbate existing class inequities. Some people in Killeen spoke resentfully of the Army's dominance of the local economy and observed that the lack of alternative prospects amounted to "breeding soldiers," as one friend put it. Junior soldiers with large families or other financial burdens sometimes found their wages insufficient to make ends meet, or keep out of poverty or cycles of compounding debt. Those same wages, though, placed other soldiers in positions of relative privilege in the communities they came from. More than once, when I asked enlisted soldiers of various ranks about what misconceptions they thought civilians had of them, they answered, "That we have a lot of money."

And there is a lot of money. Truly massive quantities of cash flow into military towns—six billion dollars of direct and indirect annual input into the local economy, in the case of Fort Hood and Killeen (Fort Hood Public Affairs Office 2009). Most surprising of all may be the fact that steady increases in military pay and benefits over the last decade combined with the rise of high-paying flexible contract labor have, in the current economic decline, made military communities some of the wealthiest cities in the United States. In 2009, Killeen was more prosperous than Austin, Texas, the state capital, home to a large university and a booming tech sector (Cauchon 2010). Yet as early as 2009, the Army had also begun to cut recruitment and reenlistment bonuses, and planned reductions in force size will soon change the fortunes of military communities again.

As with other categories through which prevailing situations of inequality become apparent, I have allowed class to lie flat against the broader contours of the analysis in order to show its operation across a range of domains. It is highlighted especially in the discussion of distinction and stereotype in chapter 1, and when I explore debt, worth, and expenditure in chapter 5.

METHOD AND ORGANIZATION

One of the effects of the excessive taxonomizing of war is a profusion of geographic, experiential, and discursive domains within which violence can be safely compartmentalized and isolated from other aspects of life.[23] My arrangement here is an attempt to decompartmentalize the everyday imponderabilia of war. Soldiers may be utterly subjected to a system of extreme control and discipline, but their experience is neither reducible to nor extricable from that system. It is instead something formed in relation, and with all sorts of other elements drawn in. What I have tried to do here is identify those elements and relations empirically and express them ethnographically. I do so without direct recourse to some of the more familiar categories and metrics offered by policy, political economy, social justice, medicine, and public culture. But I hope that this work will have something to say to all these domains, for like them, it is concerned with rules and the condition of bodies, the unequal distribution of suffering, and the way that harm is experienced, represented, and recognized.

The chapters are organized around broad themes that emerged from my informants' words, actions, and experiences, and that capture the impacts of war across diverse arenas of everyday life. These themes are, by design, wide-ranging, porous, and extensible. They operate as fields within which it is possible to carve out distinctions between things that might otherwise seem identical and posit connections between things that appear remote from one another. As chapter 1 seeks to address in some depth, war and military life abound with unitary explanations that are invoked, disavowed, and then invoked again by the people whose experiences they are meant to describe. The nervous tension of these theoretical and ethnographic features suggests an object of analysis that is not a coherent whole but instead a multiplicity of tendencies and possibilities grounded in the stuff of everyday life. Over the course of this book, this object is assembled not through the revelation or ordering of things by already-established measures but rather by the generative, promiscuous *connections* that arose from the words and lives of the people I spoke to (Deleuze and Guattari 1987, 6).[24]

The first chapter, "A Site of Exception," depicts the setting for this work and the "exceptional" ambiguity of the Army's presence in everyday life—as something that is experienced as natural, but also constantly commented on and critiqued by the people who live with it. Chapter 2, "Heat, Weight, Metal, Gore, Exposure," analyzes the corporeal "feelings" that soldiers associate with being in Iraq in harm's way, and the particular bodily sensibilities engendered by the natural and material environment that soldiers find themselves in. The third chapter, "Being Stuck and Other Problems in the Reproduction of Life," looks at how vulnerability to violence takes intimate form through technology, time, medicine, and structures of institutional support. "Vicissitudes of Love," chapter 4, takes on the overlapping, conflicting forms of kinship and intimacy that exist between and among soldiers, spouses, and the Army as a whole. And chapter 5, "War Economy," examines the simultaneously bodily, economic, affective, and ideological modes of obligation and exchange that color many aspects of Army life, and that serve as a language of critique through which soldiers negotiate the various sorts of value attached to their labor. A postscript, "So-called Resiliency," briefly discusses the November 2009 shooting at Fort Hood and the rash of suicides there in September 2010 against the backdrop of the chronic strains that the community has endured over the past nine years.

1

A Site of Exception

To describe the official form and order of Army life is not actually to portray that life. But it would also be wrong to think that the regulations, orders, constraints, and earnest and straightlaced corporate culture are simply a restrictive veneer beneath which "real" life transpires. Listening to the people who live in and with the military, one could be forgiven for wondering whether the institution is the basis for normalcy or an egregious intrusion on it. So much of what I talked to people about were things that lay in the past or future, things that happened at a distance, things that were meant to be a certain way but weren't, or things that were extreme, scandalous, or tragic and that befell people like them, but not they themselves. The most dramatic and concrete aspects of war, not least the fighting itself, lay perpetually a few steps removed from wherever we were right then. And yet the idea, feeling, and possibility of violence, pain, heartbreak, loss, indifference, and death seemed to circulate everywhere.

The more time I spent around Fort Hood, the more it seemed that something in this apparent contradiction might actually be the best way to characterize much of Army life. The community is one of those domains that Michael Taussig (1992) calls a "nervous system"—shaped by the continuous, generative tension between the imposed rationality of an institution like the military, excessive and contradictory rules and regulations, and irreducible exigencies of daily life within the institution. It is a *system* because it presents itself as a comprehensive, unfeeling, and monolithic order; it is *nervous* because life within it is dynamic, agitated, and full of unruly feeling. It is the space marked out by the rule, the exception to the rule, and the practice of living with the rule and its exception. Everything is structured, but there is much that can't be counted on. There is a rule for everything, but not always a reason. What is "normal" is not necessarily tolerable, yet one lives with it anyway.

The obvious evidence of war making is everywhere at and around Fort Hood—in the oversize unit insignia gracing the windows of dry cleaners and walls of big-box stores; memorials, welcome home banners, and patriotic bumper stickers; Humvees and desert-tan trucks caravanning down the highway; uniformed bodies; jargon and common sense invoked in everyday talk; and bureaucratic processes that are both intrusive and reassuring, sustaining and punishing. All of these details that signify some unified and purposeful force at work, though, are also just ordinary. "The 'state of emergency' in which we live is not the exception but the rule," as Walter Benjamin (1969, 257) wrote. This is what war, the biggest exception of all, looks like as a normal state of affairs as it shapes and takes shape in everyday life, alternately or even simultaneously the most alien and most natural thing.

DRIVE CAREFULLY

Fort Hood is massive. On a map, you can see the sprawl of vast preserve, and the base's main cantonment rivals the size of the towns that neighbor it. But it is surprisingly hard to see as well. The first trace of it, miles away on the approach from any nearby big city, is a standard green interstate exit sign. Along the road that connects the base to Austin, these signs are complemented by others identifying the "Phantom Warrior Highway," after III Corps, headquartered at Hood, called the "Phantom Corps." It is uncanny to see such a place—home to weapons and warriors, a drama of official secrecy that one would never expect to get close enough to touch—so plainly named. But this too turns out to be part of what the war apparatus looks like up close—secured behind gates and fences, sure, but still

just another destination. More highway signs point west from downtown Killeen. The highway cuts a tangent across the southern edge
of the base's 150,000 acres. To the south is Robert Gray Army Airfield, which shares a runway with the Killeen airport, and via which
the post's soldiers depart for and return from Iraq by the thousands.
Just to the other side of the highway is the main built-up area of the
post, visible from the road as little more than grassy verge, chain-
link fence, and the shapes of low gray and tan buildings. Phantom
Corps indeed: driving right through one of the densest concentra-
tions of US military might anywhere, you can barely catch a glimpse.
At night you can see a little more, but still not much—the sky lit
with orange fluorescent glow, spangly fields of light, and the black
silhouettes of water towers.

It's actually remarkably easy to get on to Fort Hood if you want
to, though. Anyone with a government-issued identification can present it and be permitted entrance, and all you need for a temporary
pass that will let you drive your car on to the base is a license and
an insurance card. Signs shunt you toward the massive, toll-plaza-
like main gate, more than a dozen lanes wide, where privately contracted security guards inspect your documents and genially beckon
you through, only occasionally waving a car off to the side for a
more thorough search. Once you are in, you can go, it seems, just
about anywhere you please; you can drive right up to the open gate
of a motor pool full of tanks or missile batteries, and you can walk
right in the front door of the First Cavalry or III Corps headquarters buildings—or at least I could, being white, male, clean-cut, and
otherwise innocuous. The regular traffic of families, civilian workers,
contractors, and soldiers themselves flows in and out briskly through
the gates. So despite the gates, guards, fences, surveillance cameras,
and collection of personal data, the roads and the traffic on them reveal this curious porosity to the place—a nervous tension of aggressive control and seeming indifference, a dramatic incompleteness to
the Army's intrusive disciplinary grasp. The way that all this institutional apparatus makes one feel both closely monitored and largely
invisible resonates eerily with the way that soldiers, when confronted
with personal problems or breakdowns of bureaucratic order, may
find themselves "falling through the cracks" of the institution and
its mechanisms of care, maintenance, and support. Even here in the

midst of institutionalized war making's most visible, deliberate, and coherent presence, it extends into and opens itself up to—along the roads and by other means—so many other things. It is never fully contained, nor does it fully contain.

The internal landscape of the base is low, sprawling, and demands navigation by car, even for soldiers going from their barracks to morning formation. It features classically bland, modernist government architecture, like the campus of a giant, sleepy state university, but decorated here and there with decommissioned war machines—old tanks and helicopters. The low speed limits (begrudgingly adhered to), broad four-lane streets, lack of trees, flatness, and spreading architecture make the place feel both capacious and desolate as you pass through it. There is a stadium, baseball diamonds, football fields, chapels, gyms, garages, warehouses, a family life center, two movie theaters, hospital, police station, and Army and Air Force Exchange Service shops that look like any civilian mini-mart but advertise "Class Six"—liquor and cigarettes—and sport unfamiliar proprietary brands. The uniformity is disorienting; one gym with a barracks across from it and a big field behind it looks so much like another gym down the road with a barracks next to it and a big field behind it.

The most built-up area of the base is strung out along more than three miles, from the Warrior Way postal exchange (PX, a military department store where soldiers and their families pay no sales tax) and the Fourth Infantry Division headquarters and barracks at the east end, to the Clear Creek PX and the First Cavalry and Thirteenth Sustainment Command areas at the west end. Even within this place, space and people are organized by their relative proximity to war. The base is divided north–south between operational and administrative functions: the farther from the highway you go, the closer you are to the people and facilities responsible for the actual fighting. Those nearer the highway are responsible for bureaucratic management and the command of the garrison, hospital, and so on. Many of them have not deployed, according to my friend Stan, a former cavalry scout who retired as a senior NCO after more than twenty years of service and is now a veterans advocate. "Oh yeah, the war?" he mocked. "I knew someone who went."[1]

Farther north, past a row of headquarters and barracks buildings along Battalion Avenue, lie the motor pools. The base was originally

Figure 2 Humvees in one of Fort Hood's many motor pools

established in 1942 as an armored combat training center called Camp Hood, named after a Confederate general. Today it boasts "ten miles of tanks"—the world's biggest concentration of armored military vehicles (when they are not dispersed across the Middle East) in the form of a miles-long (not quite ten) row of chain-link pens full of Abrams tanks, Bradley and Stryker fighting vehicles, Humvees, and other tracked and armored vehicles. They are all painted a uniform desert tan, and look just as at home parked on arid central Texas asphalt and limestone as they do in the deserts of Iraq. Go still farther north, and other roads take you for a good forty or fifty minutes through a vast swath of rolling upland that is home to artillery ranges, training areas with tiny stage-set-like villages, a remote and spartan barracks where National Guard and Reserve units prepare for deployment, and improbably, a fishing and boating preserve.

The roads that move in and out of the base go in and out of Killeen as well. From the highway, the town reveals itself as a low mosaic of subdivisions, commercial sprawl, and largely evacuated downtown blocks. The base and the towns in its orbit, of which Killeen is the biggest, have a combined population of around 220,000, spread over many square miles. Even with the Army's overdetermining presence, in many ways this is also just an ordinary place where ordinary people live, with many of the same churches, apartment complexes, malls, chain restaurants, and pop radio stations as in countless other American cities. The place is bound by its isolation in central Texas as well as the conventionalism of Army life and the working- and lower-middle-class, middle-American populations that the military disproportionately draws from. On the other hand, the community is permeated with distinctive forms of diversity and cosmopolitanism. The military population comes from all over the country and even the world (resident aliens can enlist). Many soldiers and sometimes their families have lived for extended periods in Germany, Korea, the South Pacific, and other places with US military presences. Correspondingly, the town is full of multiple generations of migrants drawn from these same places by marriages, friendships, family connections, and business opportunities.

On the way into town from the south, a billboard advertising a local lingerie shop changes with the seasons. Guns Galore invites you to "CHOOSE FROM 1,200 GUNS ON DISPLAY." Starlight Station, a warehouse-size country music club, is done up to look like an old-timey train station, complete with railroad crossing lights and gates. There is an IHOP, a Home Depot, a Walmart, a Target, and a very popular Starbucks. There is a Korean Pentecostal church, a mall, and endless gas stations. There is a pawnshop, its sign a weathered, sci-fi starburst of painted steel and neon over the slogan "We Love to Loan Money." Down the side streets are older blocks of red brick houses from the 1940s, 1950s, and 1960s, when the base first really started to grow, with some yards neat and green, others disheveled, and all cordoned off with chain-link fences. Many of the newer blocks are basically just spurs or cul-de-sacs, lined with identical fourplexes that are home to single soldiers and young families: two apartments up and two down, eight blank windows behind a black metal staircase, an asphalt slab in front for the cars and garbage cans.

The landscape and architecture bear the imprint of a particular temporality of growth and decay, with old things dilapidated but still holding up, and other things still new but looking ragged and worn out before they have had the chance to age gracefully. There are strips of houses that look recently built and well used at the same time, their identical brick and limestone walls and concrete drive-ways gleaming white, but with shaggy lawns and decaying cars in front. On the base, too, you can see this cycling of time in the build-ings. New construction sits side by side with old barracks and ware-houses subsiding into decrepitude as their last occupants move out a few at a time. It all bespeaks an accelerated aging, like that visited on the hard-used body of a young soldier or a teenage Army bride on whom time seems to have moved too quickly. And it suggests the manifold traces of people coming from elsewhere, staying a brief while, and then moving on—their existence in a place governed by the rapid and arbitrary tempo of military prerogatives and orders that regulate life but brook no notion of making a home. So even the buildings themselves do not stand still; like the road, they resemble something solid, stationary, and knowable, yet they remain in con-stant flux.

The roads around Fort Hood may not deliver you to a single place where the traces of war offer themselves for straightforward inspec-tion, but on the road itself you can see the war moving along, in and out of the post and town. The Army uses the road all the time. One morning, I drove down a stretch where the highway was being torn up and repaired; the lanes were hemmed in by high concrete barri-ers, and a wall of metal reared up around a bend in the road in front of me: a slow-moving flatbed carrying a big, boxy rocket launcher on crawler tracks. Another day, another huge crawler-tracked desert-tan metal box, an M113 armored personnel carrier, was being hauled on a truck in the morning rush of cars past Walmart. A woman who had lived in the area for much of her life told me that for Desert Storm in 1991, they suddenly had to paint all the Humvees tan, but they didn't get the color right at first and it came out slightly pink, so there were dusty-rose Army trucks on the road everywhere you looked. Helicopters pass over constantly—Blackhawks, insect-bodied Apaches bristling with weapon mounts, and the wide whale-bellied Chinooks. They move slowly, gracefully. The presence of these things is a sign—one of many—by which to measure the proximity of war. There isn't fighting here, but there are these other things, these machines with a singular purpose.

The road's unquestioned utility and utter banality mingle with the thrill, shock, and terror of what is possible on it. People remark all

the time on the ways that the road is an uncanny place that is especially dangerous for and made especially dangerous by soldiers. It's
where soldiers go wild and forget where they are, or go looking for
some of the excitement of movement and danger to which, people
say, deployment has accustomed them. It is a featured chapter in the
conventional narrative of the challenges of adjusting after deployment: the soldier comes home flush with cash, ready to reward himself, still wired for nonstop action and dazed by the abruptness of
his arrival back where everything is normal. He buys a motorcycle
first thing—maybe he doesn't even know how to ride it, and maybe
he doesn't even put on a helmet or sort out the insurance—and then
slams it into an overpass at ninety miles an hour. Or he gets in his
car on a few hours of sleep and ten time zones of jet lag to drive to
Oklahoma, Louisiana, or Arkansas, and crashes in a ditch before he
even reaches the interstate. This tale was common enough that after
a while, I lost track of how many actual stories I had heard about it
and how many times I had just heard the generic narrative recycled.

Anyone who spends time on the base is reminded of the danger
of the road, in case they needed to be, by the signs just inside the
exit lanes at each gate of the post: "YOU SURVIVED THE WAR,
NOW SURVIVE THE ROAD—DRIVE CAREFULLY." Big red
digital numerals indicate "[X] DAYS SINCE THE LAST TRAF-
FIC FATALITY" beside a blinking light that goes from red to amber
to green as the number of safe days rises. I only saw it change from
red a couple times while I was there; often the number did not get
higher than ten before being reset by competing vectors of mass and
momentum. Positioned next to each sign, so that you can see just
what those vectors do, is a wrecked car on a concrete platform—a
car like the one you are sitting in as you drive by, maybe going a little
too fast.

With these stories of destruction and danger, the road takes on the
qualities of those other roads, the ones in Iraq that, as anyone will
tell you, are the most dangerous and unavoidable places. Like those
roads, the road here is always necessary but never to be trusted, and
people advise you to drive carefully. People talk about the signs, the
accident ticker, and the economy of violently extinguished life that
they point to. They make predictions and tell little one-line stories
about this macabre actuarial eternal flame. The "Most Emailed Arti-

Figure 3 Keeping track of dangerous roads: The accident ticker at Fort Hood's east gate
Courtesy of Dana DeLoca

cles" on the *Killeen Daily Herald*'s Web site were frequently about car crashes. Talking to an acquaintance, a retired NCO, the week before Thanksgiving, I remarked that I had just noticed the number climbing into the twenties. "Yup," he said, "it'll probably be back down to zero this weekend." Another friend told me that he had seen it all the way up above one hundred. "And then the Cav came home," several thousand soldiers—the largest division in the Army—back from fifteen months in Iraq.

What is the sign for? What is it doing? By the Army's straightforward logic of discipline, perhaps the reasoning is that the worse the news and the more dire the condition, the more necessary the warning then becomes. The sign recalls as well as multiplies the threat of violent death and the vulnerability of living in harm's way. But even as it recalls these things it retreats into the background, becoming just another piece of roadside scenery. There is no good name for this particular way of relating to sudden, violent death—a thing that just shows up some days, like the weather, and that like the weather is real, tangible, and a thing you feel all the time. It is both important enough and common enough that it is always there to talk about.

AR 670-1

Uniformed soldiers themselves are perhaps the most notable sign of war's everyday presence. The ACU is made of a digital-print camouflage fabric in an irregular pattern of tiny gray, green, and tan squares. The design is meant to confound the eye's sense of depth and outline and make the soldier less visible against a range of natural backgrounds. But the uniform makes for a striking visual impression of massed bodies wherever soldiers are gathered. In uniform, soldiers are less differentiated than they would otherwise be by their height, weight, skin, hair, or features. These regularized persons are everywhere. Soldiers stand in formation on a parade field or in front of a command building. In groups of three or four, they carry banners or cardboard boxes from one building on Battalion Avenue to another. Soldiers in T-shirts and mechanic's coveralls crowd around a vehicle in a sun-bleached motor pool. Soldiers drive a line of trucks or Humvees across the post, pick up trash from an empty parking lot or assembly room, sit around an office waiting for a phone to ring, and wait in line for vaccinations, legal paperwork, or ear exams. Soldiers pile giant canvas duffels next to a box van. Soldiers leaning on canes or crutches warily cross the road in front of the hospital. Soldiers smoke cigarettes outside an emergency exit door propped open with a cinderblock. There are soldiers in gym shorts and flourescent safety belts doing PT, and soldiers standing in line to get on a bus to the airfield. It's hard to see past the uniforms at first. Sometimes, embarrassingly, I had trouble recognizing even familiar acquaintances when I saw them in uniform for the first time—and vice versa, when their civilian clothes didn't provide me with names I hadn't yet committed to memory.

The uniform offers up a whole array of salient information—in addition, of course, to the soldier's name, printed in block caps on the right breast. The patch on the left shoulder is for a soldier's current unit. The patch on the right shoulder is for whatever unit he last deployed with. Those who haven't deployed wear no patch on the right. Many soldiers wear the insignia of Fort Hood's combat divisions, familiar from media images of soldiers deployed in Iraq: the diagonal bar and horse-head profile of the First Cavalry and the diamond clover of the Fourth Infantry Division. Then there is the thirteen-pointed star for the brigade-size collection of support units grouped under the Thirteenth Sustainment Command, the three-pointed insignia of the III Corps command group, the draped bugle of the Third Armored Cavalry Regiment, the T framed in an arrowhead of the Texas National Guard's Thirty-Sixth Infantry Division, the simple numeral 1 of the storied First Infantry Division, the improbable sea horse logo of the Thirty-Sixth Engineer Brigade, the caduceus insignia of various medical units, and others.

Like most militaries, the Army has a two-tiered rank system, the bulk of which is composed of enlisted soldiers and NCOs (the various grades of sergeant), with a relatively small corps of commissioned officers (the appendix contains a more complete breakdown). While the most junior officer, a second lieutenant, is technically higher in rank than the most experienced sergeant major, in practice the two rank tiers work in complex parallel, with junior soldiers assigned limited and specific tasks, NCOs directly "in charge" of them in various capacities, and officers generally responsible for command and administration. Rank is indicated with a small Velcro patch worn in the center of the chest. A private wears a single chevron, and a private first class a chevron with a rocker underneath it. Two chevrons indicate a corporal, and a filled-in chevron-and-rocker shape denotes a specialist, though the two ranks are equivalent. A sergeant's insignia is three chevrons, with the addition of one or two rockers and other details moving up the line to staff sergeant, sergeant first class, first sergeant, and sergeant major. Officer insignia begin with a single bar for the two grades of lieutenant, two bars for captain, and then on to the stylized oak leaf and eagle for the major and colonel ranks, and stars for generals. While soldiers are only directly accountable to superiors within their chain of command, rank entails a host of formal and informal interpersonal protocols—not just terms of address ("sir" for officers, the rank itself for NCOs) and gestures (salutes), but also posture, bodily disposition, and eye contact. My friend Danny was a staff sergeant working as a medical technician. I visited him at his office one day, and we chatted with a coworker; she was a mutual acquaintance, but also a captain, and therefore his superior. Danny pointed out to me afterward that as the lower-ranking party in the interaction, he had kept one hand behind his back in a semblance of a deferential "at ease" position throughout the whole conversation, even as he leaned casually against a filing cabinet, cracked jokes, and told us about his weekend plans.

Soldiers are perpetually engaged in reading and being read for the wealth of information offered up by uniforms, making them avid students of symbology and sartorial etiquette, alternately invested in and scornful of the abundance of rules. When I asked Danny to explain the "fruit salad" of citation and campaign ribbons on dress uniforms, he remarked, "This is what privates talk about in the barracks: getting drunk and getting laid and shit like the right way to arrange your ribbons for inspection." Even junior soldiers would talk in critical tones about seeing fellow soldiers whose uniforms were sloppy or "fucked up," while others bemoaned being unfairly judged for uniforms made grimy by long hours of hard work in the field or motor pool. The black wool berets that were mandated in 2001 in the name of inspiring morale were almost universally despised for being uncomfortably hot and difficult to shape, clean, and wear correctly. The extreme visibility of rank on the uniform shapes the nature of simple face-to-face interaction. In place of simple courteousness and mutual respect, you "see someone's eyes go to your chest" as the rank insignia on the front of your tunic becomes a barometer of your worth. Sometimes there is resentment at being told what to do by a superior who has "nothing on their right shoulder" because they haven't deployed. But all this reading is hardly a seamless or transparent practice. Many relatively junior soldiers have highly technical jobs—like driving armored vehicles, piloting drones, analyzing intelligence, or translating Arabic—and the presence of a deployment patch, even from a combat unit, might hide the fact that a soldier spent his deployment on a safely fortified forward operating base (FOB).[2]

A few days of hanging around are all it takes to see that there are intense and far-reaching standards in place that govern soldiers' bodies. These standards go far beyond the rules concerning the uniform, and beyond the not-untrue stereotype of stiff posture and high-and-tight hair. Wearing the uniform begins with the condition and appearance of the body that is wearing it; the Army grooming standard is folded into the very first pages of the voluminous (362 pages) Army Regulation (AR) 670-1, *Wear and Appearance of Army Uniforms and*

Insignia. The grooming standard governs hair, fingernails, and physical adornments—those things occupying the space between the flesh shaped by PT and the clothing and equipment that hang on the body. Indeed, the regs on hairstyle refer repeatedly to the importance of noninterference with "headgear" and length relative to the collar. Some rules are limited to when the soldier is on duty, whether in uniform or civilian clothes, but effectively extend to whenever he is on the post, or even more widely—one cannot, say, unshave one's head.

The regs are thorough. AR 670-1 devotes two full pages of dense, ten-point type to male and female hairstyles. Hair can't be dyed unnatural colors, or cut in "extreme, eccentric or trendy" styles. It must be "tapered" so that it converges naturally around the back of the neck, and short enough that it doesn't fall over the ears, eyebrows, or collar. The regs for women allow a bit more latitude, but they are similar in spirit. Women's hair must be worn conservatively, symmetrically, close to the scalp, and not extending "below the bottom of the collar." Little to no makeup is allowed. Dee, a communications NCO, told me that Air Force women were the "prettiest" of all the service branches because their hair can be longer and they are permitted to wear earrings. As the document itself states, however, "It is not possible to address every acceptable hairstyle, or what constitutes eccentric or conservative grooming. Therefore, it is the responsibility of leaders at all levels to exercise good judgment in the enforcement of Army policy" (AR 670-1, P1-8, 3). And so the condition of a soldier's hair may have less to do with his individual preference than with a platoon sergeant's insistence that it is time for a trim. Unsurprisingly, "hair that is clipped closely or shaved to the scalp is authorized" (ibid., 26), but variations on the shaved head, crew cut, and the high-and-tight abound. In general the same haircut is everywhere. People joke about asking barbers in town to leave it "a little longer" and coming out with everything buzzed to a quarter of an inch. The overall effect is a uniformity that persists even in the absence of the uniform.

There is also the diligently clean-shaven face or recognizably regulation moustache—no beards or long sideburns are allowed. (Several acquaintances who left the Army during my fieldwork immediately grew goatees.) And one starts to notice other things, none of them definitive but all of them common: dark, bug-eyed Oakley sunglasses, upright posture, a stiffness of carriage and gait, a neutral flatness of expression, and often a certain amount of muscular bulk.

Men aren't allowed to wear earrings either, as I learned one day. I was eating lunch with Danny at one of the PX food courts. I had noticed two senior enlisted soldiers in the relatively empty seating area who seemed to be watching us as we passed by, but I thought nothing of it. When we sat down a few minutes later to talk, Danny broke from the subject and said, "I don't know if you noticed this thing that just happened." He pointed out the two NCOs—an E-7 and E-8, he told me, though I couldn't even remember being close enough to them to see their rank. They had been glaring at us, he said, staring us down with the kind of look you get from a superior when you're doing something out of reg. So he mentally reviewed his uniform. Was his rank patch fucked up? Was he still wearing his medical nametag, which he was not supposed to wear outside of work? Had he left his beret on indoors? Was something else amiss? But everything was correct. And then he realized that they were looking at me: my new haircut apparently allowed me to pass for a soldier, making the rings in my ears strictly forbidden.

AR 670-1 (P1-7, 2) is exhaustively detailed and explains itself with a practical-sounding frankness: "The Army is a uniformed service where discipline is judged, in part, by the manner in which a soldier wears a prescribed uniform, as well as by the individual's personal appearance. Therefore, a neat and well-groomed appearance by all soldiers is fundamental to the Army and contributes to building the pride and esprit essential to an effective military force." There is nothing shocking about pointing out the operation of disciplinary power here where it is operating with a transparent, instrumental generativity—a straight line connecting uniform bodies and uniform uniforms to "effective military force." Its logic of appearances and their effects sits right on the surface. So that is what you are seeing when you spot a guy with a distinctively crew cut head and clean-shaven face. What merits attention is less the fact that such discipline imposes unduly on freedom or individuality than the question of what it looks like, and going off soldiers' words and actions, what it feels like from the inside, to live in a body subjected to AR 670-1's 362 pages, and thousands more pages of regulations too.

IN IT

Military communities live in the shadow of stereotypes that suggest that the people who live in them are debased and out of control. This depiction includes Army guys who, if they weren't crazy before they went to Iraq, are by the time they come back, beating up their wives and girlfriends, smoking meth and raising hell in the barracks, and not getting kicked out because the Army can't afford to lose bodies. Then there is the caricature of teenage Army brides away from small-town homes for the first time in their lives, lonely and scared, spending the paychecks of husbands who are off in Iraq, doing drugs and going out to the clubs every night, getting pregnant by other men and not looking after their kids right. And of course there's the portrait of young vets driving like maniacs on the road because they were used to doing it in Iraq, or crashing their cars racing back up State Highway 195 to the base for early morning PT after drinking all night in Austin. These are the images that were offered freely to me by relatives and acquaintances in the Army who had spent time at Fort Hood, and the friends and professors who had passed through the area.

These secondhand tales were backed up by the bleak assessment of one of my introductory guides to Killeen: an acquaintance who had worked for the county Department of Child Protective Services there for a year and a half as repayment to the state of Texas for funding her social work degree. She told me about one- and two-year-old kids showing up at the hospital with broken bones; damaged young parents, depressed, high, or both, holed up in filthy houses; twenty-year-old soldiers who came back from deployment to be dads for the first time, and couldn't do anything with a crying baby but slap and shake it. Like the soldiers, she had been brought there by her obligation to the government, and she confronted an exhausting array of double binds and unintended consequences. And like the soldiers, she had endured not only the trauma of her own work experiences but also the secondary trauma of an overstressed institutional work environment. Her coworkers all drank, smoked, and ate too much, she said. She cared deeply about her clients, but there were far too many of them. She hated Killeen and she was glad to be gone.

It is hard to know where to draw the line between describing the political economy and the experiential challenges of military life, on the one hand, and the invocation of stereotypes that fascinate and horrify, on the other hand. Indeed, there are plenty of liberal critiques of the military that traffic freely in these images of soldiers as dupes and dysfunctional lumpens. And these portrayals aren't just found on the outside. Soldiers, veterans, military spouses, and other residents of the communities around Fort Hood all voiced their own versions of every single one of them, clichés of indiscipline, contaminating violence, criminality, ignorance, and the absence of culture. In many locals' own description of it, Killeen is afflicted with racialized and class pathologies: it is "dangerous," "ghetto," "hood," "not nice," and full of "white trash" and "the kind of people"—suspect and threatening—that the Army "tends to attract." Notions that Killeen is tainted with criminality and trauma, devoid of class and politically retrograde, unlovely to look at and uninteresting to live in, all circulate with energy and vigor throughout people's own experience of the place, mixed in with other, more placid characterizations. "These people," the bad examples, always seemed to be right around the corner, but weren't the people you were talking to right then. Until, that is, you did meet a soldier who was cheated on, got high, picked fights, or was deep in debt.

Whether under the weight of these impressions or the ethnographic imperative to interpret, there is the risk that everything gets read as meaning-laden traces of war. It is as if every car crash in Killeen were about the war, every parent yelling at their child in the supermarket stressed because of a deployed spouse, and every church full because of the mortal dread lurking in desert lands on the other side of the world. And if one assumes this, is there anything to learn from this place that folklore and common sense do not proclaim already? Even a description of the landscape of Killeen—like in the passages above—can construct this trap and leave you lodged in it. It can have the effect of saying that there is a military base, so therefore there is a degraded city full of pawnshops, used car lots, and damaged people. This assertion has truth in it. But it is not particularly interesting and risks predetermining our impressions of a place like this.

It is not this book's task to confirm the stereotypes and bleak images, correct or refine them, or balance them out with uplifting accounts of courage, resistance, or triumph. Although all these things are there: the ragged and precarious conditions of life, the bad behaviors rooted in and riffing off of them, people's care and dedication, and their often-contented persistence in the midst of it all. The war and the Army are never not there. The newspaper stories report that the people crashing their cars are soldiers. Anywhere from a third to a half of the over fifty-five thousand soldiers stationed at Hood were deployed at any given time, and many of those who weren't currently likely would be soon, so of course spouses left alone with kids were stressed out. And the prayers offered in church services always included petitions for the soldiers deployed overseas and words of welcome for those who had returned.

Jessica, my landlady, was a warm and chatty woman in her early thirties who became a regular acquaintance. Her husband, Cal, was deployed in Iraq over a year, fixing helicopters. In addition to managing a couple of rental properties, Jessica worked a full-time office job. She had been raised in a military family and lived near Army bases most of her life, so in that sense there was little that was foreign or novel to her about military settings and routines. But she gave the sense as she described them to me that she did not feel fully *in* them. Near the end of one discussion I asked if the Army was an important part of her identity, and she responded, "I don't embrace it." She rarely went on post, and didn't go to family day events or FRG meetings. There was a practical dimension to this: Cal was away and he was her major link to it, and most of her attachments and obligations, like her work, were off post. Though even when Cal was around, she said, she didn't really engage a lot with the community. She didn't have kids and the attachments that children would entail—to the physical environment of the place, schools, and other parents. The other women who don't have children are younger; Jessica "doesn't fit." She contrasts this with a friend who, she said, was "in it as a wife." Their husbands were of similar rank and were both deployed, but this woman had four kids and was involved in the community, including in her husband's unit's FRG and as the "mayor" of the Army housing area where they both lived.

It was in this context that I remarked how contained, specialized, and even exotic the world of the military seemed from the outside. She agreed, but noted that especially since she had grown up around it, she had never really thought of it that way until a civilian friend made a similar observation. It is also a confining and provincial world. If you were really absorbed in it, it was easy never to leave: your job, spouse, friends, children's school, and even the place you bought groceries were all there. Her own inclinations were more cosmopolitan; she talked about moving to Austin if she could.

The military that Jessica described to me was a world with an inside and outside, and ways and degrees of being in or out of it. Jessica and I talked together as if we were both on the outside of this world, as if there was enough of something shared between us—some quantum of bourgeois worldliness and alienated detachment perhaps—that our views into it, hers guiding mine, could be aligned. This was most striking in the class and cultural analysis she offered of the "type" of people drawn to be soldiers and the spouses of soldiers: people who were young and of limited prospects and experience, people who were literally teenagers or at least "acted like" them. Her portrait—offered evenhandedly rather than in judgment, yet an exercise in distinction all the same—signaled the normative or desirable opposites of this type's characteristics: hard work, worldly experience, aspirations, financial independence (not simply living off a spouse's paycheck and free housing), and moderation. She did not "fit" with people like this, she said, but neither did she fit with the standard expectations of an ideal Army wife.

Jessica's assessment reveals not only the power of the stereotypes but also the way that stereotype itself—especially as it is deployed by soldiers—seems to place the *it*, the definitive thingness of Army life, always at one remove from wherever you are right then. Self-conscious talk of inside and outside both points to an awareness of the military's enclosing and totalizing nature, and posits the broader civilian world as a "normal" baseline against which the particulars of the Army, good and bad, are understood. It's there in the way that people talk about "playing the game" of inhabiting a military role, but not "really believing in it." There is the mocking of those who inhabit their roles too fully or too unthinkingly, who take them too seriously—who are too gung ho and thereby too far "in." There is even just the simple fact that the extent and nature of your or someone else's in-ness is there, and available to thought and feeling.

The whole business of being in, and there being a specific interior in mind—"being in *it*," "believing in *it*"—is illuminating for what it suggests about the visibility and discreteness of the Army as an institution. It is so totalizing, so obviously present, but in this curiously illusory fashion whereby one moment it is as in your face and obvious as a Humvee on the highway or the heraldic code of a shoulder patch, and the next minute it recedes into the deep background as merely the way things happen to be. This *it* seems to be defined just as much by how it flashes nervously in and out of view, from plainly obvious to invisible and back again, as it is by any putative content. It is not just a matter of the institution being naturalized and folks being acculturated to it, for even as this happens, the institution and its rules continue to seem bizarre, arbitrary, and remarkable. Even the most arcane rules are readily available for commentary and reflection—as things that the Army should improve or get rid of, or that are just especially idiosyncratic. But at the same time they are taken for granted, referred to by casual, opaque shorthand, and treated as given and usual.

The Army is more than capable of defining and redefining the boundary between its institutional obligation and the personal accountability of the individuals who labor on its behalf. For their part, soldiers and all the other people living with the Army constantly and variously assert, with words and actions, their own boundaries, their own notions of what the Army is or ought to be responsible for, what they do or do not owe it, what it can and cannot claim of their lives. They may assert that they are damaged *and* dignified, proud *and* in need of help, or cynical about *and* satisfied with their work. If such boundaries cannot be taken for granted, then it is the constantly shifting and melting, looming and receding edges of one or another *it* that calls out for attention, that actually defines the object in question.[3] This agitated and sprawling "nervousness" is central to the blatant visibility and hyperrational excess of "the system," proliferating boundaries, thresholds, divisions between inside and outside, and productive effects at every scale and level, drawing lines that bind and divide between a thing and its observer, between an institution and its servant.

EXCEPTION

I met soldiers, military spouses, and veterans in a lot of different places—in a running club, at restaurants and bars, at vet group meetings, and through volunteer groups and mutual acquaintances. But the most significant of these was a volunteer organization located on Fort Hood that I refer to here as the Foundation. The Foundation was started by a local woman named Debbie who began attending departure manifests and handing out cookies from the back of her car to departing soldiers in 2003. As she got to know more and more soldiers, she took on an increasingly complex role as a caretaker, advocate, organizer, and patriotic booster. Armed with her considerable charm, persistence, and resourcefulness, she talked the garrison commander into providing her with a permanent space on post. She wrote grants and solicited donations, which she then used to purchase everything from basic care package supplies—snacks and toiletries—to household goods and children's Christmas presents for the families of soldiers who had fallen on hard times or had to relocate suddenly as the result of injuries. Debbie secured donations of furniture, computers, televisions, and groceries to furnish the increasingly larger spaces that the Army made available to her.

When I met her, the Foundation had for the previous couple years been headquartered in a house-size building on the west end of the post. Inside there was a kitchen with a food pantry, an office, storage rooms, and lounge areas where soldiers gathered, napped, watched television, and used the Internet. Beds of decorative plants lined the narrow concrete patio outside; Debbie and some of the soldiers who hung out at the Foundation had planted them together. The Foundation was one of a few facilities on the post—and at times, the only one—that was open twenty-four hours, and this at an installation where thousands of people regularly work early, late, and overnight shifts, and depart to and arrive from overseas at all hours of the day.

These tasks testify to the basic unmet needs of some soldiers and military families. Such needs are not supposed to exist, in a sense, because the Army's autocratic pastoralism is meant to tend to them. So the way the Foundation functioned institutionally also says a lot about the mechanisms by which the Army sustains, supports, and controls soldiers' lives, and where the gaps and breakdowns in those mechanisms lie. As a civilian organization operating at the pleasure of the base commander, the Foundation was outside the military organizational structure and Army chain of command. It paralleled but was not allowed to duplicate some of the functions of the United Service Organization (USO)—another guest organization—and the Army's Morale, Welfare, and Recreation Command, which is responsible for maintaining shopping, dining, and leisure facilities on Army installations, so Debbie had to be careful to avoid stepping on toes.

This exceptionalism afforded Debbie a lot of freedom, especially in her capacity to advocate for soldiers who had been cut loose by their command, or had exhausted their available avenues for complaint and recourse in matters ranging from financial distress to medical treatment to disciplinary sanction. She possessed a vast supply of outrageous stories: soldiers in casts denied entry to dining facilities (DFACs) by civilian contract workers because they weren't wearing shoes on their bandaged feet; a soldier on crutches marooned for weeks on the third floor of a barracks with no elevator; a suicidal soldier turned away from the post hospital's Resilience and Restoration mental health clinic; a soldier with testicular cancer about to be discharged from the Army without disability compensation or health care; a soldier trying to support four kids on a salary too small to make the car payment, buy groceries, and keep the lights on; a soldier who was drowning in Army Emergency Relief loan debts because a payroll snafu had delayed his paychecks for months. As a civilian completely unattached to the Army, Debbie had no compunction about approaching senior officers to relay complaints or difficulties she had heard about from junior enlisted soldiers. Between her charisma, persistence, and obvious dedication, she amassed an impressive cohort of high-ranking allies and supporters, so that when a distressed soldier asked her for help, she was often got results by skirting entire layers of bureaucracy—the midlevel functionaries who, it seemed, were frequently as helpless as junior soldiers to intervene.

Debbie's own personality and operational style mirrored this sort of exceptional logic—her nonformalized capacity to invoke rules and go around them at the same time. Her attention was prone to wander, and she sometimes seemed deliberately to refuse any gesture at standard organization. Instead, she relied on a near-constant font of affective intensity and personal conviction. She would switch from task to task at a moment's notice, dropping everything to attend to someone in crisis who showed up at the door or giving twenty dollars out of her own pocket to a soldier who was hard up. Debbie radiated maternal warmth, and those soldiers who knew her well and weren't afraid to appear sentimental would call her "Mom," waxing poetic to me about her loving presence. She ignored her own health problems to stay at work. Sometimes she slept at the office, though at other times she would not answer her phone, keep irregular hours, or stay away from the base for days.

Because the Foundation existed and operated by exception, it was also a sort of collecting place for things that had overrun standard categories and procedures, and for people who, as Debbie and many others there would say, had fallen through the cracks. Some people warned me that Debbie's credulity and generosity had made the Foundation a magnet for "troublemakers" and "bad apples," and vulnerable to exploitation by the unscrupulous or desperate; to work outside the usual order of things was dangerous. But by the time I began to hear these warnings, I had already become acquainted with the ways that the categories of the sick soldier, the hurt soldier, the simply unlucky soldier, and the "bad" soldier all bled into and mutually produced one another (a phenomenon discussed in depth in chapter 3). If the exception proves the rule, the Foundation was a place to see the rules along with their effects and excesses, a place where rules were experienced as having full, formative force but also as alien to any sense of normal life, and where, as a result, they were talked about constantly.

Much of the Foundation's work was oriented toward disconnects between technocratic institutional prerogatives and the priorities and burdens of "real" life, like family, debt, and health. It was a place that seemed at times to lend itself to cynicism, not to mention a violent suspicion of Army solidarity and fictive kinship, but its very existence was motivated by the desire to care for and value soldiers and their work. This was mirrored in the way that even the most jaded and embittered soldiers I met there remained invested in, even devoted to the Army, their leaders, and their fellow soldiers. People came to the Foundation when they had problems or when they didn't fit comfortably into other structural domains; inevitably, then, it was a place that threw the contradictory dynamics present throughout all of Army life into sharp relief.

There were so many thresholds and distinctions that seemed to define life at Fort Hood, and they so often hinged on differential exposure to harm, violence, and the vicissitudes of power—distinctions between soldier and civilian, enlisted and officer, those who had deployed and those who hadn't, the injured and the healthy, the green and the experienced, the ignorant and the wise, the dedicated and the lazy, those who saw combat and those who stayed inside the wire, soldiers and spouses, and men and women. These categories didn't line up or nest neatly; they sat uneasily with one another from moment to moment and circumstance to circumstance, with claims of often high-stakes difference carved from shared possibilities. The Foundation was perched on many of these distinctions—not just the life-and-death, illness-and-wellness, struggle-and-survival thresholds of the soldiers who it served but also between civilian and military, guest and gadfly, cynicism and devotion, disrepute and celebration. The Foundation took its form not from being one thing or the other but rather from the uneasy force generated at the site of exception, the passage from one space into another.

The Foundation was easy enough to get access to, yet it was so permeated with distinctions, and with people riding the edges of those distinctions, that getting access did not translate into being straightforwardly "in" anything in the classical immersive ethnographic sense. Being at the Foundation—and much of my fieldwork in general—was instead like constantly skating along an edge of inside and outside, an edge that tracked across multiple sites, people, encounters, and indeed ways of being in. Nervously positioned in a nervous system, the Foundation is illustrative of the problem of making war an ethnographic object in this place. It's not at all coincidental that this ethnographic close-up of the everyday work of state power should be so brimming with exception—that power's defining feature.

2

Heat, Weight, Metal, Gore, Exposure

When I went to meet Chad for our interview, he was waiting for me on the porch, antsy because I was ten minutes late. "Grab you a hat," he told me. "We're going fishing." Chad is short and compact. His buzz cut and bristle of regulation moustache are the same length and the same shade of light brown. He had a lot on his mind. He was a "geographic bachelor": his wife lived several states away, kept there while he was in Texas by a bitter custody battle with her ex-husband. She was having medical problems, and was jealously inquisitive about how he spent his time and with whom. He was working odd landscaping jobs in addition to his Army duties so that he could support her and her kids from a previous marriage. His unit was being reconfigured—he was a 91-B, a mechanic—and he was searching for a billet with another unit that would potentially move him to Fort Campbell in Kentucky, closer to his family. Chad was taking classes to get his civilian mechanic's certificate, thinking ahead to his planned separation from the Army in a year and a half, but the instructor kept getting on his back. His tight-jawed and cautious way with words—letting out a few at a time and then pausing as if to consider the next ones—seemed to telegraph the weight of these stacked-up worries.

It was a Sunday afternoon, and no one was around. Fort Hood was all quiet and dusty. Late winter sunlight slanted across empty lanes of asphalt. Chad needed to get to the creek and just sit there, he said. So we hopped in his truck, and he drove us to the post's rod and gun club to pick up some bait. And that was when it happened. We parked, and he trotted across the lot ahead of me. As I was getting out of the truck, I heard the "pop-pop-pop" of small-caliber fire from the sport shooting range just on the other side of a fence from us. Before I even registered the sound or processed it as something remarkable, I saw Chad's startled response: a sort of jig in which he appeared to leap into the air and pull himself into a crouch simultaneously. As his feet found the ground again he didn't even break his stride but instead just shook his head and gave the air a halfhearted punch with his right hand. "You OK?" I called after him. "Yeah," he said without turning around, registering discomfort or embarrassment perhaps, I wasn't sure what. A second later I caught up to him inside, waiting in line to buy night crawlers, and he told me about the right way to prepare chicken liver and hot dogs for catfish bait. I left it with that small talk. We headed back out to the car, and again there was a shot, two shots, and then half a dozen, but he didn't jump. "This time I knew what to expect, I was ready for it," he said without looking up. "I saw you jump," I told him as we buckled our seat belts, my tone light, unsure of where to go from there; I just wanted him to know I noticed, but that I didn't see it as something freaky or shameful.

Then, as we pulled out of the parking lot and headed for the creek, he pointed to the corner of a building about fifty yards away. "In Iraq, where we slept to the edge of the FOB was from here to there." They heard shooting routinely, several times a day. Sometimes it was the FOB being attacked, and sometimes it was insurgents fighting with US patrols, the US-trained Iraqi police, or each other. It became familiar enough that they learned to identify who was shooting at whom just by the sound and direction, whether it was US 5.56-millimeter rounds, or the insurgents' AK-47s or rocket-propelled grenades (RPGs), and where the fire and counterfire were coming from. Sometimes there were the loud booms of bombs in the distance, and then the rattle and roar of Black Hawks taking off to evacuate the casualties. He heard it every day, the sounds of people, unseen yet nearby, shooting and getting shot at, and nothing but a high wall and some empty space between you and them. You would go to your room after working all day and be ready to relax, "and then you would hear this: 'Bam! Bam! Da-da-da-da-da.' And all you could do was sit there and listen to it." At first they would throw all their gear on and go charging back outside, but there was nothing to do, no one to shoot at, and so they stopped.

Was this his explanation to me for his sudden startle in the parking lot? Especially after what I had just seen, I don't think you could say he had ever become at ease with the constant shooting. His body retained a preconscious vigilance and sensitivity to danger that had made sense in Iraq, when it pointed to a concrete, identifiable stimulus, even if it was oddly deadened. Now, here in Texas, he may not have been thinking about Iraq. In fact he was thinking about everything but Iraq—stress, loneliness, boredom, wife, money, and of course the future. All these things had plenty to do with the Army and the burdens it placed on him, but little to do directly with the war itself. In the midst of all that, though, his body was reminding him of it anyway. His physical response was one stress among many, out of place, misdirected, unruly, and socially confusing. And his response to that remembering twitch was to offer me a story—one short on feelings yet long on detail: this is what it was like there, in the place where his body's sudden rebellion came from.

VULNERABLE BODIES

The conventional image of the US soldier at war is of a lethal, heavily armored agent of violence: feet in rugged, calf-high boots, legs in pocketed canvas, a sidearm holster strapped to one thigh, torso bulked out by body armor and a harness called an LBE laden with pouches of ammo and equipment, a face hidden by black wraparound ballistic sunglasses and recessed, turtlelike, behind a bulky armor collar and the shadowing dome of a Kevlar helmet, and all swathed in the obscuring, broken grids of digital-print camouflage. These soldiers travel around Iraq in armored vehicles: retrofitted Humvees with boxy, shielded turrets; tanklike Bradley and Stryker fighting vehicles; and mine-resistant, ambush-protected trucks (MRAPs), newly designed for the specific conditions of counterinsurgency warfare in Iraq, with extra layers of armor and high-riding, V-shaped undersides that deflect the force of IED explosions. Soldiers sleep in FOBs

protected by checkpoints, gates, perimeter towers, and massive barriers of concrete and concertina wire—modular buildings bunkered
behind tiers of steel and earth HESCO baskets. They carry powerful
weapons; their trucks are mounted with .50-caliber machine guns
and MK-19 grenade launchers, and a quick squeeze of the trigger
can rip a human body in half or level a building.

Infantry platoon commander Paul Rieckhoff writes in his memoir, *Chasing Ghosts* (2006), that at the beginning of the war, Iraqis
attributed supernatural capabilities to the protective items girding
soldiers' bodies: supposedly their sunglasses gave them X-ray vision
and their boots could disarm mines. Physician Ronald Glasser (2006,
38) describes a scene in which an armored Special Forces soldier
was shot in the abdomen by an insurgent sniper, fell to the ground,
and then, "like Lazarus," got up a moment later and killed his at-
tacker. There is something supernatural to what soldiers are capable
of. They can see in the dark, with their enemies offering themselves
up as glowing green shapes against black. They can get up and walk
away from powerful explosions. They can call bombs and artillery
from the sky to destroy targets that their scopes have helped them
identify in the far-off distance.

But as Benjamin (1969) observed in the wake of World War I, the
technological "progress" evident in modern warfare does not ensure
the protection of the human body so much as it subjects it to previously unimaginable forms of harm and exposure—levels of violence
that confound past experience and present description. In an echo of
Benjamin, military historian John Keegan (cited in Asad 1996, 298)
notes that it was the beginning of the twentieth century that saw
the rise of "'thing-killing' as opposed to man-killing weapons"—
antitank mines and armor-piercing and explosive munitions—that
"invalidated the restraints" of previous agreed-on rules of war.

Since then, these new killing technologies have not only directly
subjected soldier bodies to intensified destructive force but also
served more generally to organize the tactical and strategic conditions in which soldiers are variously exposed to and preserved against
harm (Glasser 2006). In the lives of soldiers and those close to them,
there is a falseness or precariousness to the technomagical invincibility afforded by body armor, high-tech sensors, and lifesaving military medicine. Perhaps it should not be surprising that despite or

even because of these technological marvels, the inescapable fact of biological precarity is an essential feature of war and its insinuating, contagious effects. Soldiers, as I outlined in the introduction, are the agents and instruments of sovereign violence, but also its objects: equipped and trained to kill, kept alive in extreme circumstances, and placed deliberately in harm's way. In the doubly exposing zone of war violence and military discipline, terrible power and terrible vulnerability hinge on the soldier's body. Great lengths are undertaken to keep soldiers alive, but these measures are fundamentally linked to the logic that endangers them in the first place.

Talking to soldiers, I would often learn about the thickness of the ceramic small arms protective insert plate (abbreviated SAPI, and pronounced "sappy") in a body armor vest, the number of layers of armor surrounding the passenger compartment of an MRAP, or the ceramic-steel composition of the front slope of the Abrams tank through a story of how it had failed to stop a sniper's bullet, been ripped apart by an IED blast, or was drilled through by a white-hot kinetic penetrator. "The more improvements we make to the Humvees, the more these guys make to the IEDs," an infantry senior NCO told me of the insurgent bomb makers. In photographs, in the news, and driving around Fort Hood, one sees the Humvees' fresh paint, glassed turrets, and armored solidity, and they appear whole and normal. But the soldiers talk about the bombs that reduce the trucks to knots of smoking black metal. They have seen those knots firsthand, or been stuck inside them, or know people who have. They have seen the pictures and videos that these people brought back with them. To the outside observer, weapons and armor signify invulnerability and lethal capacity; their technological magic reassures us that soldiers are shielded from harm as they go about the business of exercising national military might—an exercise that is more politically palatable the less it is thought to endanger soldiers' lives. But for soldiers these objects are material, bodily environments through which they understand their *vulnerability* to violence just as much as their ability to produce and withstand it.

New protective and medical technologies have made previously fatal traumatic wounds survivable, and many soldiers returning from Iraq confront complex brain and orthopedic injuries that in previous wars they would likely not have lived to experience. I met soldiers who were the sole survivors of catastrophic IED strikes—bombs powerful enough to totally destroy a Humvee, tank, or Bradley. Their armor plating, Kevlar helmets, and fireproof Nomex coveralls, along with the quick action of their comrades and the Army's cutting-edge trauma medicine, had kept them alive through the concussion, fire, and flying metal. But mortality is only a "weak proxy" for the conditions soldiers are subject to as they survive to confront unprecedented conditions (Gawande 2004, 2471): damage to whiplashed joints and limbs that is difficult to diagnose and treat; the psychic shock of being the only one left alive of a crew of four or six, or more; and perhaps most pernicious of all, TBI, the symptoms of which are oblique, complex, and debilitating, yet often unmarked by physical pathology. The conflicts in Iraq have produced such elaborate constellations of orthopedic, neurological, psychic, and other forms of injury as to prompt military doctors to coin the term "polytrauma" to describe them (Veterans Health Administration 2005). Between the technologized destruction and psychic overload of such conditions, as Benjamin commented, the body itself, sensate and vulnerable, remains the only constant ground, even as it is yanked into disconcerting new domains of experience.[1]

As I heard soldiers speak again and again of their experiences of deployment in terms of endangerment and vulnerability, it was frequently through the body—through various felt dimensions of military life and deployment to the combat zone—that these things materialized. They were there in the sheer physical burden of working long hours in a hot climate while wearing heavy equipment; in the intimate, ambivalent relationship of the laboring, fighting body with the weapons and armor that both protect it from and expose it to harm; and in the vivid, often-tactile firsthand experience of gory dead bodies. Some of these sensory impacts are sudden; others are chronic and persistent.

These impacts and the body's responses to them are not just automatic, natural, or reflexive but rather, as Nadia Seremetakis (1996, 6) puts it, "involuntary."[2] You put up with them because they're there and you can't avoid feeling them, and you may feel them without even thinking much about them. It's in the nature of how we think about senses and feelings that they are involuntary. They come to us unbidden and unwilled, as a kind of constant, distracted, everyday knowledge (Taussig 1992). And yet the distinction between sensory information, passively cultivated responses to it, the rallying of will and effort, and forces outside ourselves that compel us to act is not always clear. When we feel, we are usually also obliged to do something *about* our feelings, and so they both incite and constrain us. In this way, the involuntariness of the senses is paralleled by and intertwined with the involuntariness of military discipline and hierarchy. There are orders that must be obeyed, functions that must be performed, and information that comes in and must be responded to, but none of it happens automatically.

Arguably, the most important of these functions is to persist in whatever you're doing in the face of discomfort, pain, and the threat of imminent harm. Soldiers are equipped with armor against harm, disciplined to ignore pain, and made strong enough to endure difficult conditions. Their continuous willed struggle against the involuntary impositions of discipline and environment is also a willed struggle to manage or even banish feeling itself. Feeling can be a kind of vulnerability, an obstacle to remaining rational, effective, and anesthetized to the hostile surrounding world (Buck-Morss 1992). But feeling does not ever go away, and so the soldier is pinned between involuntary sensory impacts and involuntary institutional compulsions.

THE FEELING OF BEING THERE

At Fort Hood at the time of my research, things inexorably revolved around time in Iraq. Some soldiers who enlisted in their teens or early twenties after 9/11 and remained in the Army had spent a third of their lives regularly deploying to Iraq. Deployment was the thing from or toward which life was moving—even if only virtually or potentially, and even for folks who had not or would never actually go. It was not the only force impinging on and producing bodily experience but it was the largest-looming entity around which so-called normal life was periodized, structured, and conceived. Deployment was at least a background for the more far-reaching effects to be described and analyzed later on in this book, even if it was not the sole origin of these things. Like Chad's leap in the parking lot, the speci-

ficity of these broader effects is only intelligible through the specificity of the sensory and material entailments—the lived affects—of the
body's direct exposure to war.

Chad and almost every other soldier I met repeatedly told me that
people don't know how it feels to be there. They meant physically,
on your body. It's hot. The breeze is like a blow-dryer in your face.
When the plane lands in Kuwait or Baghdad and the doors open,
you feel the heat waft in and up the stairwell. "That's when you know
you're there," one soldier told me. To understand what it's like for
soldiers, he continued, "you have to look at 'What makes the war?'"
He listed a long series of things: the tiny anxieties and uncertainties
of preparation and travel, the loss of control and individual autonomy, and the heat and weight.

Soldiers would say that for someone who hasn't been to Iraq, one
of the hardest things to understand about what it's like is the grinding
physical burden of simply moving around. Long hours of demanding
work—fighting, driving, patrolling, and building—are aggravated by
the relentless heat, routinely over a hundred degrees Fahrenheit, and
the mass of body armor and other gear. Stan had been in charge
of logistics for an entire combat battalion, building a patch of bare,
dangerous desert near the Iranian border into a functioning base for
several hundred soldiers. There are a lot of hard times, he said, but
even the good is shaded by the fact that everyone is "miserable for
long periods of time." This register of everydayness, lodged deeply
in the privacy of individual sensoriums, elides easy representational
framing, and the soldiers know this.

The heat is deceptive because without sensing it for yourself, it is
difficult to describe, imagine, and see. Perhaps this is what makes it
so difficult to understand from a distance. Sometimes photographs
of Iraq at least show a stereotypically hot desert scene—blue sky,
sand, camels, palms, men in blindingly white dishdashas, and sun
flaring across the lens. But most of the time they don't; instead, there
is vegetation, a busy city street, or maybe the sky is overcast. You see
US soldiers and Iraqi civilians wearing long pants and long sleeves,
and women in head scarves and abayas that reach the ground; often
people aren't close enough to the lens, or the light isn't quite right, to
be able to see darkened armpits or a sheen of sweat on skin. Soldiers'
ACUs are made of a nylon-cotton blend that is supposed to breathe

and wick sweat away better than the old cotton desert combat uniform (recognizable by the older three-color desert-camouflage pattern), but it's easy to imagine how any extra layer of fabric close to the skin and its wear mandated by rules, no matter how carefully engineered, becomes just another annoyance in the unremitting heat. Or so I gathered when Dime caught my eye one afternoon while he was in the middle of a rant about something else and disgustedly pinched the front of his ACU blouse between two fingers. "By the way, put in your book that these things are fucking retarded!" They sucked in the desert, he said.

The obvious practical effect of the heat is sweat and the moldering of the body's drenched, suffocated corners and crevices. It is the friction—the rasping heat of the strapped, swaddled, and loaded body's own mechanical action on itself, in the armpits, between the toes, in the crotch and the cleft of the ass, in the scalp, or on the shoulders, the lower back, the waistband, or any other place that the gear presses fabric against skin with no room to breathe. There is foot fungus, blisters, sores, rashes, and insect bites that fester for days. I heard this litany various times, including in an Army doctor's predeployment hygiene lecture. Between every line she admonished, "It's the desert! It's hot!" The soldiers, many deploying for the first time, laughed; of course they knew the desert was hot. But what does this mean for your body, after a week, month, or year of such abuse? They tell you to change your socks as often as you can, always use foot powder, and carry baby wipes. For women, they say to change your menstrual pad twice as frequently as you would otherwise. And you can't forget your sunscreen. If you don't have clean underwear, you may not want to wear them at all.

As base and universal as these things are, neither are they ever far from the threat of violence. In his Desert Storm memoir, *Jarhead*, Anthony Swofford (2003, 197) describes his own body's reaction to a rocket attack during a patrol in the Kuwaiti desert:

> I stand in place and piss my pants, this time not just a trickle but piss all over and running into my boots, clear piss I know because of hydration, no underwear and piss everywhere, thighs both, knees both, ankles both, bottom of my soft wet feet both, clear piss and no underwear because otherwise chafed rotten crotch

and balls from humping because Vaseline only works to mile ten and all wars and battles occur farther than ten miles from all safe points, and bloodrottenballs if you don't remove your underwear at mile ten, and rockets landing red glare and more rockets, hitting everywhere around us, but they haven't hit us, so far they have only caused great amounts of terror and forgetting.

So heat isn't separable from the stress of combat, from the fact of having to move your body, under its own power, across vast and dangerous distances. Even as he is thinking about dying, Swofford is remembering what he has done with his body in order to keep it alive. In photographer Ashley Gilbertson's account of the war, a double-page image shows a young soldier sprawled in the back of a Bradley in Karbala in the midst of heavy fighting, with his eyes closed, face stricken, and forearm spattered with his own blood. An IV runs into his arm, but he isn't wounded; the bag is filled with saline, and he is being treated for dehydration (Gilbertson 2007, 131). The simple fact of needing to consume water quickly becomes interwoven with assaults on comfort, health, and personal safety. The thing itself has hidden properties that can hurt you. "The water they make over there—it has all those minerals in it," an infantry soldier at the Foundation told me. He had gotten kidney stones from it and was in the field for months before he could get treatment. Of course they warn soldiers about this. Still, you can't not drink it.

The FOBs have ice and cold things to drink. But for long convoys, or units out on patrol or overwatch for days at a time, such comforts are absent. The water you have to drink is bathwater warm. Dime told me,

> We lived on MREs [meals ready to eat] and hot water. And to get the hot water cold you take a sock, a big green sock that they issue you, and you put the hot water bottle down in there, and then you wet the sock and then you tie it to the side . . . of the tank so when you're going down the road the [air and] cool water would cool the water so you'd have something cold to drink.

They would pay locals five or ten US dollars for ice when they could get it.

The need to relieve a body full of water presents itself too:

> It's hot. You go to the bathroom in a plastic bottle, which takes
> a little getting used to, but once you figure it out, it's second na-
> ture. . . . You're afraid to get off the tank cause you don't wanna
> step outside, you know, step on the ground or anything, hit
> something, blow up. So you use the bathroom on the tank, you
> take a crap on the tank. You don't even dare get off of it.

Sometimes, other folks told me, you do find IEDs this way—find
them the good way, that is, before they go off. Cautiously picking
a path away from the roadside to take a dump, you spot a bomb
covered in gray-painted Styrofoam that looked like a rock from ten
yards out.

Going for a piss means exposing yourself—to IEDs, attack, and
the gaze of your fellow soldiers. Privacy is impossible, especially for
women soldiers, who have to adjust. The women learn to squat between the hulking tires of a HEMTT, behind the door of a Humvee,
or against a wall, without taking off their armor, or they cut the top
off an empty bottle and piss in a moving vehicle full of men. Because
a lot of the time the convoys don't stop. Fran, a Vietnam vet and
veterans advocate, described it to me via a hypothetical situation:
"I'm in a convoy, and we're hell-bent for Baghdad from Kuwait. It's
a long way! And at some point we're going to have to stop for a pee
break. Well, the men can all get out and water a tire. But where do
the females go?" They can't go behind a tree, because there aren't
any. So often women end up holding it in until they get somewhere
that offers privacy. Sometimes that is a day or more, and the result
can be a kidney infection. Even if you think you're sick, smaller units
don't have the medical capability to diagnose something like that.
A medic or a doctor can take a urine sample in the field, but there
is only one lab, in Baghdad, and it takes six weeks for the results, by
which time you could be seriously ill or dead. I remarked to Fran on
the contrast between the fact that you can go from being blown up
on the battlefield in Iraq to being put back together again at Walter
Reed in seventy-two hours, yet you can also die from a kidney infection for want of a place to pee and a lab. It's incredible, I said, and
such a minor thing. "It's not minor to me!" she retorted. There are

small, simple devices you can get that help women pee standing up, she continued, little plastic funnels called freshettes. She wondered aloud why the Army can't get freshettes for women soldiers. It's not like they cost a lot of money. It's just not recognized as a serious problem.

Add to this another danger that women soldiers face when going to pee: for tactical reasons, the FOBs are pitch black at night, and even among one's fellow soldiers, there is the risk of sexual assault. At the most extreme, some claimed, women soldiers abstained from water later in the day so they wouldn't have to leave their rooms at night.[3] The line between what is harmful—the heat and what it does to you—and what is life sustaining—water and medicine—blurs, reverses, and folds in on itself, a Möbius strip entwining the thirsty, chapped body. But the line shows up only if you pay attention to the heat, which, again, is hard to see.

What is heat *about*, then? One answer emerged suddenly in a conversation with Ernie, a senior NCO. Ernie is short and powerfully built, olive skinned and dark haired. Despite being in his late thirties, he tells stories with a youthful glee, peppering them with sound effects and imitated dialogue. He led an infantry platoon through countless patrols and firefights in Baquba, in Diyala Province, in the middle of the 2006 troop surge. In the midst of one of his free-associating explications, as he talked about the importance of having his conscience be at peace with the things he did in Iraq, the heat suddenly appeared.

> As long as you go to bed with a clean conscience, like I said, when I look at myself in the mirror, that's all cool. . . . 'Cause I don't wanna go to hell. I hate the fuckin' heat! [*His wife and I both laugh.*] I'd rather be out there shivering because it's cold, just put on some warm jacket or something like that. But I've been in Iraq and Kuwait. It's 140 degrees, and you're in your underwear and can't do shit else but sit there and sweat your balls off, just sit there in 140-degree weather, can't do shit about it, in the middle of the desert. That freakin' sucks. And I've been in Japan, with snow up to our waists, people getting frostbite and shit. But I'd rather take the snow and the ice than the freakin' heat. So that's why I don't wanna go to hell.

Heat equals futility. It means being in the desert, far from home, where your orders have taken you, but then not being able to do anything. Cold can be acted against—put on a coat. But heat is totally overwhelming. You've done all you can do, stripped down to nothing, and still it hammers you, with shit else to do but sit there and sweat your balls off. Heat renders you passive, which is a decidedly unsoldierly posture. It's not what you're there for. Mastery of the environment, a sense of purpose, and the ability to deny pain and the intrusion of the senses—all this dissolves.

Is it too literal minded to see an allegory here for the more general experience of the work of making war in Iraq, the work of trying to impose some form of order on conditions that appear to be ungovernable and often seem to remain that way no matter what? Because heat is part of the climate, it is natural, suggesting that there is just something about that place, an intransigence that seeps into you from the environment and is physically oppressive. The problem of not knowing what to do with or in the heat is an imperialist's malady—one that reduced the English to the idiocy of the mad dog; as Noël Coward wrote in 1931 (2011, 196), the two were the only ones dumb enough to go out in the noonday sun:

> It's such a surprise for the Eastern eyes to see,
> That though the British are effete, they're quite impervious to
>   heat.
> When the white man rides, every native hides in glee.

Heat brings out the colonizer's ambivalence, not to mention the absurdity of his endeavor.[4] Yet the soldier is not the one calling the shots, the one making the decision to be there. Someone far away, someone who himself doesn't have to go, has cursed the soldier's body with the madness of going out in the heat. His orders make no accommodation for the angle of the sun, and the soldier sweats and chafes under the imposed madness of a higher logic.

Weight and heat compound one another, forming a synergistic burden. Weight is similar to heat in its invisibility. The helmet and I-vest give the soldier superhuman proportions—a massive, powerful torso, and a bulbous head. The soldier's harness slung with gear and pouches, his bulging pockets, and the M4 carbine in hand all suggest preparedness and enhanced capacity. But the body armor weighs thirty-three pounds. The rest of his gear can easily add another thirty pounds, so the soldier labors in the oven heat under sixty-three pounds of deadweight. This weight is the same as a bag of concrete mix on your back and chest, or a ten-year-old child riding on your shoulders, all the time, while you run around trying not to get killed. It slows you down and limits your range of motion, making you, paradoxically, more exposed.

Then there are the weapons. One afternoon I chatted with National Guard soldiers at a predeployment picnic. They were doing "in-theater" training, which meant they were in uniform all the time and had to carry their weapons everywhere, even as they waited in line with their families for plates of barbecue. One guy had two M16s slung over his shoulder instead of just the one. Why? "I just got lucky, I guess." The weapons weigh eight pounds apiece, unloaded. A few other soldiers here and there were saddled with a squad automatic weapon, the M249 light machine gun. I saw a short, slender guy holding one, stooping slightly with the weapon hanging from a shoulder sling in a low diagonal across his waist, its barrel dipping almost to the ground. He smiled shyly and hefted it to show me its weight: eighteen pounds empty.

So like heat, the weight is inescapable and involuntary. Like the heat, it wears a person out, intruding on health, comfort, and safety. Advocates for the injured told me numerous times about what they saw as the absurdly high rate of degenerative disk diagnoses among soldiers no older than twenty-two. The Army slates it as a preexisting condition and tries to discharge these soldiers without compensation, they alleged, but at that age such a condition is utterly unnatural. It's from marching, crawling, driving, and shooting in training and combat under sixty, eighty, or a hundred pounds of weight.

Injuries aside, though, it's simply exhausting. In many places, soldiers had to wear their I-vests all the time, whether out on patrol, driving a truck, or even in the relative safety of a FOB or command post. Especially in the Guard and Reserves, soldiers ended up with "hand-me-down gear," older, heavier, and ill fitting. One soldier I met had a debilitating shoulder injury from this, sitting in a too-big vest while driving convoys that lasted a day or two, or more, one after the other, the axillary plate in his armpit and the collar around his neck working on his shoulder until his arm was almost immobilized with pain. The earlier generation of body armor, the stuff they had in 2003 and 2004, didn't have these axillary plates, and soldiers died from it. The chest and back plates protected the big target surfaces of their bodies from small-arms fire, but not from clouds of IED shrapnel erupting out of the ground beneath them. Again, what saves the body is wrapped up with what harms it. Even barring serious injury, heat and weight mean that you come back worn out, your body aching and abused. Kelly, a young engineer who spent her tour building bridges in western Iraq, told me, "A lot of people don't realize the toll that a deployment takes on you. Like physically, yeah. Everybody gets hurt, everybody feels like shit, they're tired." We all know exhaustion. But what do weeks of exhaustion do to you, or twelve months, or fifteen months?

As much as the gear, soldiers said that the uniform itself comes to feel heavy. They would touch their bodies when they talked about it. "The uniform adds weight to my body," one said. You feel it in the chest and shoulders, or it makes you tense up and curl in on yourself; it "presses" and makes you physically uncomfortable. It's an overdetermining, excessive sign—one that clings to you, and that you yourself have to put on. Physical burden and immobility spill over into the psychic and affective weight of responsibility and discipline—another involuntary imprint. Dime sniffed with emotion as he described it to me: "Do you know what it takes for me to put on the goddamn uniform every week? It ain't easy, brother. There's a lot of responsibility to putting that fucker on." This responsibility to higher ideals and one's fellows is also bound up with the sense of being surveilled, monitored, told what to do, and accountable for everything—compelled to act in the face of the involuntary. You cannot choose not to put it on. Again, there is the everydayness of it, the automatic sensory knowledge of the constant effort that is required to subject oneself to constant burden, and the alienation from one's own body that is required to make that body an effective instrument.

Heat and weight tell a story about the biopolitical subjectivity of contemporary war. They index the ways the soldier's body is subject to a sensory assault that is the synergistic product of the actual enemy and setting of the war, on the one hand, and the military institution's management, constraint, and compulsion of the soldier's body, on the other hand. Heat tells the story of the hostility of the foreign environment, but also of the orders and tactical imperatives that force the soldier out into that environment. Weight tells the story of the technology that protects and empowers the soldier's body, but also of the violence that body is exposed to and the slow pains of injury and exhaustion it is made powerless against by rules (discussed further in chapter 3). The physical miseries of heat and weight, which seem to end at the boundaries of the body and are therefore relegated to the private incommunicability of pain (Scarry 1987), are nevertheless linked to the soldier's utter *lack* of autonomy over or privacy in his own body, and that body's implication in an order that goes far beyond the individual soldier. Heat and weight are of a piece with this peculiar structural immobilization and individualization, with *not being able to move*. It is not quite true what they say, that "the Army owns your body," because while the Army owns the body's capacities, labor, and potentials, the soldier is forced to own its pains, breakdowns, and exhaustion. Soldiers are subjected to heat and weight as a mass, by orders and protocols. But they are then made accountable for them as individuals, through the responsibility to drink water, wear your vest and Kevlar, change your socks, don't complain, and don't get hurt. The soldier's senses remain his property even if his body does not, and those senses are inevitably too open to the harsh world that the soldier finds himself in.

THE SHRAPNEL IN BULLARD'S POCKET

The first conversation I had with Bullard was while we were loading scrap wood into the back of his truck. Out behind the building that houses the Foundation, under the semitrailer used for storing donated goods, were some old two-by-fours and damp, ragged-edged sheets of plywood; they were just sitting there, and Debbie, the director, said he could have them. Bullard is wide, carrying extra weight that came with the immobilization of serious injury, although at the time I didn't know what had happened to him. He speaks in a slow Texan drawl. He sports dark, bug-eyed Oakleys all the time against the light sensitivity that is a symptom of TBI—only once, coming into the darkened office one early morning while he hunched over a computer, did I see his eyes. His truck was new, shiny, and well cared for, with Purple Heart license plates, a chrome brush guard and roll bars, and tinted windows—the latter another measure against light sensitivity that the Veterans Administration (VA) compensates TBI sufferers for. But Bullard had been a scout, and technically still was, and he moved deliberately, with a purpose and awareness that belied his size. We loaded the wood into the pickup bed and tied it awkwardly in place with some scraps of yellow nylon line.

What did he need it for? He was building a chair that he could leave outdoors and recline in; he and his wife had a lot of barbecues, but his injuries make it hard for him to sit in regular patio chairs. He was also building a shadow box. They're big with soldiers, and you see them a lot in their homes and offices, full of badges, medals, coins, and banners. But his shadow box wasn't going to be for that, or not just that. The medics and doctors had saved the plate from the vest he was wearing when he got blown up by an IED. He was driving a Bradley, sitting up in the nose with the crew and several more soldiers riding in the boxy, armored crew compartment under the thing's turreted cannon. Shrapnel blasted through the vehicle's armor, and one piece gouged through his vest plate and came to rest in the Kevlar sheath around it. Bullard showed me with his fingers how far it had gone through the ceramic slab that was protecting his chest and how close it had come to entering his body. Another time, when he told me more of the story, he showed me where other pieces of shrapnel had pierced unarmored places on his face and arm.

A lot of the metal was still in him, and he sometimes snagged his shirt when he was getting dressed. He handed me a tiny piece of metal that he carried around in his pocket: smooth, glossy, almost black, less than three-quarters of an inch long, a squared-off rod gently rounded at one end, and cut at an odd angle at the other. That was the bit that almost got him, the one that they pulled out of the lining of his vest. It was an uncanny thing, not particularly heavy or sharp, and its carbon sheen didn't look like any familiar metal, as if the same rush of heat, velocity, and friction that had turned it from inert junk into a deadly projectile had also physically transformed it. They didn't know what it was so they sent it to a lab in Washington,

DC, for testing—perhaps to make sure it wasn't depleted uranium or something else radioactive. Then they gave it back to him, though, and he always carries it. "I used to complain about wearing gear," he said, "but no more." He has these two reminders to touch and look at: the thing that almost killed him, and the thing that barely kept him alive. They both did their job, and the latter edged out the former only slightly.

Socially embedded objects remain behind not only in narrative and consciousness but also in flesh—an object's "body persists within persons" (Seremetakis 1996, 2). Living and material bodies each find their way into one another. There is a palpable uncanniness to the intimate relationship of flesh and metal that soldiers live. The two substances are so unalike; one is warm, vital, and yielding, the other hard, inert, and cool. Their interrelation is not without ambivalence. The flesh is flesh that is vulnerable and weary, but that has also been turned into a tool and a weapon, while the metal is metal that destroys and incinerates, but that also shields, protects, and enables. This ambivalence is borne out to an unexpectedly literal extent by the shrapnel in Bullard's pocket and inside his body, and by the lesions on his brain from the concussion of the bomb blast that elude detection by MRI and CT scan yet nevertheless make their presence felt. These things are the bodily imprint of the conditions of counterinsurgency war in Iraq; they are traces of a particular formation of ordering violence written on a human body.

THE POLITICS OF ARMOR

Ever since the beginning of the war, soldiers' equipment and its limitations have been a point of fascination for whatever portion of the public was paying attention. Especially early on, in 2003 and 2004, news stories abounded of units being deployed with insufficient or outdated body armor. The New York Times published an article with charts and diagrams showing the exact number of casualties attributable to the lack of axillary plates in the vests (Moss 2006). Families spent their own money—hundreds of dollars—to send body armor to their soldiers (Banerjee and Kifner 2004). Humvees were deployed as the tactical vehicle of choice, but their thin skins did little to stop bullets and RPGs (Kurzman 2007); some even had open tops and no doors. Soldiers constructed "hillbilly armor" for their Humvees and trucks out of scrap metal. But then these out-of-reg improvisations were forbidden—no homemade armor or self-supplied vests, in case they were defective (Army Bans Privately Bought Body Armor 2006). Donald Rumsfeld came to Kuwait to address the troops in December 2004, and a junior soldier stood in front of an audience of thousands and dozens of television cameras to ask the secretary of defense why soldiers had been deployed without sufficient equipment (Schmitt 2004). The Humvees themselves, even when armored, proved to be highly vulnerable to IEDs, with their wide, flat undersides absorbing the full force of explosions underneath them.

New vehicles were designed and fielded to address the problem— the Rhino, Stryker, Buffalo, and various other forms of MRAP— although by this point the public was paying less and less attention. The state possessed the technological means to protect soldiers, it seemed, but between its own negligence and the resourcefulness of the enemy, US soldiers were being killed at a rate that the public found too high. The media and political discourses on war and military technology circled around this curious phenomenon, not only of the technology itself, but also of what it symbolized: it was a problem that could be fixed, a sacrifice that was necessary, a harvest of the government's shameful neglect, or the result of an enemy whose cleverness had been underestimated. What all these things talked around was more basic. The promise, misapplication, or insufficiency of these technologies managed to remind the public of what soldiers already knew—the bare fact of human bodies being offered up to die, via a practice shaped, managed, and mediated by the technology of armor.

From the mass ground war of Normandy and the Tet Offensive, to "peacekeeping" operations in Somalia and the Balkans, to targeted attacks like the 1983 Marine barracks bombing in Beirut and al-Qaeda's 2000 bombing of the USS *Cole*, the deadly exposure of US military bodies has always been as inevitable as it is manifestly undesirable. The fantasy of the armored body inured to pain and harm helps to quash this tension, holding out the promise of exerting military might without putting flesh and blood on the line. When pain and bodily vulnerability do erupt, they constitute a sort of "scandal" to modern liberal sensibilities (Asad 1996). Both the rhetoric and the material logic of armor is that of an impenetrable surface, a hermetic seal between inside and out. Armor surrounds, protects, and insulates a fragile, sensate body, extending that body and making it powerful as well as reflecting destructive force (Buck-Morss 1992).

The scandal of the improperly armored soldier that played out in public discourse was that there were things that could be protected and weren't, chinks and soft spots. What appeared to be a hardened, hermetic, impermeable, and reflective surface turned out to be porous, slapdash, and peculiarly susceptible. The absolutes posed by the idea of armor are like the absolutes of the dramatic language of sovereign violence: life or death, invincible or exposed. But the soft spots offered an ascending metonymic scale in which the exposed places under the arms or around the neck of individual bodies pointed to the ways that whole units were rushed off before their equipment was gathered or updated, and from these isolated insufficiencies to the notion that the entire invading and occupying force was endangered because it was too small, too hastily assembled and rolled in.

The lived experience of armor—its political charge, physical specificities, salience for military doctrine and tactics, and feel on the body—is often partial and contingent rather than absolute: partial penetration, partial protection, or partial recovery from an injury. Armor looks and feels different on the ground, on a body. Ernie, the infantry sergeant, told me that there were big improvements, "from flapping vinyl doors" on the Humvees in 2003 to increasingly hardened armor kits. But, he continued, the politicians who come to Iraq know their audience; over there, they tell the soldiers all about how they're going to get them everything they need. Then on CNN, you see them back in Washington, DC, saying that we need to cut funding and withdraw. Ernie erupted in exasperation and then trailed off: "Motherfucker, I thought you just said when you were over here." In Ernie's account there is a double elision: the politician lies to the soldier that he will be cared for and lies to the public that the soldiers will not continue to be endangered. No one has to think about the bodies ready to be ripped apart.

ARMOR AND ITS DISCONTENTS

It's not surprising that the weapons and protective gear that are soldiers' tools—and that threaten them when wielded by enemies—are objects of great preoccupation. More remarkable is the amount of anxiety and ambivalence that seems to surround these things. A lot of talk I heard from soldiers about their gear had to do with its actual, possible, or anticipated failure. Body armor, Kevlar, the plating on the Humvees, Bradleys, and tanks, and the US military's formidable bomb detection, disposal, and electronic countermeasures might, from a certain angle, appear as signs of tactical and technological superiority and the safety and inviolability of US soldiers' bodies. But in practice, and in soldiers' talk, all these things exist in relation to insurgents' armor-piercing bullets, RPGs, and the artillery shells, antitank mines, shaped charges, and triggering mechanisms from which IEDs are fashioned. Bullard's souvenir piece of shrapnel went with the gouged chest plate that let it get close to him, but not too close. It went with the five Bradleys and several more armored Humvees that his troop used up as the vehicles were blown up one after another, and the dozens of IED strikes they rolled through. His story of survival and grievous injury went with the other soldiers in his vehicle when the bomb hit—all of them were killed. This is the uneasy obverse of the invincible-looking armed and equipped figure of the soldier invoked at the beginning of this discussion.

So the spectacle of the technologically enhanced and protected body is interwoven with that of its extreme vulnerability. While the drama of sovereign violence surges just beneath the surface of public discourse, it is, for soldiers, both a far more immediate preoccupation and a matter of course—the stuff of anticipatory fears and practical concerns in a way that doesn't hold for those not facing direct and deliberate exposure to war. Take, for example, an ad in *Army Times* for Revision "Mission Critical Eyewear" ballistic glasses. Accompanying the warning "IN JUST THE BLINK OF AN EYE, YOU

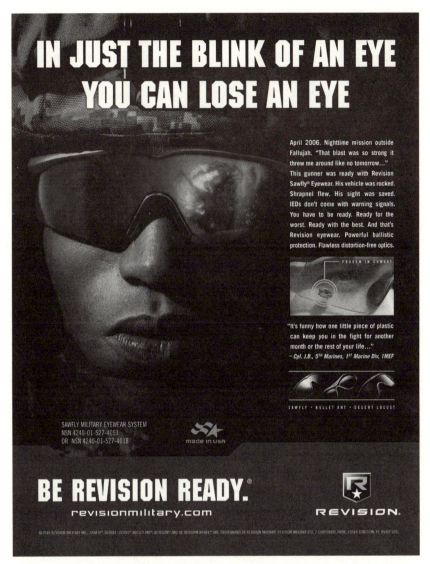

Figure 4 The promise of technology to keep you safe and "in the fight"
  Courtesy of Revision Military

CAN LOSE AN EYE" is an image of a soldier's darkened face covered by plastic lenses that reflect a menacing fireball. The text reads,

> April 2006. Nighttime mission outside Fallujah. "That blast was so strong it threw me around like no tomorrow. . . ." This gunner was ready with Revision Sawfly™ Eyewear. His vehicle was

rocked. Shrapnel flew. His sight was saved. IEDs don't come with warning signals. You have to be ready. Ready for the worst. Ready with the best. And that's Revision Eyewear. Powerful ballistic protection. Flawless distortion-free optics.

"It's funny how just one little piece of plastic can keep you in the fight for another month or the rest of your life."

—J. B. USMC, Fifth Marine Regiment

In the photo, the reflected likeness of the IED's fireball spreads across the soldier's protected eyes. We see him looking at it, apart from it, safe and shielded. A close-up image shows a piece of shrapnel the size and shape of a broken pencil tip lodged in the edge of one lens. An exhibit in the First Cavalry Division museum at Fort Hood displays a pair of Wiley-X ballistic sunglasses with a similarly embedded piece of shrapnel. On the wall next to them is a photo of the soldier who was wearing them, his face is lacerated and bloodied, but his eyes are presumably intact, and his mouth is in a tight grin. With this combination of images testifying to the impressive stopping power of military-spec eyewear, soldiers who are the market for ballistic glasses are invited to imagine themselves as invulnerable behind the reflective surfaces of high-tech armor.[5] Even as the Revision ad hails the soldier as a consumer responsible for his own bodily safety, the presence of the Wileys in the museum exhibit elides the fact that only a few years into the war, stocks of military protective equipment were being worn out and depleted at a rate that left soldiers underequipped (Isenberg 2007; Korb, Thompson, and Wadhams 2006; Stone and Moniz 2005). But both images hold out the redeeming promise of protective technology, and its ability to keep the soldier prepared, safe, whole, and "in the fight."

Sitting around the lounge at the Foundation, I would routinely hear soldiers declaiming the fallibility of body armor and voicing their skepticism of its spectacular promise. Frank, a truck driver who was getting ready for his first combat deployment, complained to me at agitated length one day about the newer, lighter, more effective armor that Blackwater private security contractors had, but that the Army was unable to provide its soldiers. Another time, I remember sitting out on the Foundation porch talking to Frank and Peters, another soldier who had not deployed either, as the two traded a series of authoritative tidbits about the weaknesses of the I-vest. Sure, they said, it would protect you from 7.62-millimeter AK rounds at range. Yet it would not necessarily stop a 9 millimeter up close, even though the fabric alone was supposed to—there had been news stories about the plates giving way—and definitely not a .45 or an armor-piercing round. And what about knives? As for wearing your vest inside the FOB while you were working or going about your business, what you had to worry about in there were mortars, and if one hit near you, well, there was only so much the vest could do for you. Even then, there were all those parts of you that weren't covered.

There was something mildly sensational about the way they handed these secondhand facts back and forth—something arguably more powerful than the precise truth or accuracy of their technical claims about the armor. It was a frisson of scandal and suppressed truth: they tell you to wear this vest to protect yourself, but what exactly it can protect you from is unclear, and at any rate probably isn't what they say it is. Like Ernie's jaded, distrusting exasperation with the visiting politician: "Motherfucker." On the other side of the government's armor and the enemy's bullets, it's your own flesh on the line, and some actuarial calculation has been made about how much pain and damage your body can be expected to endure. Even though Frank and Peters were sitting safely on a porch in Texas, months away from being deployed, all this talk about the chinks in the armor helped give shape and logic to the threat that lay over the horizon, in the future. And there was maybe a trace of excitement in it too—a dramatizing force. These guys had far more immediate problems that they talked about all the time, including anxious wives, cars to fix, bills and debts, grinding pains in their joints, and dickheaded, venal commanders who didn't treat them right. The conversation revealed the way that even then, on the porch, smoking cigarettes and bullshitting, they were already vulnerable, already exposed, with time and circumstance bringing them ever closer to danger.

Armor protects you, but not completely. Bombs, bullets, and mortars can kill you, but not unerringly. You and your body are somewhere in the middle. It is as if, when things are operating smoothly, the gear and weapons are a part of you. This is the point of the discipline after all, having always to wear your I-vest and carry your weapon. When their function is suddenly called into question, though—when they fail, when their capacity hasn't yet become second nature to you, or when they seem to be doing more to you than for you—suddenly they seem alien, no longer part of you. There is only you, naked and exposed, surrounded by indifferent or hostile machinery. And there is the uncertainty, resentment, and simple curiosity that this exposure calls up.

At least that's what I thought when I was sitting with a group of soldiers one day and Dale, an E-4 scout who had done a tour in Iraq, started talking about turning in his TA-50, the whole lot of gear that he had been issued when he joined his unit and thus was accountable for when he left. The TA-50 includes everything from rucksack to cold-weather gear. As is often the case, a lot of this stuff had just sat in his closet unused for his entire enlistment. In the shuffle between units and assignments, Dale had taken a different set of body armor and Nomex to Iraq. But now he was laughing about turning this stuff in. He and some buddies from his unit had abused a bunch of the equipment to see what would happen to it. They shot the shit out of the SAPI plates—although this barely left a scratch—and tried to set the Nomex on fire—though not much happened. One of them made his gas mask into a bong. The other guys sitting around smiled knowingly as Dale talked. It was the product of boredom, sure. They would say they were doing it for fun. At the same time, however, they were turning these miraculous technologies inside out, subjecting them to the forces they were supposed to withstand and seeing if they really could handle it: shooting what is bulletproof, burning what is fireproof, or filling the thing meant to purify your air with poisonous vapors. It's hard to imagine not having some aggression toward the technology that, for better or worse, makes it possible for your body to be exposed to bullets, fire, and fumes.

Dale and his friends' "experiments" on their protective equipment mimic a long tradition of probing the limits of what soldier bodies can tolerate, typically with soldiers themselves as the guinea pigs.[6] Whole battalions now wear sensors inside their helmets to track the force of the explosions to which they are exposed, supplying data that can be cross-referenced with TBI symptom rates or used as a basis for performing further screening when the soldiers return (Dawson 2009; Baker 2008). As Dime said as he related his doctors' efforts to manage and make sense of the TBI that made normal life impossible for him, "We are the research group." The damage to the soldier becomes more data, and thus more technology, for the instrumental maintenance of his body, for keeping him alive and "in the fight." Indeed, the current wars' devastation of bodies, revealed in military autopsies (Grady 2009) as well as surgical trial and error (McNeil 2008), has at the same time driven lifesaving medical innovations.[7] Valorized medical interventions are also "another way of making soldiers fight, of insuring compliance and deployability, and of harnessing a 'resource' for national security and policy purposes" (Bickford 2008, 6). In an inversion and extension of the biopolitical axiom that "one has to be capable of killing to go on living," the soldier has to be capable of surviving in order to go on killing (Foucault 1988, 137).

The body is an unstable, fleshy fulcrum between two apparently opposing but actually complicit forces, one aiming to destroy it and the other trying to carry it forward intact into the next moment of killing and being able to be killed. Yet this is the starting point, the condition of possibility, not the end of things. It's not a question of whether armor does or doesn't work, or whether soldiers are being deliberately neglected, unnecessarily exposed, or carelessly underequipped. The armor *does* work. Wileys protect your eyes, vests stop bullets and shrapnel, and armored Humvees can weather IEDs with nothing but a flat tire. The work these things do is nevertheless complex and contingent, enabling and constraining, and protective and terrifying all at once. Instead of protecting the soldier unequivocally, armor encapsulates him in the nervous tension between the phantasmagoric technological empowerment of the body and the felt vulnerability that technologized "invincibility" only intensifies. In this sense, it is not so much the definitive facticity of claims about equipment—by soldiers, commanders, manufacturers, commentators, or politicians—that is significant. What matters is the precarious state that it engenders. Circumstances are so changeable, so many elements are involved, and the capacities of weapons and equipment may not be known until they are tested to their limits, until potential becomes kinetic and then comes to rest again. What soldiers say with their fearful, descriptive, or playful talk is an articulation of this ambiguous, suspended, vulnerable position.

"DON'T FEAR THE REAPER"

In the combat zone, there is a balance to be struck, a cultivated operational knowledge that comes in large part from firsthand experience, about what can hurt you and what can't. If that control isn't mastered, or if it is demolished by trauma or chaotic circumstances, out comes the anxiety and terror of being utterly unprotected despite the physical burden and technosuperior claims of armor. So you need not only knowledge of what the weapons and armor can do for and to you but a kind of bodily *habitus* as well—an ability to take in the sensory indications of danger and act on them without having to think too hard about it first (Bourdieu 1987). When you hear a shot, is it passing close by? Is it accurate or random? Is it of sufficient caliber to penetrate your vest, the window of your Humvee, or the side of your tank? That RPG—they move slowly enough to see and sometimes dodge—will it come straight toward you, or will it loop to one side because its fins are bent from being carelessly stashed in some cellar? And when you don't act and you get hurt, a medic from one of the First Cavalry brigades told me, all it means is that "you forgot to duck"—the involuntary response to involuntary circumstances didn't come to you in time.

Kelly was in a small village in Anbar Province building a road the first time she heard a mortar strike. She told me the story in a tone of anxious, grinning hilarity. She had been added to her unit late, and everyone else there had been around for a while and was used to the sound. The mortar screamed in and exploded, and Kelly dove to the ground. A friend just looked at her and smirked, unperturbed: "Dude, that was like fifty feet away!"—out of range, on the other side of a wall of HESCOs and sandbags. "Dude, welcome to hell!" Kelly exclaimed to herself. She laughed as she related the anecdote, amused by her former self's overreaction even as she performed it in the telling. After a while, she said, she got used to the constant and inaccurate mortaring. Her unit would play a game, like Chad and his friends, trying to tell the incoming from their own outgoing fire. The explosions became domesticated, no longer a new and unthinkable hell. Instead they were a source of practical knowledge—when to dive and when not to—and even distracted speculation.

Lacking this knowledge can render you ineffective as a soldier. Ernie had a new guy as his driver one day when his platoon found itself charging into a firefight. Small-arms fire pinged against the side of their truck, and the kid began to freak out.

> They started shooting, and he heard "dink dink, dink dink." And he says, "Hey sarge, what's that?" And I says, "That's the engine cooling down, man." You know how engines make a noise when they cool down like "dink, dink"? [*Ernie and I both laugh.*] "That's just the engine cooling down, the metal shrinking back down." He goes "Really?" I go, "Yeah, don't worry about it." His knuckles were white. He's a dark skinned—he's a Mexican, he's like darker than me [*Ernie is Latino*], and his knuckles were white. He wouldn't let go of that steering wheel for nothing. And the rounds are going "dink dink dink." We got out, took care of business, came back in. "Y'alright, man?" He goes, "Yeah, I'm fine." I said, "All right, let's go." He goes, "OK." I go, "Let's go." He goes, "I can't move my legs!" [*More laughter.*] "All right, don't worry about it. Take a couple deep breaths, drink some water." The dude, his hands were cramped like this and he couldn't let go of the steering wheel. I said, "All right, you're no good no more."

It was important to understand the "dink dink dink" as the sound of the Humvee's hardened steel and armored windows *stopping* enemy rounds. It was the sound of safety. But Ernie's soldier didn't know that, or if his brain knew it, his body didn't. His body hadn't accustomed itself to the specifics of its enabled and vulnerable state. It was like Kelly diving to the ground because she didn't know, her body didn't know, that she was safe.

Operating in conditions of exposure demands a complex synthesis of practical knowledge, emotional discipline, and bodily disposition. Ernie said that every time he and his platoon went out on patrol, they would play the Blue Öyster Cult song "Don't Fear the Reaper" over the radio. He would play air guitar on his rifle and sing along. "If you go out there scared, you'll make fuckin' mistakes," Ernie said. "But if you go out there and you know that there's a chance, you're not scared no more. So don't fear the Reaper, baby!"

MOVEMENT TO CONTACT

Space itself becomes an objective in counterinsurgency war under tactical doctrines of "terrain denial"—making it impossible for the enemy to occupy a given area—and "movement to contact"—finding the enemy, making "initial contact with the smallest force possible, consistent with protecting the force," avoiding "decisive engagement," and maintaining "maximum flexibility" (Headquarters, Department of the Army 2001, chapter 4). Such practices entail their own forms of vulnerability for soldiers. Scouts—like Bullard, Dale, and others I met—called themselves, with no small amount of pride, "bullet catchers," and they described their terrain denial and movement to contact missions as "driving around waiting to get shot at." There's a bit of Army folklore that says that the scout's average life span in combat is twelve minutes—or five minutes, or thirteen seconds, and so on, depending on who you ask. Such statements are hyperbolic, certainly, but the point is that movement to contact is a deliberate exercise in vulnerability—a fact implicitly acknowledged by the field manual's dry recommendation to limit the size of the engaging force—the scouts—to an expendable quantity in order to "protect" the main force. Scouts are trained to operate aggressively, undetected, and in small numbers near or behind enemy lines. But the task of movement to contact is not just to survive in order to be able to find, survey, and kill the enemy. It is also, implicitly, for soldiers to put their own bodies on the line and offer themselves up as targets. The veneer of careful tactical reasoning is undermined by the morbidly absurd mingling of means and ends that plays out in decisions over how much exposure is worth risking in the pursuit of a larger objective. Scouts set out to "catch bullets" on purpose.

And they're not the only ones. The problems of vulnerability posed by small-arms fire and IEDs only *become* problems within the greater frame of how the violence in Iraq is structured, whether it is called terrorism, occupation, guerrilla warfare, asymmetrical warfare, or whatever else. The commonplace for it is war with "no front lines." In what may be the most galling and unnerving vulnerability of them all, easy targets are everywhere, as are the weapons that can destroy them, and the enemy is nowhere. This vulnerability is foundational to the kind of counterinsurgency war prevailing in Iraq—one that combines conventional combat, including armed patrols, armored vehicles, and air strikes, with "security" (the maintenance of safety and order), "force protection" (the security of the armed force itself), and the reconstruction of physical and governmental infrastructure.

Like the technologically extended soldier's body that becomes vulnerable in new ways even as its capacities are enhanced, the occupying military force needs a massive sustainment apparatus to supply, shelter, feed, maintain, and equip its "kinetic" operations at the same time as its corresponding logistical and reconstruction tasks demand a massive amount of security if they are to carry on at all. Even moving supplies and people across the landscape is essentially a tactical operation, requiring armored vehicles, armed escorts, and extensive planning.[8] And in the insurgent/counterinsurgent geography of Iraq, all soldiers become bullet catchers. Engineers, logistical personnel, and truck drivers all expose themselves to attack just to accomplish the mundane support tasks—delivering fuel, food, and water, repairing roads and vehicles—on which combat operations depend. In this sense, anyone out on the road—and not least Iraqi civilians—is engaged in a sort of movement to contact merely in the process of trying to get where they're going in one piece.

The surveillance and compartmentalization of the locals and the razor wire, Jersey barriers, blast walls, checkpoints, and watchtowers all serve the goals of security and force protection. But in spreading itself everywhere in order to control and reconstruct the landscape, the occupying force paradoxically offers a vast plethora of targets to insurgent fighters. The kinds of targets that the occupiers present are ostensibly manifold—vehicles, buildings, installations, roads, construction sites, and even intangibles like "security" itself. These things are all made targets by the presence of soldiers' bodies. Occupying space, the soldier becomes a vulnerable part of that "raw material of sovereignty" and its attendant bodily destruction (Mbembe 2003, 26). Bullard said that right in the middle of their area of operations was a one-mile stretch of road that was constantly mined with IEDs. They had to drive up and down it all the time, not only to get places, but also simply to "clear" that portion of highly trafficked road, making it, in the process, an ever-easier target for insurgents who wanted to kill US troops. He said it was stupid to waste lives in this way. "Once you leave a spot, it's no longer clear."

Elaine Scarry (1987, 12), following Carl von Clausewitz, usefully defines war as a contest of injuring. It seems apparent from all this, though, that there is a lot of important work involved not just in doing the injuring but also in being the party who is *available to be injured*— who is there to catch the bullets. The discourse of strategic warfare tends to regard injury—"collateral damage" done to noncombatants, but harm to soldiers themselves too—as something secondary to the true strategic objectives of war. Yet as Scarry points out, this inevitable damage can't be organized into a neat separation of means and ends. The injured are not "accidentally" in the way of objectives; *they are the means* of achieving objectives, and by extension, an objective in themselves (ibid., 74). Is this any less the case for soldiers than it is for civilians on the battlefield? Yes and no. Whatever the intention toward an individual target or the objective of a particular mission might be, by its broader logic, war requires bodies to hurt. There are no side effects; there is no damage that is collateral.

METAL

Soldiers are generally familiar—comfortable, even—with a certain level of instrumental objectification of their bodies and the enabling anesthesia of bodily discipline. But the kind of felt vulnerability that counterinsurgency war entails takes that shock of exposure to a particularly acute point of intensification. It finds its outlet in soldiers' preoccupation with the hardened plates and high-velocity fragments that surround their bodies and structure their vulnerability, even if metal never touches skin. Ernie's story about the reassuring, metal-on-metal "dink dink dink" of small-arms fire bouncing off the side of the Humvee, for example, segued into a second tale: the insurgents began using armor-piercing rounds, which, according to Ernie, are forbidden to US and coalition forces.[9] These rounds sound like a sledgehammer hitting the side of the truck, Ernie said, and they just go right through. One day they took apart the gunner's shield from their turret after it had been hit by one of them.

The bullet itself, the actual penetrator, is still intact. It's like tungsten [much harder and denser than the lead alloy of a conventional bullet]. You pull it out; it's not even bent. It's like, went through all that metal and didn't even bend. And they're using that against people, against soldiers, not against equipment and vehicles.

Like Bullard's SAPI plate and shrapnel fragment, one could look at the gunner's shield and the tungsten core of an armor-piercing round side by side, see the force each had unleashed on the other, and imagine the body—one's own body—hunkered just on the other side of that riven metal, or in place of it. *They're using that against people.*

Several steps up the scale of destruction is the EFP, the deadliest component of roadside bombs in Iraq. EFPs require precision manufacture, but their basic construction is quite simple: a round, open-topped canister packed with explosives, and capped with a shallow concave dish of copper, steel, or tantalum—dense metals with high melting points. An EFP looks like a soup pot with the lid on upside down. The heat and force of detonation transforms the thin metal lid into a compact, white-hot, high-velocity slug. Armor can absorb or deflect bullets and fragments of shrapnel, but EFPs go right through layers and layers of it, in one side and out the other, and through whatever is in between. They are for use against armor. Unlike the grenades, AKs, and conventional explosives that can be turned against a neighbor, thief, or sectarian rival, EFPs were specifically for killing US soldiers. No one else in Iraq was surrounded by so much hardened metal. Extension, new vulnerability, and new protection swarm and leapfrog past one another.

In the state of things that soldiers described to me, an EFP strike is a "catastrophic kill," not the couple of casualties that a conventional IED would produce. The vehicle is destroyed, and the people inside die. "Brother, there ain't nothing in our inventory that'll stop that thing," Dime told me.

After I've seen what happened to friends of mine, and what happened to heavily armored vehicles, you think you're in a suit of armor; it's a goddamn facade! Are you kidding me? . . . It goes right through an Abrams [tank]; it'll go right through it like a hot knife through butter. And I'm talking about sixty-four inches of depleted uranium, one of the hardest substances known to man—that's why we use it on a tank.[10] That goes right through it, brother. . . . [P]hew—all the way through it, and whatever's next to it, whatever's around it gets burned to shit.

The first IED that Dime lived through, sitting almost prone in the driver's hole beneath the front slope of the tank, a massive slab of ceramic and depleted uranium composite, he said he felt the penetrator slide past his legs. Everyone else in the tank, in the main compartment, was killed. As metal that cuts through metal, the EFP totally destabilizes the armored form, and turns it against itself and its fleshy, human contents. It fills the insides of a vehicle with the fractured bits of its own armor and structural members—this is called backspall, the armor that protects you becoming a cloud of shrapnel that will kill you. It ignites whatever will burn or explode—the bullets, rockets, and grenades that you would turn against the enemy cook off inside a confined space. It is a truly dire exposure.

Exposure to "thing-killing" weapons indifferent to the distinction between people and things makes the soldier himself into a thing—a sort of back-projected, highly vulnerable extension of the armor that the armor-piercing round or EFP is meant to pierce. Flesh becomes an extension of metal rather than the other way around. Or metal becomes an extension of fleshy life in ways that are uncanny and unexpected. A unit from Ernie's brigade found a massive weapons cache during their 2006–7 tour, including twenty-five hundred EFPs. The things are so decisively lethal that they said that each one they found equaled two lives saved. This numerical equivalence is striking in both its melodrama and its candid reduction of a life to a thing. It is like how Bullard's gouged SAPI plate is a life saved, and you can look at it hanging on the wall. Or the way that a pair of sunglasses with a metal splinter wedged into it is a pair of eyes that remain whole. The purpose of each bundle of steel pipe, TNT, and copper, sitting in rows by the hundreds in a dusty, secret warehouse, appears so clearly: each one equals two lives, as if they had the names of their future victims written on them already, the way that US servicemembers wrote aggressive jingoisms, dirty jokes, and patriotic memorials on the cannons, bombs, and missiles unleashed on Iraq in the first months of the war. It's easy to look at something like that and see nothing but the straightforward dehumanization of the enemy other, yet in this intimate intertwining of flesh and metal, there is something that makes these little ballistic epistles suddenly seem as personal as a postcard, love note, or epitaph.

The armor—the metal, Kevlar, Lexan windowpanes, ceramic plates, Nomex fire suits, helmets, vests, Bradleys, and Humvees—is what makes movement to contact—this intentional vulnerability, this offering up of the body as a target—a tenable exercise. In movement to contact, in the whole peculiar, technologically mediated state of vulnerability that soldiers find themselves in, apparently clear distinctions between who is doing the injuring, who is suffering it, what its goal is, and how final or effective it is against its victims all break down. Achille Mbembe contrasts the soldier to the suicide bomber, noting that conventional weapons—a tank or missile—are visible and separate from the body, whereas the suicide bomber makes this distinction impossible. "The body is transformed into a weapon, not in a metaphorical sense but in the truly ballistic sense," not a person, but moving, lethal matter that "becomes a piece of metal" (Mbembe 2003, 36–37). This metallic transformation is fundamental to the modern soldier body as well, though. And there are many ways to be made metal. The initialism GI, which evolved into shorthand for soldiers themselves, came originally from the abbreviation for "galvanized iron" stamped on pieces of Army equipment (Elting 1984). In World War I, soldiers called German artillery rounds "GI cans" after the barracks garbage cans and giant cooking pots that bore this stamp. This now slightly outdated descriptor lives on in "GI Bill" and "GI Joe," so that even these soldierly artifacts far removed from the battlefield still carry a palimpsest stamp of abject, instrumentalized, and weaponized metal. In this curious polysemy, the soldier becomes metal—the same indifferent substance that is put to work in various ways to kill him and keep him alive.

Thus while the contrast between soldier and suicide bomber is evocative, it sells short the vulnerability of the soldier's own "metallized" body as revealed in Bullard's story, or Dime's or Ernie's: the experience of being intentionally subjected to attack in the name of higher tactical demands. Clad and sheltered in armor, the soldier's body is a weapon and target at the same time; it is only one because it is also the other. And in the very act of catching bullets as an offensive tactic, the distinction between weapon and target breaks down.

A working and experiential knowledge of the capacities and limitations of weapons and armor is essentially a metric for thinking about the vulnerability of one's own body: what forces it's exposed to, what it needs to be ready for, and what it can or can't withstand. Bullard's experience took him to the limit of what a body could tolerate; everyone else in his Bradley was killed. But he himself was far from unscathed. There was no invulnerability—not even the illusion of it. And any clear division between flesh and metal, armored form and hostile world, was obliterated in the process. The shrapnel still harbored in Bullard's flesh is testament to his mastery over violence, but also to his basic vulnerability to it. In its abiding material persistence in his person, the shrapnel testifies as high drama but as something ordinary too.

At the Foundation office, Bullard would snip the tiny shafts off thumbtacks and hide them in the cushions of the desk chairs for people to sit on. I thought it a rather brutal prank until I sat on one myself and it barely even stung; it didn't break the skin, and I laughed. But it was a curious and diminished echo of the metal prickling out of Bullard's own skin.

SPAGHETTI

At one end of things are heat and weight, which are felt but cannot be seen, and which therefore are thought to be nebulous and mute in their meaning. They aren't talked about because you had to be there for them. At another end are those things that are talked about cagily or held back because they are too easy to see, too easy to leap to a false understanding of, their meaning too obvious and too terrible. They are the things that everyone, civilians and soldiers alike, already knows about war yet would never bring up in polite conversation, though maybe they do anyway: the dead bodies in all forms, things meant to remain hidden that you cannot help but see.

Dead bodies in general are so charged with significance that they cannot *not* mean, even if that meaning is unstable and fiercely contested (Verdery 1999). Through image and imagination, the dead are assimilated into narratives and morally salient scenes of suffering. From the safe, mediating distance of the news, a movie screen, or political talk, even the most gruesome death in war can be redeemed as sacrifice.[11] The grotesque body's gaping wounds and yawning orifices, literally open to the world, are figuratively open to all manner of subversive interpretation (Bakhtin 1968; Stallybrass and White 1986). The spectacle of abused and destroyed bodies is capable of inciting terror, or serving as a basis for critiquing the wrongness and inhumanity of war itself.[12] The grotesque, in this framing, moralizes and politicizes dead bodies.

But for the soldier, there is no neat division between what gore might mean for a perpetrator and what it might mean for a victim, because he is both at once. He is stuck in the middle of this relation, because this relation is the empty, undetermined center of the play of sovereign violence: sometimes the terror is meant for the soldier, sometimes he is merely an incidental witness to it, and sometimes he, or his side, is the one responsible for it. Even though gore and bodily destruction are not to be spoken of in polite company, ideas of taboo or transgression don't fully capture their force. As they appear on the battlefield, in the zone of exception, gory bodies do not carry a meaning that is mysterious, transcendent, or sacred; instead, they are a vulgar illustration of the material subjection of life.[13] The soldier in Iraq lives in a body that is stuck in the messy, often-horrific middle of things—a place of simultaneous opposites.

Like heat and weight, being face-to-face with dead bodies and their parts is a difficult thing to understand. Not many people have to see dead bodies, spectacularly ripped apart. As Dime put it, not many people *get* to see them. But even for soldiers for whom it becomes routine, gore is a spectacle, albeit a morbid one, or at least a point of interest. One soldier, Tim, told me somewhat abashedly one day that seeing bodies in the street relieved the boredom of long, uneventful patrols: "It sounds fucked up, but you're like, 'Cool!'" It's dramatic and in your face, in contrast to the silence, invisibility, and banality of heat and weight. It's far easier to describe, given the vocabulary of images and associations available for death and violence, but it must also be kept back from others, and is perhaps best enjoyed as secret knowledge among those who have seen it firsthand.

Soldiers say that a body that has been blown up looks like spaghetti. I heard this again and again—the word conjures texture, sheen, and abject, undifferentiated mass, forms that clump into knots or collapse into loose bits. Chris, a scout NCO who looked and carried himself like a professional athlete, said flatly that "it was all Spaghetti-Os" inside when they went into a blown-up Bradley to pull out one of his guys. We were drinking beer as he flipped through photos on his computer: "This is Baquba." Click. "That guy died." Click. "That's the grove I told you about." Click. "He's dead." Click. "He's dead." Click. These are—were—his friends.

Ernie kept his calm and jovial tone as he related some pretty gory stories—stories skating along whatever line separates humor and horror, fascination and fear. Suicide bombers trapped inside fortified checkpoints would just "paint the walls with red" when they exploded, he said. "And then you go through and clear and spray 'em off, and twenty minutes later you're back in business again." When an Iraqi police officer standing next to him got shot through the chest, Ernie saw "ketchup" squirting out of him.

Dee was responsible for checking and recovering the electronics from vehicles that had been hit by bombs. She pulled open the door of a Humvee in which everyone had been killed by an IED blast and found the whole rack of radio gear splattered in gore. She vomited on the spot, doubled over while one of her fellow soldiers held the strap on the back of her I-vest, and then got back to work. That night in the DFAC, some of the guys from her unit brought her a plate of pasta with red sauce—a joke. I thought it seemed cruel, but she said no, they did it to let her know it was OK. They only fucked with her because they considered her an equal; it was what they would have done to anyone. Confronted with a disintegrated dead body, a living whole body turns its own self inside out for a moment and vomits. In a perverse way, the plate of pasta closes the gesture and gets everything moving in the right direction again. But maybe the spaghetti gets transformed too, having its name attached to this other thing—a reminder of the body's capacity to invert or come apart suddenly and without warning. And it lingers, because in the wake of such destruction, nothing will ever be the same again.

Why this talk of spaghetti? Does it domesticate the violence and loss? Is it a critique? Gallows humor? Is it a reminder, perhaps, that you are ultimately nothing more than the dumb matter that you eat, made whole and held together only by changeable circumstance? Despite all the armor, the body is open to a hostile world and can collapse into bits in the blink of an eye, at the speed of radio waves, electrons, pressure plate springs, and hot metal. The pasta and red sauce are reminders that nothing is normal and everything has become possible. Some body—one's own body—has been placed in a position where it is allowed to die. More than this, though, it has been made into a thing—a thing draped with ceramic plates, a thing inside a metal box, a thing through which a cloud of shrapnel passes, or a thing served up on a plate.

Dime invoked spaghetti too, the pure horror of it, when he told me through tears about what had happened to his friend. "He hit an IED, and it was a considerably bad one. And the whole goddamn tank went up. And it turned him into goddamn mush." As they left the FOB, they had raced to the gate, and the friend's tank was just a little faster. Otherwise Dime would have been in front and would have taken the hit.

> And that was supposed to be my tank. He ran over it, and it hit right underneath his driver's hole, and everything above his knees was turned into fucking spaghetti. Whatever was left, it popped the top hatch, where the driver sits, it popped it off and it spewed whatever was left of him all over the front slope. And I don't know if you know . . . not too many people get to see a body like that, and it, and it . . . . [The IED] destroyed the fucking tank, if you can imagine that. It was sitting on its hull. It blew the goddamn road wheels off, blew the fucking skirts off the side of it. . . . We went up there, and I can remember climbing up on the slope, and we were trying to get everybody out, 'cause the tank was on fire and it was smoking. And I kept slipping on—I didn't know what I was slipping on, 'cause it was all over me, it was real slippery. And we were trying to get the hatch open, to try to get Chris out. My gunner, he reached in, reached in and grabbed, and he pulled hisself back. And he was like, "Holy shit!" I mean, "Holy shit," that was all he could say. And he had cut his hand. Well, what he cut his hand on was the spinal cord. The spine had poked through his hand and cut his hand on it, 'cause

there was pieces of it left in there. And we were trying to get up, and I reached down and pushed my hand down to get up, and I reached up and looked up, and his goddamn eyeball was sitting in my hand. It had splattered all up underneath the turret. It was all over me, it was all over everybody, trying to get him out of there. Trying to get him out of there, you know, before the tank burned up. We put what was left of him in a bag. And I don't know if you've ever taken a trash bag, and just taken like a wad of shit and just put it in the bottom of it and then tied it—and that's what we sent home to his mom and dad. Everything that was below his kneecaps was there because it was sitting down in the nose of the tank, but everything that was above it was pretty much mush. It was just shredded mush.

There is nothing comic or subversive here; only horror. Even in the middle of the event, it's insensible, unspeakable: *and it, and it . . . , I didn't know what I was slipping on.* The person is still there, and you have to "get him out of there," but he's everywhere and he's gone at the same time. The whole is gone, and the parts—the eye, the spine, and everything else—aren't where they should be. A person reduced to a thing: *it* was slippery, *it* was all over, *that* was what we sent home. *He* wasn't simply killed; he was literally destroyed. Through a grisly physics, there was somehow less of him than there had been before, transformed from person into dumb and impersonal matter.

Death itself is different, with the dead having been altered so dramatically. Dime was going to a funeral the next day.

It's bad enough it's a closed casket. Most military funerals are closed casket. They don't open them up anymore 'cause there's not a whole lot there anymore, brother. If there is, they don't even look like . . . they don't even look right. They look like dolls with as much makeup and stuff that they put back on 'em to make 'em look sorta human.

It might or might not be true, Dime's claim that "most" military funerals are closed casket (since he was in combat arms, he likely saw more than his share of them). But what matters is the overwhelming impact. Even in death, one can't be human. The artifice meant to cover the excess of the body's destruction—the mortician's makeup—takes on an obscene and inhuman excess of its own. What does this say about life?

Gore is about the horror of a person being replaced by stuff that just a moment ago was a person. Ernie described the first time out on patrol for one of his soldiers—a guy so young he turned eighteen on the flight to Iraq. A massive car bomb went off in the middle of Baquba, and

> we go up to the roof and start securing the area. And my boy Getz is like trying to throw up. 'Cause he says, "What's on the wall?" I said, "Don't worry about it, just calm down." "Is that a person? Is that a person?" 'Cause you know it looked like the outline of a person just got thrown against the wall like this. It was just . . . all it was, was wet. There wasn't nobody else. It was just wet. So when you got up to the roof, you could see everything that happened, 'cause from the roof you could see a like perfect circle of just body parts and just explosions everywhere. And that was the first time he went out with us, [and] the kid was throwing up. He's a hard-core infantry, Getz. . . . He came back, "Hey, I don't wanna go out with you guys no more. I don't know how you do it! I don't know how you do it!" 'Cause he knew. He knew we'd been hit before.

And then he trailed off. "Is that a person?" is the question, and Ernie doesn't really answer. It looked like a person, "but there wasn't nobody," just sheen, texture, and liquid. Getz's shock, his other question—"How do you do it?"—isn't just about the horror of witnessing something like that, to the extent that it's about that at all. It's not about the grief of Dime's story. It's about being exposed to the same kinds of forces that did it, because "he knew we'd been hit before." In this sense it doesn't matter if the body is Iraqi, American, or whatever; what matters are the questions. If that can happen to you, are *you* still a person? Will you still be one once the bomb goes off? Again, it's the zone of exception: anything can happen, and it can happen to you.

The soldier inhabits a bodily reality in which his own physical form could be extinguished at a moment's notice, and in which, under the burden of heat and weight, every step and breath is a further reminder of that destructibility. There is no symbolism or allegory in the disintegrated bodies that the soldier sees, acts on, or finds himself suddenly touching. They just happen, unceremoniously, and the only narrative to which they can be assimilated in the immediate context is one of continued movement, action, and perseverance, because grief and mourning are not safe, desirable, or even possible there in the moment. The abjection of the spaghetti'd body, the entropic raw material of ordering violence, does not symbolize anything. In this incoherence, a certain type of madness takes hold. Soldiers routinely invoked insanity to depict what being in Iraq was like: "Crazy is the best word for it"; "It's crazy—anything can happen." This madness is present, for example, when a carful of civilians speeds directly into a checkpoint and the terrified US soldiers kill everyone inside. Neither party to the encounter can make sense of the other's reasoning, and any sense of rational agency at work disappears into the "absent center" of this relation (Aretxaga 2004). The destroyed bodies are evidence of such craziness and the things that can happen to you for no apparent reason.

Spaghetti is a way of mediating this madness in order to live with it. *Standing for* nothing, spaghetti *is* the soldier's abjection in the face of the lawmaking violence in which he participates. Spaghetti is that ejected other matter that threatens the stability of the good soldier-subject's impenetrable, anesthetized boundaries—except that instead of spitting it out, the soldiers take it in.[14] As Begoña Aretxaga (2004) writes of the Basque police officers who, even in full-body riot gear, feel themselves profoundly vulnerable to rock-throwing youths, soldiers both embody the law and are alienated from it. They can be punished for breaking it, while those who seek to harm them—criminals, civilian collaborators, or enemy combatants—remain protected by it. Soldiers' abjection, like that of Aretxaga's police, is necessary for the order of the law to exist. And in that abjection, they are beyond its recognition and on the other side of its protection.

"OUR JOB IS NOT TO DECIDE"

I have made a deliberate decision here to steer clear of direct engagement with the subject of killing—what soldiers say about it, how they feel about it, what it might mean to them, and so on. In a way this is simply an outgrowth of the ethnographic material: soldiers spoke far more about feelings of vulnerability and exposure than they did about killing. It makes a certain kind of sense as well, for while only some soldiers find themselves in the position of exercising the right to kill, they all experience the defining condition of being able to be killed merely by virtue of being in or some day being sent to a combat zone.

But the right and responsibility to kill also carries within it a form of vulnerability that stems from the soldier's abjection from the law—another peculiar involution of the calculus of bodily expendability for which the soldier is the currency. Chip, a retired scout and military police officer who did two tours in Iraq, explained to me that he would always tell his soldiers, "'Don't never fear,' because that's the number one thing that gets soldiers killed." Unlike Ernie's injunction to not "fear the Reaper," however, it wasn't fear of the enemy that Chip was talking about but instead the fear of sanction and punishment from one's own side. Soldiers were afraid to shoot when their or their comrades' lives depended on it since they feared violating one or another rule of engagement or law of war. "Soldiers are getting confused because they're scared they're gonna get prosecuted," and officers second-guess what's going on "because of the politics." Soldiers cannot be afraid of the consequences of their actions. Just as Ernie spoke of the habitus of operating effectively while exposed—that you have to develop an alternative sense of your own bodily vulnerability and ability to be killed—Chip suggested that this habitus also demands a certain detachment from any excessively strong sense of moralistic consequentiality about your ability to kill. Soldiers have to be able to do the mission without thinking twice about it, he said. Of course you take precautions. Chip described cordoning off a building where two shooters were hiding and clearing the whole surrounding area of bystanders so they could level it with an air strike. Still, the soldier's job is execution, not choosing the right targets or right way to take them out, let alone the right time and place to make war. "Our job is not to decide," he remarked.

All the same, you can't just make yourself into a cog in someone else's machine. All these involuntary embodiments entail a subjection that knows it's being subjected. The curious vulnerability of killing brings us back to the notion that "the spectacle of decision" is an inadequate model for how people actually inhabit their own actions and sense of agency (Berlant 2007, 755). Even if ultimate authority lies elsewhere, as a soldier you're still invested with more than a little of that power. You might be a docile, disciplined body, but you're not an unsentient instrument. As that power flows through you, it leaves something behind—some excess or remainder that is not captured or fully dissipated by the sovereign mechanism. It may not show up as anything as obvious as guilt, remorse, or regret. Yet it is there, and it lingers, as in Ernie's preoccupation with going to bed "with a clean conscience." "You dream about the targets you were issued," Chip said, his flat, earnest, run-on talk shifting not at all. "I have night-mares because I've killed people because that's my job." "Sovereign is he who decides on the exception," declares Carl Schmitt (1985). Sovereign is he who has no fear and no bad dreams.

3

Being Stuck and Other Problems
in the Reproduction of Life

As crazy as things were in Iraq, as soldiers would often remark, they were simpler there than they were back home in Texas. And that old saw about war being composed of long stretches of boredom punctuated by brief episodes of terror applied as much to the home front as to the combat zone.

The terrifying vulnerability of the human body extends beyond the individual soldier and the foreign battlefield. It is not just the deployed soldier who endures the vagaries of exception as agent, instrument, and object of state violence. This precariousness also afflicts the soldier who has returned home, and the spouses, lovers, parents, and friends who remain bound to soldiers while they are away. The logic of such precarity lies not just in the sensory imprints of bodily exposure, as elaborated in the previous chapter, but also in the affective proximity of death as it travels through intimate attachments and institutional interventions, and the sorts of responses that this proximity provokes. The bodies that are the currency of the state of exception are always social, always attached, and always intimately implicated with others. Even—and perhaps especially—when it is thousands of miles away from home, the soldier's vulnerable body exists like all bodies "out in public," as Butler (2004, 26) writes; it is on its own, but also the possession of intervening, dependent, and caring others. We are "attached to others, [and thereby] at risk of losing those attachments" (ibid., 20). In its relation to others, a body communicates by its visible presence, its terrifying absence, or the humming waves of tension it telegraphs along intimate bonds. It offers itself up as a source of contested moral and medical information. And it announces itself to its owner in stubborn and unruly impulses that point to other times and places. A body does not necessarily have to be subject to extremes to be vulnerable; it is vulnerable simply because it is biologically and socially alive. The peril of vulnerability spreads outward from the soldier to those linked to him in a sort of generative contamination (Stewart 1991). The Army's management of that peril reflect it back onto the soldier. Attachment and exposure mingle to the point of indistinction.

HEAVINESS

I asked my friend Jessica if her husband seemed changed by his time in Iraq. Cal had just finished a fifteen-month tour. When Jessica and I first met, his tour had just been extended, meaning he'd be home by Christmas instead of by Labor Day. She said she could tell that certain things bothered Cal more, that certain things stressed him out, even though he hid it well and didn't talk about it. He could be pretty quiet anyway, so she didn't worry about it much. But she remembered that a few weeks after he got back, they were at the science museum in Chicago, where they had gone to visit his family. They crowded into a huge, dark room with dozens of other visitors to watch an elaborate new weather simulation exhibit featuring wind, lightning, and sudden peals of thunder. She didn't see him move, start, or do anything, and it was only minutes later, after they had left the exhibit and were walking down a crowded corridor, that she noticed how uncomfortable he seemed—tense, jumpy, and extra quiet. Was something bothering him? Yes. Was it the sound from the exhibit that did it? Yes. And she left it at that. I asked her what it made her think. She said she just didn't want to think about what it was that he might have been reminded of. She didn't want to know what had instilled that lingering, disruptive bodily sensitivity to signs of violence and danger.

By way of contrast, she told me about a close friend, also a spouse of a frequently deployed NCO. Every time this woman returned home from work or running errands when her husband was gone, as she rounded the carefully planned curve of her street in an Army housing subdivision, she would picture in her mind a car with government plates parked at her front door, and a couple of soldiers in shiny shoes and class As there to notify her that he had been killed. Every time. "Why would you think that?" Jessica wondered aloud to me. "Why would you do that to yourself?" Invoking the notion that a feeling is something that one "does" to oneself, the question highlights the uneven and partial sense of agency that obtains when it comes to feelings. The emotions, like the senses, are involuntary, unleashed as one "comes up against the outside world," provoking the will and demanding a response (Butler 2009, 34). Jessica kept herself on an even keel by assiduously not allowing herself these kinds of horrific fantasies, not thinking the worst, or indeed trying not to think about the whole thing at all—no simple feat. "I'd rather not go there," she said.

Army spouses like Jessica and her friend say that "they also serve" and invoke their status as "the silent ranks": there is a state of war that happens in the sudden sense that your easygoing, imperturbable husband is silently crawling out of his skin as he stands next to you, or that violent death may reach you through the thing you value most and find you out of nowhere on the way home from the grocery store. This vulnerability is as constant a preoccupation as the durability of a Kevlar helmet or the white-hot kinesis of an EFP. When I met soldiers and told them about my project, they would routinely enjoin me to talk to the spouses—theirs or anyone else's—because "they have the harder job."

When I spoke to Army couples together, they would typically remark that while the burdens were different for the soldier and the spouse, it was difficult to say who had it worse. Lena, a soldier who worked in media and public affairs, said that deploying felt like leaving everything behind, including her relatively new marriage. When she got up from the table and left the room for a moment, her husband, Harry, told me, "She said she left everything behind. But *I* lost everything; she was *everything* to me!" Not that his end of things was necessarily worse, he said, but still, it was impossible to convey the stress of knowing that she was about to go run missions for five days and not be reachable by phone or email. "How do you not talk to someone for five days when they're going to war?" he demanded. "She knows she's alive, she knows I'm alive," but when she was out of reach, he had no such assurance. Kristen, whose boyfriend, Stewart, was a truck driver, said the same thing: "You know they're going on a mission, they can't tell you where. 'I'll call you when I get back.' 'Well, when are you gonna get back?' And if they don't call . . ." The possibility of loss—of a loved one's life, of the reliable connection that lets you know you can expect to hear from them, of, indeed, *everything*—hovers constantly, compounding the more immediate loss of separation and absence. Kristen told me, "In regular everyday life, you don't have to sit around and wait to hear whether or not your husband's dead." Except that in this regular everyday life you do.

The main vector of this vulnerability, paradoxically, is knowledge and information. What information do you seek out about what is happening where your loved one is? What information does he or she share or hold back from you when you speak? What do you hold back from them? And more than anything else, how long do you have to wait between the moments of affirmation that let you know that everything is OK, the phone call or online chat message that lets you know, *I'm alive, nothing happened today*? How do you manage your anxiety and imagination in the vast spaces of everyday life in between those brief moments? This endurance of separation is a major feature of Army life, whether it's waiting for a call, an email, a visit, leave, the end of the tour, or a move to another installation that will bring you closer to home. We all know what it is like to wait, of course, or endure an absence. But my informants said that even they themselves didn't know "how long" a deployment of twelve or fifteen months really was—how it felt—until they were in the middle of it, or until they were preparing to face it for a second or third time. Normalized and stretched over this length, and indefinitely repeatable, waiting becomes something qualitatively different, as a defining feature under which life is reproduced rather than the unremarkable dead time breaking up the steady unfolding of meaning and eventfulness.

The soldiers in Iraq can call, but they can't receive calls, so wives, husbands, girlfriends, brothers, and kids wait to hear from them. In a *Doonesbury* cartoon, one of the soldier characters, Ray, gets yelled at by his wife for missing their chat date because he got caught in a firefight out on patrol. During Desert Storm, there weren't even affordable phones. Soldiers who were around then described sending faxes or facing thousand-dollar phone bills. Now there are Defense Switched Network phones set up in Iraq, Kuwait, and Afghanistan that call through a switchboard at a stateside installation, and then go out to the handset hanging on a kitchen wall down the street in Killeen. There are phone cards, burning through eighty-five cents a minute. Gene, an NCO who had done a couple of tours, spent thousands of dollars to call his fiancé, Danielle, three times a day from Kuwait when he was there. For the lucky few, there are satellite phones. And there are Skype, instant messenger, and various other text, audio, and video Internet chat options.

Even on big FOBs with established infrastructure, access to all these things was often limited. You had to find time in your own schedule, and then you had to wait in line for the phones or computers. If there was an emergency—if a base in Iraq or one of the units stationed at it had been attacked, and people had been hurt or killed—there was a communications blackout for several days while the Army established the identities of the dead and wounded, and then notified the families. The blackouts were especially scary, because the sudden lack of communication lets everyone at home know that something bad happened without revealing what. You could call up the unit rear detachment, but they wouldn't say anything. You could watch the news and speculate about what might have happened. Rumors abound. Nothing in these accounts was as terrifying or exciting—or both at once—as the sound of the phone ringing or the new message chime of the chat program or the email in-box.

Other technologies can bring only bad news. The if-it-bleeds-it-leads television news, they say, tells only of IEDs and ambushes, scenes of disaster and body counts; it cannot tell you anything good. The doorbell is similarly overdetermined, for in the right (or wrong) frame of mind all it suggests is the arrival of a notification detail to let you know that your soldier is dead. Charlotte, married to a combat arms NCO who did three tours, served as the community-elected "mayor" of her military housing area. She worked at home, and people were always stopping by, but when her husband was away she was adamant: call before you come over. The worst were the military police officers, who would stop by to check in during their rounds of the neighborhood. Charlotte couldn't bear the brief moment of terror that came with having a uniformed soldier as an unexpected guest.

In its ambivalence, though—its ability to bring good, bad, or simply boring news—the telephone is a potent avenue through which power's indifference to human vulnerability is apparent. The anticipated phone call exerts a kind of thrall. "The lover's fatal identity is precisely: *I am the one who waits*," as Roland Barthes (1979, 40) writes. "To make someone wait [is] the constant prerogative of all power." This temporality of power is different from any quick, showy spectacle of violence and decision, although it is still "fatal," it is still death that is awaited. And it compels the lover to take on the immobility of death too, "sitting in a chair within reach of the telephone without doing anything" (ibid., 39). There is no agency, "resistance," or effectuality to be found here. Other categories are needed, such as the ability to defer, endure, make oneself forget that one is waiting, or maintain oneself in the empty space between irregular episodes over which one has no control.

You're waiting whether you want to or not, keeping yourself alive in what can be a killing state. The excess of waiting can eat you up, binding you to another in a way that makes you not yourself. The hardest part of deployment is that you can't just sit by the phone, explained a woman whose husband's battalion was about to deploy. She and I were sitting on the front steps of the auditorium after a predeployment meeting for families, with the setting June sun making long shadows across the landscape of vast, dusty lawns and sharp-edged brick buildings that faced us. It was his third tour since they had been together. During his first tour, she was at home with her family in Ohio, and their first child hadn't been born yet. But during the second, she was at Hood with a toddler and another baby on the way. "I was isolated. It was bad. I hadn't made many friends. I would just sit around. I wouldn't leave the house." I imagined her clad in pajamas, hunched under a blanket in an unlit living room with the midday sun creeping around the edges of the drawn shades—

cocooned. But you can't just do that, she said, you have to get out. Now she always tells people, you have to make sure you have time to do things, time for yourself, time with people who understand what you're going through. You have to have time that is not waiting.

This attendance is always a delicate territory. Sometimes you don't hear from a soldier for weeks—because they are busy or have no access, or maybe because they are freaking out. Sometimes there really is a problem. But most of the time, it's waiting itself that is the problem. Everyone is waiting together, so you have to be careful with what you say. Lydia is married to a senior NCO who had just finished up his last tour in Iraq before retiring. After almost two decades as an Army wife, she had certain ideas about how such dilemmas should be handled, and because of her husband's rank, younger wives often turned to her.

> You don't ever ask, "Have you talked to your husband?" You have a lot of [spouses] that [say], "I talk to my husband every day!" [And someone else will say,] "Well, I haven't heard from mine in three weeks, shut up!" 'Cause it depends on their job, and it depends on their location. Yeah, that's like an Army thing, you don't. The young ones will ask you, "When's the last time you talked to your husband?" I won't even tell 'em really. I might have talked to him yesterday, but she hasn't heard from her husband in a week. So [I say,] "I haven't talked to him yet. When was the last time you talked to your husband? Oooh, OK. Well, it's OK, he'll call soon." That's all that they need. . . . It's my rule.
>
> And you know what? It will ease them down. It will calm them. Just the knowing that, OK, she's like me. And I know, Ken, that it will not be three weeks for them. I know it'll probably be about a week, week and a half, tops. But if they knew that I had spoken with [my husband], first of all they'd be pissed at me, and they'd be pissed at their husbands. But I don't know what Steve has the guys doing. Or . . . you just don't know. Maybe your husband doesn't wanna call you! It happens! . . . And I always tell them, if something happens, you're going to know. You're going to know. The only difference is, do you wanna know? And I told you this earlier—do you wanna know for every little frick and frack? My husband hit an IED. . . . I didn't know. Which was the best thing

he could've done for me. I'm pissed he didn't tell me, don't get me wrong. But he didn't want me to worry for a whole year and a half. He did good.

It wasn't that Lydia herself was indifferent to Steve's calls. She would wake at four in the morning to await a call so that he could go to the phones when the lines were shorter and not waste time standing in line. In her account, the problem of waiting for the call, talking about the call, and what the call might be about all slide into one another in a muddle of medium and message. Telephonic communication is not just about the words and thoughts traveling up and down the wire; it is about the way that everyone—all the soldiers and wives—is "jacked in" to this same "central nervousness" (Massumi 2005, 32). The affective currency of nervousness and reassurance is shared over the phone along with the conversations and professions of love and longing. We say that these things are "transmitted" and "communicated," employing the same terms that one would use to describe the spread of a contagious disease. And contagious dis-ease is indeed what comes out of it, spreading in a web of vectors that are both transglobal and densely intimate, zigzagging wildly between and within camps in Iraq and neighborhoods in Texas and countless other installations, living rooms, and anxiously monitored cell phones. Everyone is connected and everyone is in the same situation; if it wasn't your husband who died, it was someone who could have been your husband, or it was someone in his unit, a similar unit, or a unit in the same area, and someone whose wife might be your neighbor or best friend. The pressure caves you inward to your own individual horror of loss and at the same time it spreads you out—your hurt and fear cut you off, but someone else's hurt and fear are yours also.

It was only with hard-won experience that Lydia exerted some semblance of control over the radiating and rebounding waves of anxiety and fear. Information is as much the cause as it is the cure for this uncomfortable condition. While Harry was dogged by the possibility that Lena might not be alive when he didn't hear from her, Lydia found virtue in having been protected from the knowledge of her husband's brush with death. The solution for Lydia was to barricade herself from many aspects of the news that she so desperately craved, dealing with the uncertainty by knowing less, and accepting the silence—in itself a bad thing—as a sign that nothing bad had happened.

In this way, Army life forces a studied attention to the hundreds and thousands of moments of selective sharing and embargo that arguably are present in all intimate relations. Like Lydia being angry yet pleased that Steve had not told her about the IED that hit him. Like Jessica seeing her husband quietly freak out in the museum, but not pressing him on what was happening both for his own good and hers. One's own exposure to information as well as its release to others is carefully policed. There is no perfect management of this vulnerability, and in fact its management is built around inevitable transgressions and slipups, overheard rumors or glimpsed news stories, and all those things you later wish you did not know. Like the systemic vulnerability it nervously responds to, it is a collective phenomenon. Lydia's friend knew about Steve hitting the IED and didn't tell her. Jessica's friend bent her ear about a rocket attack near where Jessica's husband was. Soldiers try to persuade their parents, spouses, kids, and girlfriends not to watch the news. If something happens, if they have a close call, they wait to talk about it or they don't say anything at all. They try to keep the vulnerability to themselves. The emphasis is on *try*, for circumstance, overactive curiosity, and slips of the tongue make it so that everyone perpetually breaches these boundaries.

Civilians take for granted the ease of living without this looming, daily shadow of loss, waiting for news of death, or news that it has been forestalled a few more days. They don't understand the "heaviness" of such constant constraint, Cheryl told me. Her husband had been in for a while, but was only now about to leave on his first deployment. I asked her what she meant by heaviness, and she said that "the Army has a lot of control over you," and that people in the military and their families "give up a lot of freedoms to protect freedom." Just as the Army "owns" the soldier, it "owns you" too, said Cindy, whose husband had done a couple of tours. Just as it weighs down the soldier's body with arms, armor, equipment, and responsibilities, making the soldier's body not his own, it also weighs you down.

The Army explicitly controls where you live now and where you will go next, the house you will live in, and the people you will live and work with. As it moves you around, isolating you in its communities and installations, it controls your opportunities—you can have a job, for instance, but not necessarily a good job, and only rarely a career. The Army holds sway over your privacy, comportment, and conduct, your access to the rest of the world, and your sense of what's possible. The very pace and transience of Army life makes you vulnerable as it imposes both an intense intimacy and a sense of bunkered-off isolation. You meet new people and bond over your circumstances, but you fear the loss that comes with moving on again, and so you close yourself off to new friends. As a soldier's spouse, you, like the soldier, "operate under conditions of fear" shaped by the pace of bureaucratic decision, ponderous one moment and quick as an ambush the next. Both the speed and slowness have a dulling effect, because in all this waiting, you are ultimately waiting for the next shock, the next moment when "the rug will be pulled out from under you," as Cindy put it, with a change of orders or deployment extension. Jerked along in these fits and starts, there is no opportunity even to come to terms with the ways that you are being exposed. Instead there is endurance, maintenance, attrition, and opting out—protecting yourself so that you can carry on.

The *weight* and *wait* are bound up with each other. There is no transcendence in living with loss in this way. It is a kind of discipline, perhaps, but not an ascesis, mortification, or anything else that promises peace at the end of it. Rather, it is a constant and incremental labor, accomplished in the endurance of loss—"I lost everything"—one moment at a time. Cindy put it thusly: "We don't get a break." Heaviness gets at something beyond the vulgar literalness of fear and control. Fear can be overcome, and control can be resisted, but heaviness must simply be borne even as it wears you out with a labor of endurance that is punctuated by the ringing of the phone. So waiting is a temporality of power that can be interminable and sudden, chronic and acute, as it moves through a variety of relays and intermediaries. Its slowness is made crueler still, maybe even defined, by the lightning-speed "jacking" of the phone call. In all cases, there is power: your husband may be too tired to call, say, and the civilians may have no clue what you're going through, yet as you wait for the phone to ring or not ring, it is the Army that makes you wait. That heaviness is a feeling of the Army.

If these circumstances confuse any effectual understanding of agency or resistance, they also wreak havoc on the linear eventfulness of trauma. Does it even make sense to talk about this exceptional condition of vulnerable life as a pathology or problem, when it is so persistent and ordinary? Can one even speak of trauma in any meaningful way when to be soldier or to be attached to a person who happens to be a soldier is to subject oneself to an often-terrifying psychic drama that plays out all day, every day? For at the same time that death is there, life goes on; husbands, wives, parents, and friends love each other, and most of them love the Army, too—in their own ways and with qualifications. This is not redemption; it is just the way things are. It is a daily reproduction of life and death, and bodies bound together whose liveliness is shaped by the ways that they might die.

WORN-OUT BODIES

The various modes of power that operate on soldiers generally possess a certain consonance, even a synergy, but they sometimes work at cross-purposes to one another. Beyond and before the extremes of combat, routine soldiering in garrison and during deployment can take a massive physical toll. In the service of the greater goal of combat and its exigencies, soldiers spend weeks, months, and years exercising, marching on rough terrain, lifting heavy loads, operating loud and dangerous equipment, performing repetitive tasks, climbing in and out of tanks and the backs of trucks, sleeping on the ground, enduring heat and cold and the elements, eating miserable food, and going without sleep.

The physical wear and tear of these obligations can naturally, and sometimes suddenly, work against the capacity of the body to fulfill them. In performing the labor of soldiering, the soldier can work his bodily equipment to the point of ruin, pitching himself into a state of precarious unsoldierliness. The possibilities of such ruin are built into the conflicting, concordant regimes to which the soldier is subjected. The soldier's relentless labor can jeopardize his ability not only to perform his job but also to support himself and his

family economically, and understand himself as a physically and socially whole individual. The same tasks that make and prove the soldier's body are, in turn, liable to undermine and destroy it, and being
hurt confronts soldiers with a series of double binds. Claiming to
suffer from pain and discomfort typically earns a soldier little more
than the suspicion of his commanders, fellows, and doctors. Routine
bodily burdens get transmuted into and recirculated as illness, injury,
complaint, bureaucratic control, psychic and emotional stress, and
the retelling of stories that make sense of present conditions. The
bodily toll of soldiering is a preoccupation not just for soldiers but
also for the institutions that manage and support them, and the inti-
mates with whom they share their daily lives—all of whom depend in
various ways on the lability and integrity of the soldier's body.

One sunny June afternoon, I chatted with Stewart out in the
Foundation parking lot. Stewart served three tours in Iraq as an
88-M, a truck driver, but now he was on medical hold due to a busted
knee. The knee wasn't what brought him home from Iraq, though. In
a fit of pique one day during his most recent tour, he made a passing,
sarcastic reference to slitting his wrists, and the next day he was on
a plane back to Fort Hood. It seems a telling biopolitical irony that
the Army would be so quick to respond to this nonexistent crisis and
so slow to treat Stewart's damaged leg.[1] We perched in the slanting
afternoon sun on the front of his car, which a fender bender had
folded into a cockeyed beak. Peters sat facing us on a bench with
a broken slat, the remaining three narrow boards bowed under his
bulk. Stewart is skinny and rangy, with an angular face, shorn scalp,
and efficient, dark bristle of regulation moustache. The combination
of him and Peters has an almost Laurel-and-Hardy aspect to it, but I
don't know that they would appreciate the comparison; their bond is
one forged in boredom, circumstance, and shared discontent rather
than any sort of mutual affection. Stewart breaks the filters off his
cigarettes before he lights up, having acquired an idiosyncratic taste
for unfiltered menthols; Peters has recently quit the more conve-
nient tobacco high of dip.

Like a lot of the other soldiers who worked at and patronized the
Foundation, Stewart and Peters were injured, and had been assigned
to the Fort Hood Warrior Transition Unit.[2] The WTUs were set
up across the Army in the wake of the 2007 Walter Reed neglect

scandal in a much-publicized bid to intensively manage the care and treatment of injured soldiers.[3] Walter Reed Army Medical Center in Washington, DC, and Brook Army Medical Center in San Antonio, Texas, treated many of the most gravely injured soldiers—those with missing limbs and severe burns. But across the Army, soldiers are transferred into WTUs at their home installations when they suffer from any of a range of physical and psychic injuries as well as illnesses that prevent them from being able to perform their normal duties, including everything from PTSD and shrapnel wounds received in Iraq, to back injuries from training, to cancer and respiratory conditions, to broken bones from car accidents just down the road. In the WTU, these soldiers' "mission is to heal," in the words of the Army's often-repeated motto. Separated from their old units, they perform none of their previous regular duties, and instead follow a tightly managed and sometimes confusing schedule of briefings, meetings, and appointments with physicians, specialists, and case managers. Through these interventions, their conditions are evaluated and treated. The system serves military readiness, because removing the temporarily or permanently disabled from the ranks of active line units means that they can be replaced with the able bodied, and the units can stay ready to deploy. Eventually, WTU soldiers are found fit and returned to duty, or they are pronounced disabled, their worthiness for compensation is judged and quantified, and they are discharged from the Army.

The default length of a WTU assignment is ninety days, but I was told almost no soldiers make it through in that amount of time. Many I met had been in the WTU for months, and it was not uncommon for the entire process to take a year and a half. During this time, WTU soldiers are nominally required to perform some sort of useful labor if they are able, which is what drew many of the Foundation's volunteer staff. But they cannot do much of anything that they or other soldiers recognize as worthwhile work, and with cynical and frustrated humor they would refer to themselves and one another by Army epithets for slackers and malingerers: they were "turds," "broke dicks," "shammers," and "shitbags."

For the bulk of the wounded soldiers I met, even those proceeding through the WTU and medical evaluation processes at a relatively reasonable pace, their jobs and therefore their lives had become

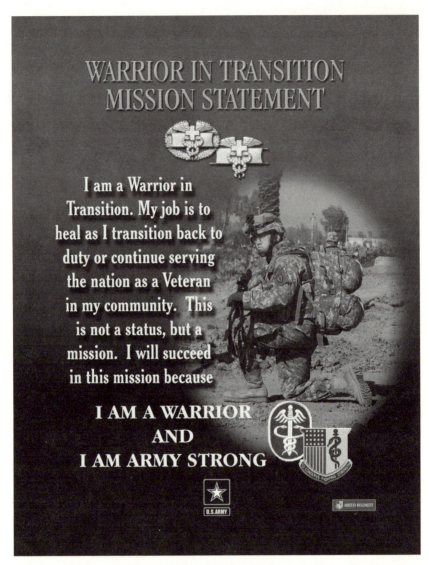

Figure 5 The *Warrior in Transition* mission statement: Healing as a willed undertaking
    From US Army Medical Department

organized around the institutional management of their injuries and
the nervous anticipation of an uncertain future. Would they be able
to heal and return to duty? Would they be treated with sympathy or
suspicion by their caseworkers? Were their agitation and stress the
product of a frustrating system, an unsympathetic spouse or friend,
undiagnosed posttraumatic stress, or all of these things? Would one

doctor consent to approve the treatment that another doctor said was necessary, and would it be successful? Would the Army recognize its culpability for an otherwise-healthy twenty-two-year-old's ruined ankle, bad back, or illness exacerbated by the stress of deployment, and provide them with medical retirement, prorated pension, and continuing medical care? Or would a soldier struggling with physical pain or psychological trauma find himself cut loose with only a few thousand dollars in severance pay, no health insurance, few marketable skills, and maybe a family to provide for on top of it all?

That afternoon, Stewart had just been to the doctor for his knee and was worked up about it. As he complained, I began furiously taking notes. He pulled the leg of his fatigues tight around the knee to show us what it looked like; even with a brace on it, the joint appeared puffy and inflated, especially on his lean form. His right anterior cruciate ligament was practically torn, but the Army deemed the necessary surgery to be elective. The medial collateral ligament of his left knee was injured too, and he had a torn rotator cuff and TBI. So he had been consigned to the WTU. Running, walking, and getting in and out of his car were all painful activities. He was on a so-called "dead man's profile." Profiles are the Army's "system for classifying individuals according to functional abilities" (AR 40-501, 7-1), providing an official set of medically recommended activity limitations. With his profile, even if Stewart wasn't in pain, which he almost constantly was, he was not allowed to do anything. He had bought a motorcycle, but in order to ride it on the post he had to take an Army safety course, which his doctors forbade him to do because of his injuries. "If I were to throw my back out I'd get an Article 15!" Article 15 is shorthand for the nonjudicial punishment authorized by Article 15 of the Uniform Code of Military Justice— the punishment Stewart would face for violating his profile limitations. There is a lot of apocryphal soldierly folklore about Article 15s for ill-gotten sprains, sunburns, hangovers, or other minor injuries; soldiers joke that unduly messing yourself up constitutes "destruction of Army property." Such stories, like Stewart's theatrical claim of possible prosecution, may be hyperbole, but the larger point holds. For Stewart, as for all soldiers, his hurt body and the institution both constrained him—the latter in the name of protecting the former.

Nothing about Stewart's medical treatment seems logical or straightforward to him, and he shared the complaint of some other WTU soldiers I met that their doctors only focus on injuries one at a time rather than treating them comprehensively. The result, Stewart said, was that "I feel stupid on a daily basis because of the Army." Nothing seems to have gone his way, he complained with his typical acidity. "I've earned everything I've gotten in the Army, including not getting surgery! I don't wanna make it seem like, 'Oh, the Army medical system is against Derek Stewart.' But it feels like if there's a shitty doctor, I've had him." It's soured him on the whole enterprise, including the war itself. On a recent trip home, a family acquaintance told him that he was thinking about enlisting. He "told them not to do it, because you'll never be the same. People see the soldiers coming home, getting off the planes, [and they say,] 'Oh, you're so great!' But we're all thinking, 'This shit sucks!'" How many of you are thinking that? I asked him. "Oh, a good 60 to 70 percent," he responded assuredly.

Peters agreed. He griped about the weight gain that resulted from the steroidal medications he was on, exacerbated by the PT limitations occasioned by his back and shoulder injuries, which were painful, sometimes to the point of immobilization. He had gone from 195 pounds when he completed basic training to 285 pounds. Jimmy, a senior NCO from the WTU who helped run things at the Foundation, called him "Big Country" and "Corn-fed." Peters was from a decidedly rough East Texas background. Both his parents had drug problems, and his brother is in prison for assault. His father once sold a classic Thunderbird they had been working on together to buy crack and liquor, and Peters missed his own high school graduation because his brother had recently given Peters's name instead of his own when he got busted, resulting in a warrant with Peters's name on it. His stories of relatively recent adolescence (he was twenty-two) often revolved around scenes of intense racial avarice—times that "these black guys" or "these Mexicans" started a fight with him—but he was genial, warm, and funny, if indelicate, and got along with everyone.

Peters joked, as I had often heard him do, about his breasts: "I got bigger tits than my wife, man! I hate it! I used to love to take my shirt off at the pool. Now I'm embarrassed." His injury and medical care had literally feminized him. He showed me a picture on his phone from when he enlisted: he is dressed in Class As, his body a hulking, broad-shouldered V, and his legs slim and proportional, all of it so unlike his present massive roundness. In the photograph his babyish face is distinctly recognizable, but dramatically different nonetheless, with his jaw more defined and set in a theatrical snarl. He squints menacingly at something or someone just outside the frame, leaning slightly forward, his arm in the middle of a sweep and a cigar or blunt in his hand leaving a wreath of smoke. The picture was taken in a bedroom, maybe; there are hospital-white walls, a milk crate on the floor, and a full-length mirror propped against the wall. Despite the low-light graininess and harsh fluorescent tones, he looks good, and quite different from how he looked that afternoon at the Foundation.

Peters was approved for surgery when his injury occurred, during infantry training. But then he came to Fort Hood and the doctors there denied the operation. He got assigned to the Fourth Infantry Division and then they kicked him into the WTU. No one doctor or administrator has his complete medical records. When he complained, the surgeon told him, "It's not all about you." Stewart chimed in sarcastically, "Yeah, it's not all about you!" Other doctors refused to look at the MRIs that showed how damaged Peters really was, he said. "I went to get a second opinion and they didn't even look at my MRIs! They're just a bunch of dicks, man." He said this sadly, with a shake of his head and a wistful, almost sweet tone of resignation. I heard him talk this way a lot. "I haven't even been to Iraq, but I feel like I have," he remarked. He felt like he had PTSD just from having to deal with bullshit of the WTU. But perhaps being stuck here was for the best; he speculated that maybe "God hurt my back, because if I went to Iraq I would go crazy. I wouldn't be the same person if I went." Or maybe it was too late for things to be properly sorted out: "From how I grew up, my mental state is messed up." He had taken three loans to cover the debt he incurred with his landlord when his housing allowance was delayed by an administrative error. Nothing he did seemed to work out right. "I'm a bighearted guy, but my life is always full of getting yelled at. I'm already stressed out from life completely. I knew the Army was hard on you, but I thought it was only if you are an ass, but I'm nice! I help people! I still get yelled at, get into trouble. I don't wanna go to Iraq, shoot people, and blow them up, get blown up, do stuff that don't make any sense."

The incoherence and apparent hostility of Army medicine have thrown Peters into a double bind that is both grave and unremarkable. Things ought to proceed logically; the Army should evaluate his injuries and treat them. If he recovers well enough, the Army should return him to duty. If he doesn't, it should decide how disabled he is and how much of that disability the Army is responsible for, and then it should compensate him accordingly and pass his medical care along to the VA. The system should decide for itself how he is to proceed and what is to become of him. Yet in both Stewart's and his own case, and in the cases of many other soldiers I met, this was not happening. Encountering Army medicine made their conditions and treatment murkier rather than clearer (cf. Mol 2002). Some combination of doctors, physicians' assistants, and caseworkers refuse the treatment that other doctors, physicians' assistants, and caseworkers told them they would need to be whole, functional, and free of pain, leaving Stewart and Peters caught at the beginning of this process and its long list of hypothetical *shoulds*. The way forward from there was a tortuous labor of bureaucratic box ticking.

The skepticism and suspicion that soldiers are subject to, however—from the dicks and shitty doctors—means that this is only the start of the problem. The experience of being injured is decisively shaped by the idea of "healing" as a willed undertaking for which soldiers are responsible. For even as the system simultaneously pronounced Stewart and Peters unfit for their old jobs, failed to decide what should be done with them, and prevented them from taking any action on their own behalf, it also questioned the legitimacy and the very existence of their debilitating pain. The Army had decided that their injuries were real enough to make them useless, and merit the prescription of opiates and steroids, but not necessarily real enough to necessitate the trouble and expense of surgery—or so it seemed from their end. Peters in particular felt himself faced with an untenable choice: because the Army would not recognize the legitimacy of his injury by either treating it and keeping him in, or compensating him for it and letting him out, he was considering how to address the situation on his own terms. As he saw it, he could suck up the pain, tell the doctors it didn't hurt anymore, get back in shape, and return to duty. Or he could allow himself to be judged unfit for duty, get processed out, and get a civilian job. The former option probably meant going to Iraq, and the latter to Houston or the Gulf coast for decent-paying work in a chemical plant or refinery, but his wife had just started nursing school nearby in Waco. Either option, though, demanded living with pain that most of the time prevented him from being able to lift things, kneel, or hold his arms above his head. If he was discharged without a service-connected diagnosis, the military would no longer be responsible for his condition. In the meantime, the Army would medicate him, keep him busy going to physical therapy and doctor's appointments, and leave him feeling bullied and neglected.

Frustration was equally high on the other side of things. Irene, a physical therapist recently retired from the Army and now working as a contractor, described her work as a combination of, on the one hand, treating soldiers expeditiously and aggressively so that they could get back to their units, and on the other hand, educating unit commanders about how to prevent unnecessary injuries. If she could get platoon and company commanders "in tune with what needed to be done for soldiers, then they could decrease the amount of soldiers who had to go to sick call" with aches and pains. But it was a delicate balance to strike. Given the urgent operational tempo of continuous deployments and the concomitant strain on time and resources, it was difficult to get commanders to attend to injury prevention.

The results are perverse. Units train harder because they are getting ready to deploy; more soldiers get hurt with easily preventable stress fractures and other repetitive strain injuries, and have to go to sick call. The medical system gets swamped; the nurses and physicians' assistants are already overwhelmed, and lacking the time and resources to attend to each individual case, I was told over and over again, they send hurt soldiers on their way with a bottle of Motrin and a xeroxed sheet of instructions for stretching exercises. The soldier continues to get hurt, misses work because he has to go to sick call, receives little or no care, and incurs the suspicion and ire of his commanders and fellow soldiers. All the while, the medical system generates a backlog of potentially preventable cases that distract from more serious problems. Some of the prevention measures are striking in their microtechnicality and apparent simplicity. For example, arranging marching formations by height, shortest to tallest, prevents stress fractures because soldiers of different heights don't have to unnaturally lengthen or shorten their strides. Or it's just a matter of not working soldiers quite so hard.

> [In] the *Fort Hood Sentinel* . . . a commander was actually bragging about doing twice-a-day PT. Twice-a-day PT! And talking about how important it is to basically run these kids into the ground to make sure they're physically fit so that when they go to Iraq and have to deal with the temperature, then they've been trained so that their body can adapt. Well great concept, but you and I both know what happens. And yeah, we're we seeing a lot of their soldiers in physical therapy from that same unit. . . . They thought what they were doing was a great idea. And then they wondered why all their soldiers were going [to sick call]. Well, part of it was that their mentality was that if their soldiers were going to sick call, their soldiers were weak, and what did they need? They needed more PT.

As Stewart, Peters, and Irene all indicate in different ways, the Army is a hard place to be hurt. From basic training onward, Army life cultivates and encourages suspicion toward claims of nonvisible injury as well as a tendency to equate injury with deception and moral failing. "They told us in basic, 'Anything that's not life, limb, or eyesight, suck it up. If you say you're hurt, we're gonna assume you're faking.'" All other complaints will be regarded as malingering or deception. Soldiers would often report this stance to me ruefully or with irony, making a sort of public secret of its unreasonableness. But still the abject slang stuck: shitbags and brokedicks. Injured soldiers are broken soldiers. That it is frequently the basic bodily labor of being a soldier that has caused this undesirable, individuating decay does not protect the soldier from the confusion, skepticism, and hostility that his condition will provoke. The hurt soldier becomes a problem for everyone, usually despite anyone's best intentions. For his sergeant or commander, the soldier is failing to properly fill his slot, and for the RN, physician's assistant, or doctor, he may be another potential shammer or malingerer taking the place of a worthier or more cooperative patient.

These imputations collapse back on one another and produce their own unintentional structural effects. By providing a medical alibi for lassitude and incompetence, sick call and the WTU do in fact offer themselves as "dumping grounds" for "bad" soldiers. A medical officer I met was adamant about this: she would never say so to her friends in line units, but it was simply true that it was easier to send a problem soldier to the WTU than it was to kick him out. Because the WTUs were instituted specifically as an internal safeguard against the scandal of neglect, all complaints have to be taken seriously. Or rather, they have to have the appearance and provable bureaucratic substance of having been taken seriously, although medical personnel sometimes dismiss overly demanding soldiers as manipulative "barracks lawyers" overplaying their special status.

Perversely, even as WTU soldiers' treatment and diagnosis is delayed for months and months, the high priority accorded WTU patients bottlenecks the post's entire medical system, extending the wait time for appointments for regular patients—including deployable soldiers—from days to weeks. I heard more than once, and always in a tone that combined cynicism with a whiff of taboo, that "malingering does not exist in the WTU"—which is to say, it does or it must, but it was not to be spoken of. The bureaucratic apparatus and institutional culture literally—and often despite themselves—turn injured soldiers into bad soldiers, and bad soldiers into injured ones. The soldiers feel bullied and infantilized, and the doctors and caseworkers feel manipulated and overwhelmed. The whole thing spirals into degrading subjectifications, displaced responsibility, and a sort of mysterious vacuum that sucks up misdirected effort and resources. The soldiers and the people charged with healing them are divided from one another by a gulf of antipathy and suspicion. All parties, however, tell stories of bad faith on the part of some spoiling it for the honest others—stories that are antagonistic yet ultimately parallel.

Thus it is that injury thrusts whole sets of actors into positions of exception that are sticky and entrapping, and that do not resolve along any predictable timeline. Injuries are exceptions, after all—accidents that should not have happened (Jain 2006). Stan told me that "the Army is very good at taking care of large numbers of people, but when someone becomes sick or injured, they become an individual, and the Army is not good at taking care of individuals." Indeed, the chief goal of military medicine is to maintain the interchangeability of individuals by restoring their broken bodies to a uniform standard—a goal that has its depersonalizing dark side even in the best of circumstances. Soldiers refer to the depersonalizing bureaucratic machinations by which they are shuffled from job to job, or post to post, as "making a number," "filling a slot," or even just "needing bodies," and this characterization is not inaccurate.[4]

Under this pressurizing logic, medical categories become just another system by which the Army can leverage maximum utility from soldier bodies. What results is a confusion of means and ends. Instead of the categories being instruments that serve the healing of bodies, the bodies become raw material for the satisfaction of the categories (cf. Petryna 2002). And otherwise-unsuitable bodies can be, as it were, rewritten in order to accomplish this satisfaction. You can fail a drug test two weeks before deploying and still be sent to Iraq, soldiers would tell me, but if you fail a drug test two weeks after you get back, you'll be kicked out. You can be spared deployment because of severe sleep apnea, but then the Army can decide that sleep apnea is a deployable condition and give you orders to go. You can be scorned for weakness or malingering if a sprained ankle forces you to sick call and then made to labor in pain if your unit needs you to deploy. A constellation of symptoms can be pronounced PTSD, and therefore worthy of medical discharge and compensation, but a second (or third, or fifth) diagnosis can rename those same symptoms as an anxiety disorder and thus a preexisting condition. This was not just the grumbling of a few malcontents. In the middle of the war, the Army's own inspector general found that it had deliberately lowered disability approvals more than 60 percent to save costs (Kennedy 2007).

Of course the soldier's job *is* to be a number, fill a slot, or be interchangeable, at least to an extent. And while soldiers may occasionally chafe at this, it is a familiar condition of their world. When a soldier gets injured, however—when he is so encumbered by discomfort or pain that he can no longer perform to the uniform standard—he no

longer constitutes that number or fills that slot. He has become, as
Stan says, an individual—not in the liberal sense, suddenly coming
into positive possession of autonomy and individual identity, but instead in a negative sense, as an exception, a bodily unit with nonstan-
dard and undesirable properties, mired in feeling rather than coolly
detached from it. This is, as Lochlann Jain (2006, 7) observes, the
American culture of injury, of which the Army's clinical and bureaucratic logic is merely an especially acute manifestation; injury exists
"in isolation—as an event that could have not happened." This logic,
Jain writes, regards injury itself as unjust (once proof has cleansed it
of suspicion), but it naturalizes the injuring structural, disciplinary,
and market conditions to which injured bodies have been subjected.

Stan's observation and the general cynicism of soldiers about
filling slots and making numbers testify to the acuity with which soldiers feel the threat of this individuation, and how it both batters
the emotions and leaves the body stranded in pain and dysfunction.
This is what comes through in Stewart's sardonic remark to Peters
that "it's not all about you." It's not about you from your perspective.
But from the Army's perspective, it *is* all about you and it ought not
be, for in the disembodied eyes of a total institution there is nothing more useless or contemptible than an individual. And yet there
is something distinctly liberal about the embodied experience of the
hurt soldier. Even though your decrepitude is often inseparable from
the burdens that the Army has placed on you, your injury thrusts
you into a particular zone of exception that is, ironically perhaps,
paradigmatic of modern liberal subjectivity: you are at once "buf-
feted and controlled" by power, and "starkly individuated, stripped of
reprieve from relentless exposure and accountability" (Brown 1995,
69). It is freedom without care (Mol 2008). In the previous chapter,
I referred to the ways that armored soldiers' exposure to violence
constituted a sort of experimental probing of the functional limits of
the human form. That same logic operates in the WTU, albeit much
less spectacularly. Indeed it functions in a way that is not so different
from the logic of injury in society at large, making the body a rhetorical and literal "placeholder" for the limits of corporate and state
behavior (Jain 2006, 28), except that the decision, as it is parceled
out in an endless schedule of doctor visits, briefings, rounds of paperwork, and persisting pain and impairment, never seems to arrive. In

the meantime, as they say, the Army owns your body, but you alone are obliged to own its pain.

A DRUG FOR SOLDIERS

Juares explained to me that soldiers should be given stimulants when they return from deployment. It was another conversation out on the Foundation porch. The day was quiet. Jimmy, Bullard, the other regulars, and Cindy, the Foundation director, were all gone. As I sat eating my lunch, Juares had come striding out of the building, and then I had half heard the fragments of his screaming phone conversation as he sat in the cab of his truck across the parking lot. He ended his call with a loud declamation, and then walked straight to me across the asphalt and introduced himself. Cindy had introduced us briefly a couple weeks earlier. Juares was in psychological operations and had been in a small unit working to train Iraqi Army soldiers.

Juares was in his ACUs. He held a tall silver-and-green can of energy drink down at his side. He has olive skin and his black hair was on the long side for a soldier. He looked to be somewhere in his early thirties. He was in the Texas National Guard, but had been on active duty for two years: first on a tour in Iraq, and now at the WTU. His speech was rapid, jittery, and just kept coming once we began talking. "So are you going to write a book and sell it to the RAND Corporation or something?" he asked when I told him about the project. I was a little taken aback. No, I told him, not really that kind of book. Had I read a book called *Downrange*? It's a sort of PTSD primer coauthored by a psychologist and Vietnam vet, and rich with bullet-pointed lists of warning signs, symptoms, and coping strategies (Cantrell and Dean 2005). It's about healing. There were dozens of copies of it sitting around the Foundation lounge and offices. "It's shit! It's not worth the shit it's written on!" he declared. I hadn't read it at the time and asked him what the authors said. "Well, I'm not gonna tell you what it says. You have to go and read it for yourself."

His tone was snippy and flat—angry without being hostile, fussy and matter of fact, and refracted through the jumpiness that seemed to have a hold on him. I tried again: What did he think the authors had gotten wrong? They didn't get into the details of real life, the little things. "It changes you permanently," he said emphatically. He launched into a haphazard list of details of daily life, swerving in and out of experiences from before, during, and after deployment. He described daily, taken-for-granted amenities of predeployment life, like going to work for regular hours, waking when you want to, and driving your own car. He veered from the everyday luxury of running water to its absence in Iraq, where there were port-o-johns and open latrines for sanitation. This led to his current preoccupation with the smells of trash and cigarette smoke; they bothered him back here because of their association with constant and overwhelming odors in Iraq. He worried about how the polluted, unhygienic conditions in Iraq were affecting his body and those of his fellow soldiers. He talked about desert heat and the physical toll of wearing armor—how your body hurt and was worn down from carrying all this weight.

Your behavior after you return is also altered. You are still used to ways of behaving from over there. For instance, you are on post, and you see the Black Hawks and Chinooks, or hear gunfire and explosions from out on the ranges, and sometimes you want to hit the ground. Cops pull you over and don't understand why you were driving fast down the middle of the road like you had to do in Iraq. You try to make yourself drive slow, and sometimes you drive too slowly or erratically, looking around at innocuous objects that could be IEDs or keeping your distance from other cars. Juares didn't like to be around people, so he went shopping at night. In the store one time, he was startled when he backed into a shopping cart that some-one left behind him, "and I just"—he threw his leg out—"kicked it away. It pisses me off! A guy came up behind me in the airport and clapped me on the shoulder to say 'Thank you for your service,' and I"—again he twisted and raised his arm to demonstrate—"almost punched him. You don't do that! It pisses me off!" In restaurants, he sat with his back to the wall to scan constantly and find the exits.

Laying these things out, Juares moved back and forth in time, so that the sense of causality became both diffuse and overwhelm-ing, with all the details woven into the fabric of the most banal things. The ones from before his deployment were filtered through the awareness of imminent departure and interruptible momentum, the stress of embarking on a multistaged journey toward a fearful destination that could be indefinitely interrupted at any time—a temporality of anticipation at once relentless and fragile. The ones from during deployment traveled into the future to affect him even now, after his return.

With all these things, Juares was adamant: *they were not psychological symptoms*. Symptoms were what therapists talked about, he said with scornful dismissal. "I hate these fucks!" They saw behaviors, and mapped them onto some idea of war and trauma that made them signs of an invented entity called PTSD. Civilians and nondeployed medical and psychiatric personnel couldn't understand this sensory and bodily dimension or its persistent and overwhelming quality because they hadn't been to Iraq; their bodies hadn't been there. They offer talk therapy, biofeedback, acupuncture, "and all this other shit," but none of it accounted for how you actually feel, how *soldiers* actually feel. If someone got in a car wreck here—Juares pointed out toward the road—these therapists would diagnose them with PTSD and prescribe them antidepressants. But they want to give this same civilian diagnosis and civilian drug to soldiers, whose experience is of a whole other kind. Soldiers get special medications, like vaccines for anthrax and smallpox. Why not military-grade drugs for stress as well? And forget antidepressants anyway; they didn't make any sense. Soldiers are full of surging endorphins set off by everyday stimuli. It was a state to which they had become accustomed, and antidepressants just masked it, suppressed it, and didn't address the authentic nature of the problem.

What soldiers really need, Juares explained, is a powerful stimulant. Here I looked at the energy drink in his hand but said nothing. This would help them come down gradually from the hyperactivated state in which they dwelled. He gestured with his hand to show the ascending levels of arousal of a regular civilian, a noncombat soldier, a soldier trained for war, and at the very top, a soldier in combat or who has been to combat. There was an ideal spot to inhabit near the top of the range. "Soldiers are very high-strung. I'm very high-strung." Being a soldier means being on edge, a constant state of bodily activation. A stimulant would help soldiers come down gradually from the very top, and relieve them of the stress and exhaustion that came with it, without dropping them so low as to become militarily ineffective. But such a drug does not yet exist.

Juares was describing a condition that is persistent, pervasive, and perhaps even desirable. But PTSD, like the concept of trauma more generally, is organized around a linear etiology in which an isolated, exceptional event unfolds into a neat chain of cause and effect. Trauma is something "outside the range of usual human experience," to use the language by which PTSD was first formalized in 1980 in the third volume of the *Diagnostic and Statistical Manual of Mental Disorders* (*DSM-III*) (American Psychiatric Association 1980, 236). The memory of the traumatic event is not fully processed, and so it intrusively returns, over and over, prompting emotional numbing, persistent avoidance of things that trigger it, and physiological arousal. The refusal of the traumatic memory to be safely synthesized is what adds *disorder* to routine posttraumatic stress. Sufferers are "stuck" on their trauma, to use the therapeutic language. PTSD is a disease of memory.

The generally accepted mechanism for how PTSD works is that sufferers steer clear of those stimuli in their everyday life—triggers—that resemble the sensory imprint associated with an original traumatic event, and thus precipitate not only intrusive and upsetting memories but also intense physiological arousal. Avoidance is thought to be pathological because it prevents the successful processing of the traumatic memory, and indeed some of the most demonstrably effective therapies for PTSD involve exposure to the traumatic memory (Institute of Medicine 2007; RAND 2008), whether through talk therapy and the narrative revisiting of the event, controlled in vivo confrontation with triggering stimuli, virtual reality simulation (National Institute of Mental Health 2008), or other means. A clinician might be inclined to understand Juares's elaborate model of war trauma as a justification for avoidance behavior or even itself a kind of avoidance, and would probably also take note of his symptomatic objectless anger and vigilance, intensity of affect, and abundance of triggers. These things, combined with his having been in a combat zone (which he refused to tell me anything about), are the stuff of which PTSD diagnoses are made.

Juares's account of PTSD as a purely civilian affliction contravenes the actual history of PTSD as a medical category in the United States, Canada, and western Europe: the disorder's nineteenth-century roots are in the recognition of "hysterical" responses to both industrial accidents and warfare, and its contemporary medicalization in the *DSM-III* came directly in response to the traumas suffered by US Vietnam War veterans (Caruth 1995; Young 1995). US war veterans, in this sense, were the raw material for the invention of PTSD. But Juares is correct in his exasperated observation that PTSD makes a single object out of a whole range of experiences. As the disorder has been defined and redefined over the last several decades, it has come to include the psychological dimensions of sexual assault and abuse, genocide, industrial accidents, and imprisonment. And the category of clinical trauma has been expanded so that it assigns equal recognition to the sufferers, perpetrators, and witnesses of violence (Fassin and Rechtman 2009). The soldier potentially occupies all three of these roles, making him both the archetype of trauma and its special case. Unlike the refugee or rape victim, the soldier's training prepares him for violence and his work exposes him directly to it as a matter of course. Juares's rather occult formulation has at its heart a kind of critique of the understanding of posttraumatic stress, "disordered" or otherwise. The problem he describes is both structural and phenomenological. Juares was not the only soldier to suggest that many of the phenomena that signify this condition are simply normal features of soldiering, even if they are also disruptive and discomfiting. Nor was he alone in his emphasis on distinctive, unwanted bodily sensitivities, rather than on strictly ideational, mnemonic, or emotional upset.

Juares normalizes the putative symptoms of PTSD as simply the way things are, and even valorizes them as the part of the capacity and constitution that make someone a normal, good, effective soldier. In military health care as in wider public discourse, stigma is repeatedly cited as one of the most significant barriers between troubled soldiers and the balm of medication and psychotherapy: the shame of emotional frailty and debility, the more general stain of mental illness, and the imagined (and false) link between the posttraumatic stress and violent behavior. While such institutional and cultural stigmas are real concerns for soldiers, Juares's account doesn't seem to be a direct reaction to any sense that the condition is the result of weakness. He was not alone in his normalizing assertions. For example, all soldiers seem to know the posttraumatic stress screening questions that they will be asked in their mandatory Post-Deployment Health Assessment (PDHA), and what answers to give. "Did you see dead bodies?" "Did anyone you know get hurt?" With these questions, they want to know if you're crazy, Ernie, the infantry platoon sergeant, told me, "but I've been like this as long as I can remember." Ernie joked with the woman who administered his PDHA, and his entire account of it is punctuated with laughter.

> The psychologist lady comes up and asks you questions. . . . This lady said, "Did you ever have any dreams of shooting people?"
>
> "Well, do I ever dream about shooting people?" I said, "You don't have to dream about it when you do it in real life."
>
> "Good point!"
>
> 'Cause you know, when they ask you those questions, some of those questions are personal, and you don't . . . want people to think you're crazy, 'cause then they might send you to another unit or something like that. . . . I don't want people to write shit down in my medical records for anything. So they ask questions: "How do you feel about being home?"
>
> "I feel damn good!"
>
> "You ever have any suicidal tendencies?"
>
> "Never." . . .
>
> And then everyone goes, "Do you guys feel invincible? Do you have feelings of invincibility?"
>
> "Invincible? No. Unbreakable, yeah." I did a lot of stupid shit and was OK. I wrecked a motorcycle and was OK. All the cars I've blown up and totaled, I've been OK. Every time, thank God [*knocks on table*], I've never been hurt. All the times that we've been hit with stuff [in Iraq], I've never been hurt. So when the lady said, "Do you have feelings of invincibility," I go, "Unbreakable, yeah; invincible, no."
>
> And she looks at me like I'm crazy and stuff like that, and she asks me other questions. And I say, "Do you want me to answer them the way you want me to answer them, or do you want me to tell you the truth? 'Cause I don't think you wanna hear [that]; they'd take me away in a straightjacket." [*He laughs.*]
>
> "Oh forget it—good sense of humor, you're feeling good? OK, we're done."

"I was asking a serious question! Do you want me to answer you the truth, or do you want me to tell you what you wanna hear?" She thinks I'm joking. But I'll tell the damn truth. . . . [E]veryone says, do you think you have any mental conditions from any—what's it called, PTSD? Do you have any posttraumatic stress disorder? Do you have any PTSD? "Naw, I've been like this for as long as I can remember."

Soldiers know what all of the questions in the PDHA point toward, and they know that answering them truthfully in the affirmative could, at the very least, keep them tied up with doctors and counselors when all they want to do is go on leave and see their families. Even worse, it could stick with them in their medical records, rendering them (officially or unofficially) unsuitable for their jobs, ineligible for a security clearance, or unfit for promotion. Aside from these structural disincentives, there is a basic cognitive dissonance to norms implied by the PDHA questions: if you answer them truthfully, they will make you seem crazy, but all the contextual cues of your own experience say otherwise.

During his Desert Storm deployment, Ernie was assigned to clean up body parts along the "Highway of Death," the road connecting Baghdad to Kuwait City where thousands of retreating Iraqi soldiers were bombed to cinders. "And they never gave me no counseling for that shit! So I figured it wasn't a big deal." Civilians and civilian clinicians simply don't understand what war is like, and it is only on contact with the civilian world that the experience of soldiering is made to seem crazy. "Everything you go through, you go through with the same people you see day in and day out," Ernie said. "So when you're talking about it, it's perfectly normal because you were doing the same shit I was doing, so you're talking about it like it's nothing." Worse than merely misunderstanding, civilians offer diagnoses that judge the soldier. "Combat is fun," a recently retired soldier who had done tours in Iraq and Afghanistan told me one night at an American Legion bar. Combat isn't what gives you PTSD, he asserted. "Being subliminally told by a twenty-seven-year-old woman therapist that 'you were in a terrible situation' and you should feel bad about what you did is what gives you PTSD!" In this perversely apt inversion of normal and exceptional, an archetypal catch-22, it is the experience of diagnosis and therapy that makes you crazy, both fitting you with the label and upending your own felt sense of normalcy. And diagnosis here also becomes the foil for articulating a highly particular sense of normalcy against the feminized naïveté and medicalized morality of those who have not been to war.

The problem of normalcy is woven into the heart of PTSD as a diagnostic category. PTSD was first defined in the wake of the Vietnam War as a "normal response to an abnormal situation."[5] The "normalcy" of the response and "abnormality" of the circumstances were crucial to placing the onus for soldiers' mental distress, and therefore for their care and compensation, squarely on the government. The *DSM*'s definitions of traumatic stressors are incredibly broad.[6] The events and memories assumed to produce these stressors are essentially impossible to verify (Young 2010), making the diagnostic category so widely encompassing as to risk being meaningless. This referential vagueness is especially vexing in the case of combat. Exposure to violence is a routine condition of being at war. But in the genealogy of PTSD, combat is treated as the paradigmatic traumatic experience. Subsequent revisions to the *DSM* have cast the net even wider but left this fundamental contradiction intact: the diagnostic category meant to help soldiers depends on exceptionalizing and pathologizing the routine work of being a soldier at war.

Given these conflicting standards of normalcy, the apparent remoteness of PTSD diagnosis—how Juares rails against therapeutic platitudes, and Ernie names all the disorder's connotations yet gropes for its name, and then only to dismiss it—is not surprising. This sense of wildly misunderstood normalcy all goes to Juares's more basic assertion that what soldiers experience is too qualitatively complex to fit under the abstract diagnostic label with which it is saddled, too visceral to be called merely mnemonic or cognitive, and too fundamental to be called pathological. Trauma's language of shock and eventfulness makes less sense, and generates less useful understanding, when these feelings are the routine and shared result of training, soldierly disposition, deployment, and combat.

Juares didn't want drugs for his emotions—antidepressants—but for his body. Plenty of the soldiers I met would mention traumatic memories, nightmares, and intrusive thoughts. But I was surprised over and over again by their emphasis that it was as much their bodies as their minds that refused to calm down. You're going about your business at Fort Hood, and you hear a helicopter or the sunny-day thunder of artillery fire rumbling in from the ranges, and before you even realize you heard it your guts turn to ice, your palms get clammy, and your whole body is arched and alert, ready to go. You might even suddenly find yourself on the ground, with your body having thrown itself to the dirt before your brain has a chance to think about what's going on. One soldier described being at a party when a friend took out a handgun and fired it into the air. She was on the ground before she knew it. She seemed to brush off being startled, but she was angry that it aggravated her knee injury.

The way that soldiers talk about these bodily responses brooks no narrativization or translation into a temporality of recollection. The sound of the helicopter does not necessarily recall an unpleasant image from Iraq that then provokes an unpleasant feeling, nor do soldiers necessarily think all of the sudden that they are somewhere else. Soldiers' emphasis on somatic manifestations arguably belies some need to segregate mind from body, but in practice it makes a muddle of both terms and the distinction between them. What soldiers describe is far less a matter of meaning than of *feeling*—a feeling that is a memory, but that follows a direct line from sensory stimulus to neuromotor response, bypassing consciousness, thought, and interpretation. In this way, Juares's conception of trauma suggests an affective conception of soldierly embodiment that is keyed less to the bright-line breaks between viscera, nervous system, brain, and conscious thought, and more to the indistinctions within that continuum.[7] It's less concerned with an arbitrary criterion of normalcy, and more with a rebellious, unruly body that has now developed a personality and gotten out of control, "retain[ing] an affecting agency all its own," as Katie Stewart writes (1996, 132). "I just want to get off this roller coaster," Dime told me, miming a swoop of hill and valley with his hand. That morning in formation he had heard a helicopter fly over "and all of the sudden I feel like I have to take a shit!" Dime had nightmares, depression, and spikes of anger as well as an ex-wife who had taken his kids away. He had seen his friends die in front of him. But with all that, what he felt he needed was to be able to domesticate his body again, calm it down and balance it out.

Dime's reaction suggests that PTSD diagnosis misunderstands something fundamental about soldiers' vulnerability—not only what their "usual human experience" consists of but also what that normal experience *feels like*, both in normal and disordered forms. With its emphasis on disorder, there is no space in the diagnosis PTSD in which to say, as Ernie does, "I've been like this as long as I can remember," or rather, "I've *felt* like this as long as I can remember." In this context, the typical therapeutic focus on memory and cognition as a way of confronting PTSD may be simply too mentalistic. Why fixate on how it's all in your mind when it's not just in your mind but also in your life, and in everyone else's life too, and what is giving you trouble is your body? All that talk lacks the hammer-blow efficacy of Juares's fantasized military-grade upper. It can't compete with the way the body takes over in response to innocuous situations, sounds, smells, and talk—the way that "the organism itself is beginning to think" (Wilson 2004a, 82).

This unruly body tells a story about power, but perhaps a less familiar one, for the inclination to narrativize and textualize the body can do injustice to its vagaries, agentive capacities, and affective intensities (Csordas 1993; Haraway 1991; Scheper-Hughes and Lock 1987; Wilson 2004a). In this story, the body "is and is not mine," to borrow a phrase from Butler (2004, 26). It is attached to others and available to their scrutiny, it is subject to the institution in every detail, and now it has become actively traitorous even to the soldier's conscious command. This third dispossession plays off the other two: the soldier is bound to his loved ones, and their vulnerabilities are his, but his discombobulated body deprives him of the pleasure of merely "being himself" with them. The same disciplinary power by which the Army "owns" the soldier's body also empowers that body, crafting it into an instrument whose capacities are a source of pride and self-worth for the soldier, but that are called into question when the body rebels. As with the binds of heat, weight, metal, and gore, the soldier's body becomes the instrument and raw material of sovereignty, and the soldier himself loses sovereignty over it.

None of this is to say whether Ernie, Juares, Dime, or any of them do or do not have PTSD, or whether the disorder is real. As Ian Hacking (1995, 7) suggests, it is always important to ask, in response to the question of whether a thing is real, "A real what?" PTSD names real sets of symptoms that have real effects on people, and in the process it does describe a kind of shared experience. And it links these things to real institutional and social consequences.[8] If the diagnosis is alienating and "tyrannical," it is also an indispensable medium for linking individual ills to collective systems of healing and redress (Rosenberg 2002). At the same time, the category PTSD is not always meaningful for soldiers in the ways we might expect it to be, especially when, too use the argot of PTSD, they are "stuck" in some liminal state between traumatic eventfulness and a stable diagnostic constellation.

But I would argue that they are stuck not merely because they need to move on and adjust, or because they haven't been properly diagnosed. They are stuck because there is little conceptual language for this field of normalized posttraumatic stress that they inhabit—a field overdetermined though often insufficiently described by PTSD diagnosis. Soldiers know that posttraumatic stress is real, in both its so-called normal and disordered forms. They bond over its intensity and note its pathological excesses in themselves and others. Many of them do have nightmares, intrusive memories, and emotional scars that they link to precise events. Yet their emphasis on the somatic dimension makes it clear how, when it comes to labeling things, the pieces have not been arranged so that they make sense to soldiers. Or perhaps it is that soldiers are not interested in that kind of arrangement or convinced of its importance. For even if this state is something that they must "move through" and mediate with narrative and carefully reformed cognitive-behavioral mechanisms, it also has the stubborn autonomy of the flesh. In their talk it is an immediate and grounded thing—this is what they *feel like*—while the diagnosis remains artificial, abstract, and arbitrary.

These soldiers are stuck in another way: stuck at the very point at which psychiatry, medical anthropology, or trauma theory are inclined, at the same time as they provide valuable bases for therapeutic intervention, to move perhaps too quickly to consolidate fragmentary and even dubious collections of symptoms under a single label, and explain, narrativize, and synthesize them just as they would encourage the afflicted to do. Most psychological, literary, and medical anthropological literature on trauma focuses on individuals and groups that have been diagnosed, or as in the instance of Holocaust survivors, are otherwise widely recognized as having been traumatized. The soldiers I am talking about here were variously hesitant, cagey, and strategic when it came to taking on any such mantle of victimhood or medical pathology, and in various ways they kept PTSD diagnosis at a cautious arm's length, even when it was applied to them.

One day I asked several of my acquaintances at the Foundation if they had been diagnosed with PTSD and if they thought that they had it. Some said that they thought maybe they had something like it, but not as bad as other people did, so they didn't think it was a big deal. Those who were contemplating leaving the Army talked about the importance of getting it on their record—so that it could be factored into their disability compensation and they could get VA care for it—and those who were staying in cited the need to keep it off, so as not to jeopardize their promotability down the line. Juares was getting out, and he said he was happy to have the diagnosis, since the Army was going to pay him for it. "But I'm normal," he insisted. He didn't think he had it. "I'm not gonna kill somebody. I'm not gonna rob a bank."

The diagnosis exists separately from the lived condition, not just because it fails to encompass soldiers' experience adequately, but also because soldiers know full well how readily the Army will bend and reshape diagnostic categories to suit its own purposes. The symptomatology of PTSD overlaps with several other diagnoses, including various anxiety, depressive, and personality disorders, and there have been numerous accounts over the past several years of individual and coordinated efforts by Army and VA personnel to reclassify PTSD cases as these other, nonservice-connected maladies (Finnegan 2008; Hunter 2010; Maze 2007). This is not to take anything away from the crucial, dedicated work going on in military and VA medicine. But diagnosis inevitably overlaps with disciplinary control and material value, especially in institutional settings (Petryna 2002; Rhodes 2004), and this only compounds the ambivalent unreality that PTSD seems to possess for many soldiers. On the one hand, the label PTSD often does not accord directly with soldiers' lived experience, and on the other hand, the diagnosis is inseparable from institutional structures that soldiers are suspicious of and dependent on. The diagnosis has so much attached to it in terms of material value and stigma. While the feeling of posttraumatic stress makes the body into a traitor, or at least a rowdy and unpredictable nuisance, a PTSD diagnosis makes it into a pathologized commodity. As with a physical injury, the body becomes an instrument of another kind—one that the soldier is obliged to demonstrate is broken.

To the extent that soldiers' mental distress is the product of fundamental features of modern war fighting and not simply the result of structural flaws, leaders and policymakers also remain in a sticky position when it comes to mitigating PTSD. On the one hand, they are obliged to acknowledge the tremendous toll taken by long and repeated deployments. On the other hand, their proposed interventions will help alleviate soldiers' suffering but cannot stop it at its source. Recent Army statements on psychological health, for instance, including two massive and widely publicized survey reports (Department of the Army 2010, 2012), have made a point of emphasizing so-called PTS—posttraumatic stress without "disorder"—along with a positive psychology-based concern with resiliency and "posttraumatic growth."[9] (These new trends are explored further in the postscript.) Such rhetorical gestures toward the destigmatization and de-medicalization of traumatic stress mean little, however, if they do not address the full complexity of soldiers' experience and take honest account of the constraints by which soldiers are bound.[10] Scholars in a range of disciplines have observed the potential iatrogenic effects of PTSD diagnosis: being told that one has a disease can ultimately hinder a return to normalcy more than it helps (Horwitz 2012). At the same time, caution about overdiagnosis is inevitably entangled with the massive amounts of money on the line in questions over who will get treated and compensated for disability, not to mention the even weightier moral economy of who bears responsibility for the effects of violence. What Juares, Ernie, and others describe here is a free-floating condition that is intimately familiar to them and that they will surrender to larger interpretive schemes—the schemes that decide fitness for duty and promotion as well as the level of disability payments—only on their own terms.

AT HOME

Dee, the technician who got pranked with the plate of spaghetti, volunteered for guard duty on transport convoys. She rode as a gunner, sitting behind the .50-caliber machine gun in the turret of a Humvee, and went out almost every day for six months. She had been home for nearly two months when she, her husband, and their three-year-old daughter went into town Christmas shopping. They stopped at a Red Robin for lunch. It was busy, and they sat down by the entrance to wait for their table. The hostess gave Dee's daughter a balloon. The guy next to Dee, a man in his sixties, was wearing a Vietnam veteran cap, and she struck up a conversation with him. As they were chatting, the balloon got away, floated to the ceiling, and popped on a giant metallic Christmas ornament right above Dee's head, and she instantly ducked her head down between her knees. The vet put a friendly hand on her shoulder and told her dryly not to worry. "It'll only take fifteen years for that to stop." I asked her how it made her feel to hear that. "It made me feel normal," she said.

Things in her marriage weren't normal, however. She couldn't be close to her husband. She was used to sleeping alone, she said (intense sensitivity to personal space is classed as a symptom of PTSD). One night Dee rolled away from him, sat up, and said, "You need to get out of the bed, now." He was furious with her the next morning, but she didn't even remember it. They didn't have sex anymore. They rarely even touched. Enraged one night, she yelled at him, "I'm sorry you're not getting laid, but I'm still seeing my buddies get killed in my head!" He felt resentful and emasculated; he had been in the Navy, but he had never been in combat, and he had gained weight while she was gone. She internalized his criticisms of her distance and thought that she wasn't doing enough to make things right again.

Dee had traumatic reactions to unexpected things. One night, months after getting back, she was watching _Transformers_ with her husband and daughter. The opening scene shows a desert military base being destroyed by a malevolent robot. She watched it, knowing it was just a movie, but even as the dramatic tension in the scene was building, before any of the destruction actually started, she could feel the hyperarousal coming on—her heart raced, and cold sweat ran down her back. Dee left the room and sat on the kitchen floor with her head between her knees. Her daughter came up to her and offered her apple juice. "For the first time in my life I couldn't sleep," she told me. Her Army friends used to call her Cat because she would curl up anywhere—in lockers or under vehicles—to take a nap. But now her mind would zip through a chain of relentless associations that always ended up somewhere dark. "It was not hard to connect taking my daughter's Christmas pictures with .50 cals," she remarked.

They were working through it a little bit, Dee and her husband. But a month from when we spoke, she would be leaving for a couple weeks of field training. And another month after that she was slated to leave the state for an NCO training course, and more likely than not she would be deployed to Iraq again before long. "This is how our marriage works," she said. She and her husband were both used to deployments and being away from one another. Except that now it wasn't just the separation that was hard; it was all this other stuff folding back on top of it. Being apart wouldn't save them, yet it would make it possible for them to carry on.

After Bullard got blown up, he woke up in the hospital. His buddies told him he had gotten out of the demolished Bradley and was wandering around babbling, but he didn't remember it. He was in the hospital in Balad in central Iraq for a couple weeks, and then Landstuhl for a couple more, and then Brook Army Medical Center in San Antonio for an additional month. When his wife came and met him there, he said, and he was utterly emotionless. His responsibility as a Bradley driver had been to bring everyone home safe, and he had failed. They hadn't gotten to come back. "I felt like I shouldn't have come back. I was trying to keep myself from coming back." There was lots of stuff he hadn't told his wife about what it was like. He still didn't tell her about the IEDs, all the vehicles getting destroyed, and his soldiers getting killed—anything that would have made her worry when he was there, he told me, he still kept to himself or talked about only to his buddies.

So it was hard for her to understand, he said. And it was hard for him to feel dependent on her, to feel taken care of. With his TBI, he had to stick to a really regulated routine and double check everything. And she had to double check it too, which he didn't always like. It was like she didn't trust him to do it. "You feel like a kid." At other times, though, she acted like there was nothing wrong, like there was no injury. She was still getting used to what he was like, the things that bothered him, and what he could and couldn't do. But she was patient; she read the medical literature when there were things he couldn't explain. "She tries so hard," he said. "She's really, really understanding."

One last story is worth mentioning here. Childs was a Texas National Guard chaplain in his early sixties. His office shelves were full of philosophy texts in French and German, but because of his TBI he can't read them anymore. The forms and meanings of words slopped around in his brain like a bowl of noodles, he said. He would try to grab one, and it would slip away. He was at Camp Slayer, a luxurious former Ba'ath Party compound at the edge of Baghdad International Airport, and a 122-millimeter rocket hit the chapel where he was conducting a service on the morning of the first Iraqi elections, in 2005. The TBI came on slowly: mood swings, memory loss, and Tourette's-like swearing fits. Then he had a stroke—a mild one, but scary.

The stress doesn't just go away the day you come home, he said. When he was home with his family, he was solitary and withdrawn. His kids could relate to him all right, but his wife didn't really believe anything happened to him, that he ever saw any action. One day she noticed a dark stain on his boot. It was the blood of a soldier who Childs had been with when he died. "That's Browning's blood," he told her. "No it's not," she said. "You don't love me anymore," she told him. He was still deployable. He wanted to go back.

This all sounds grim, and so I want to emphasize that there is abundant good feeling here too. The reunions are joyous. Soldiers are happy to be back, and their families are happy to have them home. People describe how every smile, touch, and common comfort swells with fresh significance and value. Sometimes, I was told, the adjustments are seamless, or close to it. There are countless points at which the wounded do heal up, the stressed out do relax, and the neglected, bullied, lonely, and bereaved begin to find some solace. But again, this usually happens in increments, by slow labor that most of the time resembles nothing so much as waiting out the feeling of being stuck. And the current temporality of Army life is short on opportunities to allow time to pass without new stresses coming to bear. The stresses of exposure and separation do not end with reunion, and they are not necessarily reversible. Just about everyone is changed. In that transformation, vulnerability extends itself into these intimate spaces, asserting itself in moves of isolation, withdrawal, and holding back. Where before it made its presence felt through absence, now it works in the barriers that people raise, or spaces they carve out between one another and within themselves. The soldier blocks out his injury, swallows his anxious thoughts, and works to perform the limited roles afforded him by the rules that make his world. The spouse seeks only certain information, is granted only certain information, and is even distrustful of information altogether. And the Army itself looms over the whole scene—what it demands and expects, what it gives with one hand and takes with the other.

UNCOMFORTABLY NUMB

What unites the accounts and examples above is the labor of *not feeling*, the self-conscious mastery of affect, emotion, and physical pain by soldiers and spouses, and the institutionally imposed haze of medication, emotional and bodily discipline, and compelled endurance. There is a whole range of gripes about Army life that revolve around the stress of managing or suppressing feelings, along with more neutral or positive commentary that valorizes such discipline as a way to empower oneself, protect others, and maintain one's efficacy and capacities. People live with this ambivalence.

But numbing is the bad side, the critique. I met a helicopter pilot who had become a massage therapist after her service ended. "Everyone in the Army walks around all hush-hush," she said, because there's so much you're not supposed to say, so much you're just supposed to take. It blocks your throat chakra, she explained, and stops you up. She mimed a hunched posture, her body curled in around the imagined point of blockage in her throat. All that restraint builds up in the body. When she was stressed out, her Army psychiatrist just wanted to give her antidepressants and redeploy her. That was "the Army solution," she said—chemically inhibiting the feelings instead of addressing them. In this sense, it is important to understand anesthesia as something more complicated than simply the absence of feeling; it is the imposed compulsion not to feel. It can be accomplished equally by foisting Prozac on one soldier and denying Percocet to another, demanding that physical or psychic pain be shaken off, or pathologizing injury as weakness or a failure of character. The result is not the banishment of feeling but rather the "benign brutality" (Povinelli 2006, 204) of having to actively ignore it. This is an anesthetic that never quite takes hold and never fully wears off, and so you remain perpetually aware, even if only at that proprioceptive level where feeling fades off into a tingly fog, of the feelings that you aren't feeling, which lie buried between brief punctuations of consciousness.

4

Vicissitudes of Love

The departure and return events for deploying soldiers are called manifests. They are a bureaucratic roll call combined with either a prolonged, devastating farewell or a quick, joyful reunion. They have a sort of folk-mythical significance in military communities as scenes of eventfulness and intensity that define the collective experience of absence, anxiety, separation, strained attachment, the stone-faced inhumanity of the war apparatus, and the extravagantly painful human frailty of the people caught up in it. People wanted to know if I had gone to one; they wanted to make sure that I did go.

A lot of the time the manifests are held in gyms, of which there are several on post. Indeed, the gym is such a familiar scene of imminent absence and endangerment that its bleachers and brick walls often provide the setting for the ads for military life insurance that appear in *Army Times*. It seems both odd and appropriate that this wrenching ritual of departure should be set in a place laden with youthful associations of sex, competition, discipline, play, humiliation, and burgeoning bodily prowess. The gyms look like normal, good-size high school or YMCA gyms, with patriotic slogans and icons—soaring eagles or geometric designs of stars and stripes—on their cinderblock walls above stacked bleachers. Yet they do so much duty for manifests that there are signs hanging up permanently with big block-letter messages specific to the occasion, but serving as constant reminders, it would seem, to soldiers playing basketball or lifting weights. Above the doors out to the parking lot there are ones proclaiming "COME HOME SAFE"; on the opposite wall, so that it is the first thing you see when you enter, is a large "WELCOME HOME" sign. The rooms are configured for coming from and going to war.

For whatever reason, this manifest is outdoors, on the lawn and parking lot next to the unit headquarters building on Battalion Avenue. There is a long line of battalion headquarters buildings stretching for a mile or maybe more through this part of the post, and like all the others, this one is square, bland, and tan, inside and out, with not much to it but a long linoleum-floored corridor, a reception desk, a conference room, and a handful of offices. The walls are mostly bare. In front, a parched yet well-kept lawn slopes to the street; behind, there is a long stretch of parking lot—filling now with cars—and then a barracks; and next door is a narrow, equally nondescript warehouse, where in a couple of hours soldiers will line up to receive their weapons. Sometimes these buildings have a sleepy feeling; on the few occasions I've been in them before, privates on desk duty kill time while they wait through a long afternoon for the phone to ring. But today this place is lively, with soldiers and civilian family members moving in and out the doors, calling to one another from one room to the next.

The manifest is for several hundred soldiers, a good part of a field artillery battalion. Some others from the same unit are deploying the next day, and a smaller number have already gone ahead. Field artillery is the only combat arms branch with positions open to women, but still the soldiers are mostly men. An acquaintance, Danielle, invited me. Her husband, Gene, is a senior NCO who has already served two OIF tours, so he got assigned to the unit's rear detachment, the part that stays in garrison while the rest is deployed. When I first met Danielle, she was adamant about steering clear of military wives during deployment, avoiding what she described as the pointless drama and hassle that came with life in a military community. She singled out the FRGs, which are organized by the Army to foster communication, mutual aid, and social connection among soldiers' spouses, for special scorn: nothing but gossip and bad energy. Originally, when it looked like Gene was going to go, Danielle had been planning on moving back to Georgia, where she is from. But now, somehow, in spite of her previous reluctance, she had ended up in charge of the FRG for Gene's company—FRGs are organized parallel to their Army counterparts, and it is typical for the spouse of a senior NCO to serve as the corresponding company-level FRG head.

Danielle—tall, broad-shouldered, and with a disposition at once cheery and forceful—had spotted me in the parking lot of the Foundation a few weeks previous, told me the unit was deploying, and then shepherded me along to a whole series of events leading up to their departure. First there had been a mass FRG meeting in a giant, nondescript auditorium, a briefing for all the spouses and families of the soldiers in the battalion; there were handouts, PowerPoint slides, and a series of presentations outlining basic details of the deployment. The soldiers would be at Camp Anaconda, a massive base in Taji, Iraq. There were pictures of the white vinyl-sided trailers mounted on cinderblocks and studded with air conditioners where they would be staying. They might be incommunicado for a bit after getting there, but then they would be able to keep in touch via Internet, phone cards, and the Army's Defense Switched Network phones. They discussed Red Cross messages, which bear emergency notification of sick or dying family members to soldiers, and the limited circumstances that would merit emergency leave—the Army was taking these soldiers to Iraq, and it would not bring them back until it was done with them. There were specific people that spouses and parents should contact in the rear detachment with questions or problems. Before the meeting, Danielle and the other FRG section leaders stood at tables in the crowded lobby, handing out deployment care packages for the soldiers: heavy, purse-size plastic bags of toiletries, sunscreen, candy, stationery, and pamphlets on stress management and communication skills. These were either assembled by the FRG itself or donated by an outside group like the Foundation; the Army does not provide them.

The next event was a family day, a couple days later, a sort of company picnic for the entire brigade that Gene described as "mandatory fun." There was barbecue, furnished for free by a host of chefs from all over central Texas, served under tents on a wide, bare field watched over by the facade of the post's stadium and a giant water tower. There was a flag football tournament with teams drawn from the deploying battalions, and speeches, award presentations, and some impromptu line dancing to Steve Earle's outlaw ode "Copperhead Road" blaring tinnily over the PA system.

The manifest, in contrast, isn't about getting ready or getting together; it is about saying good-bye. The soldiers will gather, wait, attend to a few last duties, and then, with little fanfare, assemble in formation and board the plain white school buses that will carry them across the post to Robert Gray Army Airfield, where they will board a plane to Kuwait and then drive in convoy to Baghdad. The wives, children, friends, and parents of many of these soldiers will gather and wait with them, passing an uneasy last couple of hours together before a sudden and painful good-bye; they will watch the buses depart and then they themselves will disperse.

Around 10:00 a.m., soldiers show up in uniform, toting massive bags: big rucksacks that they will carry with them, and even bigger duffel bags, which get dumped in a pile and loaded into a plain white box van. The soldiers cluster in groups and stand in lines across the parking lot, lawn, and loading dock next door, waiting on squad or platoon leaders or comrades with clipboards, who then check their names off one or another list. They pass in and out a back door of the headquarters building that opens on to a strip of sidewalk and the parking lot where the buses will pull up before long.

Just inside that door, in a vacant-looking lounge area—windowless, high-ceilinged, with a wall of vending machines and the furniture pushed into one corner—I stand with Danielle along with some other FRG ladies and a group of civilian volunteers who have come to help see the soldiers off. They have laid out a couple of folding tables with red-, white-, and blue-frosted cupcakes decorated with the unit's informal dragon crest (all artillery units are nicknamed after dragons of some variety), little bags of snacks and candy, and sodas and bottled water. They also hand out stuffed toy bears that the soldiers can take with them and, the idea is, give to Iraqi kids, or to their own kids here, now, before they leave. Soldiers and their kids come up and avail themselves of these things, and Danielle and the other wives and volunteers all chat smilingly with them. The volunteers work for a big telecom company; they tell me that they stuff and stitch up the bears on their lunch hours. They are in their fifties or sixties; some of them were in the military themselves, or have spouses who were, and several of them come regularly to manifests at Fort Hood. The bears, done mostly in brightly colored print fabrics, are small and squishy enough that they stuff easily into the side cargo pocket of ACU pants. Before long, in the gathering crowd of milling soldiers, you can see the little button-eyed faces and fabric arms and legs sticking out of pockets and the side straps of backpacks, vivid against the drab ACU camouflage. One lady explains to me she makes sure the privates and privates first class (PFCs) all get one. "I tell them they can use it as a pillow." Privates and PFCs don't have pillows because they can't afford them, she says, but then adds, "They're for the kids. I really hope they make it to the kids."

Outside, the soldiers settle all over the lawn, joined now by wives, kids, parents, siblings, and friends, forming a field of drab olive and crew cuts interspersed with blue jeans, T-shirts, sneakers, bare limbs, and long hair. Two little girls in matching Supergirl shirts alternate between messy bites of cupcakes and clinging to their dad's camouflage-clad legs. A teenage boy holds the leash of a little pit bull puppy with sores on its back. The crowd grows and spills across the lawn, around to the front of the building. It is a summer day in Texas, mostly overcast but still hot, and people crowd into the scant patches of shade. Soldiers without family or visitors to see them off sit in groups by themselves. Families sprawl in big, multigenerational packs. Little kids run around playing tag. Couples hold each other as closely as they can in public. It is an exercise in waiting, as everyone sits through these precious and agonizing last couple of hours. As I skirt the edge of the crowd, it seems, from the outside, surprisingly upbeat, not much different than the family day the week before. There is the same mix of soldiers with soldiers, soldiers with families, and families with families, as well as the same odd combination of tedious official obligation and the pleasure of socializing. The tension of the looming deployment is surprisingly *not* palpable, or at least not to me.

Danielle introduces me to the wives of the other NCOs, a couple of the officers, and the battalion commander. For many of them, this is their third deployment. One of these women, married to an E-5 and in her early thirties, tells me, "A lot of young couples won't make it." Another one of the women gestures out to the crowd of soldiers and points out that almost half wear no patch on their right shoulder, indicating that they have not deployed before. They have all been told to expect the deployment to last fifteen months, and though they will end up coming home in twelve instead, this preemptive extension, a whole year plus another season, weighs on everyone's mind. "Just stay busy," the sergeant's wife says—that's how you get through. An acquaintance tells me, "I've already cried once," at home, in private. When we talked a few months earlier, she mentioned she preferred to stay away from the manifests, that she and her husband and kids didn't want to be around other people's negativity—crying, fighting, and recriminations—when they were trying to say their own good-byes. People who have been through it before have already done their talk at home. Maybe that accounts for the sense of relative calm. Earlier this morning, she read the notes that her middle- and high-school-age kids had written to their dad, and she packed them in his gear for him to discover later. She was proud of them; they're old enough to express themselves really well now. Her daughter quoted Psalms 31 in her note: "Angels will watch over you."

Time passes, relatively uneventfully. After a while, a couple dozen soldiers are called into formation, then a couple dozen more, and then they disperse again. Two buses arrive; they look innocuous, but they are icons of despair. Danielle jokes that the FRG should have a fund-raiser where wives could pay money for a chance to smash the hell out of one of those buses. The buses sit a few feet from the curb with their engines off. There is another formation, and then another. Everyone keeps telling me to just wait, because I'm going to see a lot of crying any minute. They have said this a lot, as I have met them over the past couple of days, and now all morning long. "Just wait a few minutes, that's when all the boo-hooin' starts," Gene says to me, his voice conveying some feeling between scorn and a put-upon uneasiness. They, the women, have brought me there to see the crying, I suppose.

The families and little kids continue to mill around. And then, at some signal that I miss, the soldiers begin to shoulder their packs and weapons, and move toward the buses. Little kids, half comprehending what's going on, are hoisted up again by their dads and put back down. Here and there, couples twist into final, desperate clenches and hold on for dear life, for minutes. One by one, the soldiers pull themselves away from wives and kids, arms stretch out, and hands grip, slacken, and then release. The soldiers walk across a few feet of asphalt to form a long, orderly line along the side of the bus and slowly file on. I look for the crying, and there is a little, here and there. It won't really start until they drive away, Danielle murmurs to me. Minutes drag on as the soldiers board the buses. Nothing about this melodrama happens cleanly or quickly, or even particularly dramatically. Some women dash up to the line to steal one last embrace. One couple lingers, holding hands awkwardly through the bus window. There is a constant racket of squads and platoons being summoned, questions shouted, names called off, jokes exchanged. The soldiers are not crying, or not that I can see. Some of them are smiling, and most look at least a little dazed—and tense. But they are with each other now, on the other side of this strip of pavement. And on the sidewalk and lawn, the families, wives, and girlfriends are with each other. The obligations and boundaries that for the previous couple of hours could be foregone and forgotten have snapped cleanly back into place in a kind of intimate social alchemy. One moment the man in the ACUs belongs only to the people who have come to see him, to their embraces, smiles, and last words, and the next moment he belongs only to the Army.

Again without preamble, the buses drive out of the parking lot and away. The soldiers are now deployed. I look around for the deluge of tears, afraid to look and then doing it anyway. I see wet cheeks and eyes and the women hugging—hugging each other, hugging kids, and hugging dads, brothers, and in-laws. But there is no spectacle. Indeed the crowd has thinned, and many people are already gone. It seems like a classically liminal moment, a ritual of passage and resolution, but for everyone who didn't get on the buses, there is no passage to the other side, no clear ending. There are signs, protocols, and all that, for sure, but no pomp, regalia, or ecstasy of *communitas*; there is no flood of tears and no closure. Does the closure come in twelve months, or fifteen, when the soldiers return? Can it, when they know they will be headed out again after a scant twelve months at home, with even that precious and far-off time filled in with long days of work and weekends in the field? There is no closure; only whatever quantity inheres in persisting with daily life, with normalcy, in the face of the burden of fear, anxiety, and absence that now lies before the wives, girlfriends, parents, children, and even, in different form, soldiers themselves. Instead of closure, there is the daily work of not coming undone.

I say good-bye to some of the women I met and wish them well. Danielle looks around for Gene. He disappeared inside minutes ago and missed the entire departure. A moment later he emerges, his giant action-figure frame striding out the back door of the building. "You left me and Ken out here with all the bawling wives!" she snaps at him.

"I know," he replies. "Why do you think I went back in?"

"You needed to see that," she retorts, and then walks off.

Gene turns to me. "My wife doesn't understand that if it's hard for them, it's even harder for the man, because you feel like you're abandoning your family! You're in a mind-set, and if you look back, you're gonna get out of it. She called after me when I left last time and I didn't look back. She was mad. She didn't understand." His voice has more its aggressive edge than usual. Other soldiers have told me this too—you feel like shit when you get on that bus, you look around and see everyone else on the verge of breaking down too, wiping their eyes, looking away, but you don't let it take you over. The women wanted me to see the crying. Gene wants me to know this other side. They each want me to know what the other, I think, cannot help but know, but which they each insist the other somehow fails to understand.

From the outside, this event looks oddly flat and anticlimactic for something so intimately wrenching. From the inside, it looks totally different depending on who you are and where you are in it. It's an exercise in solidarity and affection, but its strongest features are pain, loss, grief, misrecognition, and the tight control and suppression of emotions. Then on top of all that, there is the anticipation and recollection of all these things, as they have happened before and will happen again.

The manifest appears to be a break of some sort. It gets built up and reacted to as a break. And of course it is. But it is also just an extreme scene in an ongoing condition that moves in longer, slower waves. The pain and absence are both problems of anticipation, duration, waiting, and being stuck; the way through is at worst attrition, at best endurance, and in fact probably some combination of the two. This is what it means to cry beforehand at home or to know you will need to stay busy. This duration, the slow movement through time of these attachments, is arguably the feature that makes such a mess of them. It poses the dilemma of which moment should matter more or less than another, or another, or another.

All different forms of attachment seem to be in full flower, all the different things that share a family resemblance under the name *love*. There is the soldierly solidarity, the leaders giving orders, the benediction and encouragement, the parental affection and worry, the romantic and conjugal bonds, the sentimental volunteers, the wives who lean on each other, the kids half scared and half oblivious, the single soldiers with no one to say good-bye to, and the looming presence of the Army and the war—these inhuman forces that just go rolling arrogantly along, *thank you for your cooperation*. These things all knot together against a background of work, sex, death, loss, danger, absence, duty, and money—the reasons for making one attachment that then places another one in jeopardy.

Classic liminality means that some surface splits open and truer, more fundamental things are exposed. Here it is more as if the significance of all these relations is revealed as they variously combine forces and turn against one another. There is no subtext. The conflicts and synergies work right there on the surface, and everyone is talking about them—waiting for the tears or trying to avoid them—so that as you attend bit by bit to this knot of attachments, what you get is decidedly not a sense of what is "really" going on. Rather, any claim to normalcy, any claim that any one of these attachments naturally or necessarily comes before the others, and the others merely exert a deforming influence on them . . . well, it all begins to seem pretty arbitrary. Does Gene's dedication to his job hurt his marriage? Or do Danielle's expectations of him interfere with his ability to be a soldier? Is it worse to experience the pain of departure alone, as one wife of one soldier, or in a group, as one of many wives, some of who behave in unsettling ways? Are the men soldiers first, or husbands, sons, boyfriends, or fathers? Are the women women first, or wives, or Army wives? Which attachment is more basic? Which comes before and which lasts the longest? Which is left when others dissolve and fail? Which is called into being only by dissolution and failure? Which rules apply? Which ones get broken? And are these attachments separate kinds at all? Are they not, even as one struggles to give specific and appropriate names and forms to them, always excessive and always ready to collapse into nameless flatness? Could it be the chronic uncertainty, the high-stakes mutability, and the dull, mundane ground of attachment as much as a promise of no-matter-what-forever-and-ever that give love its charge?

LOVE IS THE ANSWER

Soldiers and those close to them endlessly invoked love by one definition or another to explain one thing after another. People say that they love their country, the Army, their fellow soldiers, their husbands and wives, their jobs, and where they live, and sometimes they say that they hate these things too. War raises the stakes on the ability of love to conjure so many different feelings and attachments. Or perhaps it merely helps reveal what the stakes always already were. After all, violence and politics are always hovering over the question of "how one loves what one loves" (Dumm 1999, 3).

People endure and do the unthinkable out of love for those they are bound to protect or support. War is full of things that are overwhelming, that cannot be balanced out, or that cannot be justified or adequately explained—things, in short, that beg for something sentimental and transcendent, certain and unarguable, to intervene and sort them out. And people turn to love, in one form or another, so that the unthinkable becomes livable, or at least sensible. Love makes some things easier and other things harder. It is the reward for work, or it is the thing that itself has to be worked on. It is the thing that must be explained, or it is the explanation for things. As it alternately empowers and compels people, frees them to decide or holds them in its thrall, love, I argue in this chapter, is a form of sovereignty. It is not a set of rules so much as a basis for making, breaking, and being subjected to rules.

Like so many other aspects of social life, part of love's power lies in its capaciousness. Indeed, it is surprising how bereft the English language is of vocabulary that specifies the various kinds of attachment

conjured by love. That this banal bit of language deliberately ob-
fuscates the boundaries between categories of attachment may be
precisely the point. David Schneider (1980, 50) writes in his classic
study *American Kinship* that love is an "enduring, diffuse solidarity"
that conventionally applies to two very different kinds of attachment: the erotic, conjugal bond between men and women, and the
filial bond between parents and children. As a symbol, according
to Schneider, love bridges differences—between generations and
sexes—and affirms the unity of the people thus differentiated. It di-
vides and binds.

The narrowness of this formulation—limited as it is to heterosexual coupling and nuclear reproduction—hints at love's regulatory
power. Sigmund Freud (1989), whose description of the term's odd
plurality in *Civilization and Its Discontents* is echoed in Schneider's
book, says that we are "obliged" to distinguish between these types
of love as well as among a whole welter of muddled, misdirected,
sublimated, and often wildly inappropriate desires. Love can indicate
so many things and attachments that we are supposedly obliged to
keep separate—friendship, filial loyalty, sex acts, patriotism, the pleasures of money and material things, well-being and goodwill, duty
and responsibility, care for pets and children, and so on. And as Michel Foucault (1988, 103) points out, intimate relations between and
among people are "an especially dense transfer point for relations of
power: between men and women, young people and old people, . . .
an administration and a population." That these relations have the
feeling of personal and autonomous obligations is what gives them
their regulatory force. In the Army specifically, obligation takes
proper and often highly explicit form as heteronormative love, domestic coupling and marriage, children and parental love, carefully
bounded platonic love for one's fellow soldiers and military spouses,
the homosocial filiation of Army corporate culture, and the ideolo-
gized love for the Army and country. Love is called on to organize
and reproduce military labor, animate the overbearing uniformity of
the "Army family," and give meaning and purpose to horrific, violent
death.

This frame is crucial to understanding the myriad ways love is
talked about in the community around Fort Hood, and how it is
that it seems to be and do so many different things at once. As in the

culture at large, heterosexual love and the nuclear family appear as powerful and self-evident goods that justify difficult choices and motivate the endurance of hardships. People experience the obligations and attachments of their actual families in direct tension with the Army's intrusive demands and impersonal coldness. Soldiers comment on, valorize, and complain about their families and significant others—citing them as sources of inescapable stress, undue drama, immeasurable reward, and limitless devotion—almost as much as they do the Army itself. Supporting wives, husbands, and kids is the reason for joining the Army, getting up every morning in the dark to go to work, and enduring misery in Iraq. That sort of love is the highest good, the thing that seems able to redeem everything else. But it is also incredibly fragile. It is severely tested by war and Army life, and has to be looked out for, protected, and "worked on," as many folks told me. Frequently it is painful in its transience, mutability, and susceptibility to betrayal. Tales of infidelity and broken marriages abound, and many of them are even more painful than the comparatively straightforward challenges of bureaucratic discipline and the traumas of war violence. Love appears as an other to and victim of the Army, as an alternate and vulnerable system of value.

Just as often, the language of love is invoked to metaphorize the intense homosocial bonds among soldiers, or to talk about how these bonds overspill their institutional boundaries and take hold of other areas of life. This love is epitomized in a bit of the Gospel according to John (15:13) that appears in speeches, pep talks, eulogies, and newspaper columns, and is inscribed in emblems and on walls: "Greater love hath no man than this, that a man lay down his life for his friends." The friends cited here could be read as the national populace that the soldier has sworn to defend, of course. Yet it refers as much to fellow soldiers as it does to fellow Americans. Terms like brotherhood and friendship hint at this solidarity, but they don't tell the full story. It is the attachment between people who would die for one another, who have exposed themselves to harm for one another, who have seen others who were helping them befall harm as a result, who have so much confidence in their leaders that they would follow them anywhere, or who care so deeply for their subordinates that they would do anything to protect them.

More prosaically, love is the attachment among people who have passed significant portions of their lives living and working in extremely intimate proximity with one another. Though perhaps not so prosaic, for in the Army it is precisely the potential for harm and death that demands an unparalleled level of attention to and involvement in other people's lives. The emotional quantities known by terms like cohesion, morale, and esprit de corps earned these technocratic names exactly because military logic understands them as instrumental matters of life and death. This kind of love can be painful too, when it is lacking, taken for granted, or dysfunctional. It hurts when leaders don't care, when subordinates don't show respect, or when people don't look out for each other. It can spell alienation. It can mean death.

Schneider remarks that American kinship is notable for its putative autonomy from other areas of social life: family is separate from work, politics, and the nation. To label an attachment love is thus to claim an exception to all the binds of the social, as Elizabeth Povinelli suggests. It is an individual, involuntary impulse that materializes *in spite* of supraindividual constraints—in spite of distance, absence, difference, fear, betrayal, rules, and misery. "True love works against the social," states Povinelli (2006, 177). Indeed, love's sovereignty, its powerful exceptionalism, seems only to make sense against a background of constraint. In a setting as manifestly unfree as the Army, it is even more apparent how love both thrives on constraint and easily infiltrates ostensibly separate areas of social life. Notions of soldierly solidarity and Army family turn Schneider's segregated formulation on its head, bringing love to the heart of work, politics, and nation, even as love chafes at these other domains, and even as they trade freely on the power of love's irreducible independence.

Love, writes Lauren Berlant (2006, 20), is "a cluster of promises we want someone or something to make to us and make possible for us." Love is not simply desire but also the heady proximity of desire, the desire for desire, or the desire for a feeling powerful enough to rearrange all other priorities. You surrender yourself to it, and it makes you whole and free. Here again are the involuntary feelings, out of our control and obliging us to act even as we wait for them to oblige us. This is the curious, backward sovereignty that love's binding force seems to furnish in Army life.

"PERSISTENT TENSION"

Much of what first caught my attention about this terrain of love is described in expert detail in John Hawkins's ethnography of life at US military installations in West Germany during the mid-1980s. Hawkins—a retired Army colonel turned anthropologist—frames his analysis in terms of the immense satisfaction that soldiers and their families take from Army life, and the simultaneous alienation produced by the Army's domination of all other areas of life—its domination, especially, of domesticity and the family. US posts in Germany during the cold war were incredibly insular, both by design, for reasons of security and control, and by circumstance, since linguistic and cultural barriers divided Americans from the local German population.

In the context of this insularity and the high-alert posture of the late cold war, with the frontier of the Eastern Bloc literally a short car ride away, "The military ethos penetrated the entire community . . . , and thus, also penetrated the military families that constituted part of the community" (Hawkins 2005, 43). Military families found themselves subject to the "competing premises" of Army corporate culture and their "native" US culture, Hawkins writes. In words that my own informants echoed, Hawkins's subjects complained that the Army was full of "bullshit"; it was a "crazy system." And while the Army was—as it still is—able to make unconditional demands on soldiers, its standards and mores appeared to soldiers as well as their families as "subordinate," "contingent," and even "foreign" and "communist" against the "naturalness" of American culture (ibid., 230, 276). It is precisely this disjuncture, "the interplay and misplay of institutions," that proves "alienating" (ibid., 282). The tension between the Army and home life is most often the space and medium through which soldiers and their families experience this "misplay." It is a tension apparent in Hawkins's implicitly gendered characterization of the relationship: the Army is rational and arbitrary; home is emotional and natural. The Army is doing, hardship, and sacrifice; home is resting and nurturing. Home supports Army, and per Hawkins, the Army "penetrates" home.

Such imbalances can or ought to be justified, for Hawkins's informants, in terms of the functional efficacy of the Army. That is, soldiers and their families would be willing to live with these tensions if they seemed to serve some purpose. But because the institution was dysfunctional, the imbalances were not regarded as worth the cost in hassle and unhappiness. The problem of "competing premises" is a structural-functional friction. Hawkins's aims are straightfor-wardly practical—how to increase military efficacy by alleviating this alienation—and his book concludes with a series of nuanced policy recommendations.

Hawkins's whole approach assumes that the irrationality of a hy-perrational system can be rationalized away. But what happens if, instead, the competition between Army and family is treated as fun-damental rather than incidental, if all the effects of institutions are taken as a single whole and the undesirable ones not shunted to the side as misplay? Hawkins himself quotes Erving Goffman's insight that total institutions like the Army "do not really look for cultural victory. They create and sustain a particular kind of tension between the home world and the institution and use this persistent tension to leverage the management of men" (Goffman 1961; cited in Hawkins 2005, 277). While Hawkins's goal is to refine a means of leverage that is both efficient and humane, the "sustained tension" that Goffman points to has a constitutive power that far exceeds straightforward instrumentality, or any collateral bullshit or craziness. As I suggested earlier, the system is a nervous system (Taussig 1992), animated by this always incomplete, always in progress, always productive tension between the hyperrationality of imposed regulation, itself riven with excess, and exigencies of experience, with rules being imposed, and attachments being cultivated, stretched, broken, and forged anew.

Just as the careful regulation of the body and emotions is a starting point as opposed to a conclusion for thinking about what war actu-ally feels like, rules, orders, premises, and the organizational sociol-ogy of the total institution can all be starting points, rather than sim-ply conclusions, for thinking about how the system itself is infused and invested with feeling, how it is only effective because it is affec-tive (Mazzarella 2009). We can see the system not just in its rigidity and dysfunction but in its nervousness as well. Those features that Hawkins analyzes as problems to be solved appear differently when treated as inescapable aspects of this basic state of things. It is exactly the insolubility and excessiveness of the rules that makes the competing forms of attachment—the love—described in this chapter so compelling to the people enmeshed in them, and thus so important to pay attention to. Hawkins, like many others, regards the Army purely in terms of function, as though any negative or contradictory feeling wrapped up in it is incidental, and as though institutional rationality does not have its own perverse magic. In doing so, he sells short the generativity of things like the opposition between work and family, the Army's intrusions on private life and private time, its ability to always trump without excuse, and the absence of any recourse. The tension in these things is real, but in the context of ongoing war, repeated and lengthy deployments, and the prolonged absences and exposure to danger that these circumstances entail, does it even make sense to think of it a soluble problem?

In my ethnographic experience, this tension is a chronic condition, and the question it prompts is not how to solve it but how it is that people live with it. And what thing other than love could resolve the contradiction between the autonomy and self-gratification that Hawkins says characterize American civilian culture and the asceticism, discipline, and hierarchy of the military? In reality, the functional significance of and emotional investment in these differences swoop and swarm around each other, entangled and without a single distinct origin. Here we come back to "no greater love," the Army's most valorized "cultural premise." This greatest love belongs not to the person willing to die for his country, constitution, political leaders, or the democratic will of his nation. It belongs to the person who is willing to die for "the guy on your left and the guy on your right," as I was told numerous times. This love is the point at which any opposition of Army, war, and violence to feeling and "culture" dissolves.

ARMY FAMILY

There is of course also tension between the two senses of love as I deploy them here: as the other of the Army, and as the Army itself. And that tension takes perhaps its most explicit form around the simple fact that the Army is an inflexible, massively time-consuming employer whose workers are to varying degrees invested in, ambivalent about, and resentful of its domineering character. Thus, the soldier is desperate not to be kept late at work so that he can go home to his wife and kids, or the soldier uncomplainingly foregoes time with family or a significant other in the name of duty and obligation to fellow soldiers—or the same soldier does both. But this tension is complicated by the sprawling constellation of overlapping definitions by which the Army and the people who make it up bring their competing loyalties together. Indeed, one of the features of love in the military is that it is not necessarily possible to disaggregate practical concerns from sentimentality and dogma from authentic emotional investments. The modern US military has been a kind of social laboratory for experiments in the regulation of sexuality and appropriate modes of attachment for almost a century. During the congressional debate over sending US soldiers' families to live with them in post–World War II Germany, congressional representative Margaret Chase Smith argued that cohabitation was not only central to "the American way of life" but also that "American families could 'set an example for the natives'" of host nations. The recent contentious abolition of "don't ask, don't tell" is the current generation of the modern military's perennial sexual policing (Canaday 2009).

In the name of things like morale and esprit de corps—and hence, ultimately in the name of military efficacy—the Army institutionalizes care and cultivates an imaginary of familial and domestic love. It provides housing and health care for spouses and dependents of soldiers, and moves you to a bigger house if you have more kids. It pays married soldiers who live off post higher housing and food allowances. It officially recognizes degrees of hardship based on the separation of families and provides extensive life insurance. It builds schools, chapels, commissaries, PXs, and movie theaters so that married soldiers can enjoy the pleasures and privacy of domestic life on the post instead of the mass room and board of barracks and chow halls. The Army organizes the aforementioned FRGs. It sets up unit family days, when soldiers get to take their kids into their motor pools and firing ranges, and establishes family resource centers, where military couples can go for marriage counseling or seminars on household financial planning. And it maintains ties to older generations of former soldiers, opening its facilities to veterans and retirees.

This elaborate, far-reaching arrangement of institutional involvement, along with the ethic of care and affective investment infusing it, is glossed as "the Army family." The term has a slippery polysemy. It suggests recognition of soldiers' families as Army families, and therefore the Army's responsibility, owed compensation and recognition for their work supporting the soldier. But it also implies that the family is comparable in status to Army boots or Army regulations—at worst generic, interchangeable, and instrumental, at best still subject to the Army's control and standards, and in either case only there in support of the soldier. The phrase Army wife is the same way. It has a straightforward, surface meaning, but also suggests that its referent is a piece of interchangeable equipment, something issued by the Army; a woman who is married to the Army as a whole, rather than to an individual who belongs to it; or a wife who is herself in the Army, though "by marriage," as it were, instead of by the "blood" placed on the line by enlistment. Like Army family, the label Army wife is valorized by many of the women who see themselves in this role, who talk of their love for it or their duties within it. It also has its own subgenre of crude, misogynistic jokes. Army wives are "fat and nasty," or money-hungry "boot-chasers." An "SIAW" is a "standard-issue Army wife," and a "BMW" is a "big military wife"— sexualized figures of greed, complacency, and ugliness reduced to technobureaucratic acronyms. Such images reveal the range of relations to soldiers that Army wives are expected to have: at once valorized caretakers, helpless dependents, and debased threats.

The term Army family also goes beyond individual families to the sense in which the Army and those attached to it comprise a single Army family. Here too it has a double meaning. On the one hand, it is officially enshrined. The Web site of the Army's Morale, Wellness and Recreation Command states:

The Army Family is broad-based, and includes:
   Soldiers (Active Duty, Army National Guard and Army
      Reserve)
   Department of the Army Civilians

Retirees
Veterans
Families and their children
And Survivors

The Army Family Covenant

We recognize the commitment and increasing sacrifices that
our families are making every day.
We recognize the strength of our Soldiers comes from the
strength of their Families.
We are committed to providing Soldiers and Families a
Quality of Life that is commensurate with their service.
We are committed to providing our Families a strong,
supportive environment where they can thrive.
We are committed to building a partnership with Army
families that enhances their strength and resilience.[1]

It is perhaps not surprising that many soldiers and spouses bristle
at the earnestness, superficiality, and heavy-handedness of the Army's
"recognition" and "commitment" as well as the promises of support
that might sometimes stand in relief against a lack of real material
assistance. The official practice and rhetoric of Army family are
mocked as pointless busybodying, "mandatory fun," or intentionally
deceptive window dressing. Still, everyone attached to the Army recognizes the rules of this game of compulsory kinship, even if they resent or actively resist them, critique them, or ironically mock them.
Everyone agrees, as Hawkins puts it, on the basic premises about the
respective natures of the family and Army, their compulsory stric-
tures, and the tensions between them. Army family is one of those
formations that, in Michael Herzfeld's word (1997, 26, 19), "link[s]
the little poetics of everyday interaction with the grand drama" of the
official realm, thereby "constructing the nation-state"—and in this
case, the state's apparatus—"out of intimacy." We can take Herzfeld
literally here. This intimacy is not just mere rhetoric; it's an actively
produced fantasy of ordinariness (Stewart 2007). It is deeply felt, and
felt just as much as a fantasy as some objective, unalloyed good, binding the institution and the people who live with it together in a loose,
changeable, but ultimately inescapable sense of attachment.

Army family is not merely a slippery, labile discourse, then. It is a lived affect, thick with feeling for soldiers and their spouses, even those who are inclined to view some features of it with suspicion. It would come up in the way senior NCOs spoke of their responsibility for the care and behavior of the soldiers under them. They talked about encouraging young enlisted soldiers to think long term and consider what they would do when they got out of the Army. They talked about the importance of "bringing families in," not just telling a new soldier and his young wife about the family center or financial planning office, but rather taking them directly over there themselves. They talked about involving families in what the soldier's unit was doing and keeping them in the loop, informed and interested.

"Family and the Army go hand in hand," a recently retired sergeant major explained to me. "The Army is what we do," and the family is part of it. It's crucial for your family to be "wrapped up" in what you do—in a positive way, because they inevitably are anyway. Basic Army business—promotion or bad behavior, changes in pay or housing, extra duty or responsibilities, or a move to a different unit or different installation—can have profound effects on a soldier's family even before the egregious stresses of deployment arise. Bringing families in—getting them to come to FRG meetings, or getting them to be knowledgeable about and affirmatively invested in everyday Army business—means, the sergeant major told me, that things will go better for them when soldiers go off to war and they really are in harm's way.

Bringing families in also takes the form of the fictive kinship that many senior NCOs along with their spouses and kids extend to "their" soldiers and "their" guys. The paternalism and sense of mutual care and responsibility of the military hierarchy, metonymized as family, bleeds back into the domestic sphere. Wives of sergeants use the first-person plural to talk about the soldiers in their husbands' units—"we" didn't lose any of "our" soldiers on the last deployment, they would say. They talk about "adopting" junior soldiers, especially those who are young, unattached, and far from home, or being their "surrogate moms and surrogate dads." Though it can be a violation of fraternization rules, many sergeants invite their soldiers into their homes for parties and holidays. Lydia, whose NCO husband, Steve, had recently retired, called the other wives her "girls," and the commander's wife, the head of the FRG, was "like the mother of us all"; Steve's soldiers were "his babies." These relations of care are truly "enduring." Lydia told me,

> [Steve's] so good to his soldiers. So good. I mean, he'll go out of his way. You know Ken, we still have soldiers that call him, that he met like thirteen years ago, seventeen years ago. And they'll always call us like their surrogate mom and surrogate dad. [This one soldier is] in Chicago. . . . So he called [Steve], "Hey, so I heard my dad is retiring! It's about time! How many years? I'm thinking about going back into the Army! You know I got out. . . ." [*Lydia laughs.*] And he would tell him, "You know Sergeant Uribe [Steve] taught me *so much*. I still talk about you guys." Seventeen years later, Ken! And they call you, and they keep in touch, and they tell you—it really makes me *so* proud of my husband. That there're like *aaaall* these, our guys, I still hear them, I still hear them: "I still, I do certain things certain ways because I knew you said, 'That's the way you have to do it. You got to treat people with respect. Family comes first. God first, family second. And the Army comes next.'"
>
> It's always amazing to us how when they'd call. We have friends who were stationed here, and they got out of the Army, and now they're in Jersey. And he was a Redskins fan, Steve is a Cowboys fan, and they'll call, every day, every Cowboys–Redskins they'll call! And they've been gone fifteen years. And every day, every game, they call, or we call. It's amazing! You never forget. You never forget—your Army family.

In one sense, Lydia's portrait makes it apparent that Army family is hardly just cynical doublespeak; it also does describe a transcendent, persisting, and deeply felt sense of solidarity among many soldiers, military families, and veterans. "You sit down with any Army," she said, snapping her fingers, and "it's automatic." More instructive, though, is the way that in the space of a few sentences, her depiction swerves through a whole series of different, mutually enforcing attachments: from her love for her husband, to his care for his soldiers, to their filial attachment to him, to higher principles of faith, family, and personal conduct, to friendships that have endured across time and distance. And maybe this is why it is misleading to describe Army family in terms of mere polysemy. For as much as the term assumes different meanings in different contexts, its various definitions overlap with and feed back on one another; they can't be disaggregated. And that is arguably what is most powerful about them: not their exploitation by the military, their effective enshrinement in corporate culture, their rejection by the jaded or suspicious, or their embrace by others, but rather the whole knotty constellation—all these things and more.

CARE, VIRTUE, AND VIOLENT DEATH

Like the Gospel says, death is the measure of the greatness of love.

Fictive kinship can become the source of abiding loss and pain. I asked Randy, an avuncular NCO in his mid-thirties, what the most difficult and rewarding parts of being deployed were, and what things were hardest to convey to someone who hadn't been there? The best thing, he responded, is taking care of soldiers. "It's just the family that you feel there. When you're in Korea, you're in Bosnia, you're in Iraq, those troops are your mom, your dad, your brothers, your sisters, your kids." In garrison, you can work nine to five with the same people, but then you go home. Over there, in a combat zone, you're together all the time and you don't have anyone else to turn to. Your life is in other soldiers' hands, and their lives are in yours. This solidarity of Army family, this intimacy and sense of kinlike dependence honed by the close proximity of death, was real and beautiful to Randy. What a lot of people don't understand about soldiers, like the junior soldiers under his command, is that they're kids, Randy said. "Most of the people who are fighting are children—seventeen-, eighteen-, nineteen-year-old kids who haven't really seen the world yet." Children: the utter innocence and dependency this conjures resonates with the fact that, as Randy put it, they're "just doing what they're told."

Then I asked him to tell me about when he was injured. I had heard only bits of the story before. I knew there was a mortar blast, and now he wore a knee brace, sometimes a sling too, often used a cane, and would disappear for a day or two for surgery, or to acclimate to a new regimen of pain meds. The story, he said, "starts way before the war ever started." It began when he was at his first duty station, in Korea, as a young and inexperienced private. His squad leader "took me under his wing and pretty much became my dad. Showed me everything." Years on, Randy had been promoted several times and was working as an instructor when this old sergeant's son showed up as one of his students. Then Randy went to Iraq—volunteering at the last minute to fill a vacant slot—and there the kid was again, not working directly under him, but in the same shop, maintaining and repairing attack helicopters at the war's beginning, when things were hectic and hot. Randy looked out for him and checked in on him all the time. The guy was sharp, his work never needed to be redone, his bird was always ready to go, and the pilots loved him.

One day they got a call to go out and tend to a downed helicopter; a mechanical problem had grounded it at another base. They had been working for several hours and were almost done when a mortar hit. It landed next to the helicopter, and the explosion flipped it over, and it exploded too. Randy and his soldiers had been on top of the bird working, twenty-five feet in the air. When Randy regained consciousness, he was on the ground. There was nothing but black, and then blinding, blurry white. He couldn't hear or smell right away, but then after a moment there was the sound of gunfire, the aroma of smoke, and a sickening sweet char. Around him his soldiers were gazing uncomprehendingly at one another, slowly coming back to it just like he was. Except one of them wasn't moving. He was lying facedown near Randy, and the sand around him was stained red. Randy hobbled over to him on a ravaged leg and turned him over. It was the kid. His eyes were open, but his chest was a single giant wound. He was gone. "The medic kept telling me to let him go, there was nothing I could do, let him go. And I kept yelling at the medic to fix him. 'He can't die, I promised his dad! His dad asked me to look out for him!' . . . I was gonna kill the medic if he didn't fix this kid."

Randy's injury had affected his life in all kinds of ways. His tour was cut short, along with his career as a platoon sergeant, a helicopter mechanic, and an instructor. He needed numerous surgeries on his knee and shoulder. His leg might not ever heal, and his use of his injured arm was severely limited. He took a combination of opiates and other medications for the chronic pain from his injuries. Some of these meds left him sleepy, altered, and unable to work or drive; they tripped up his mood and wiped out bits of his short-term memory. Randy never complained, but if you so much as patted him on the shoulder, he winced in pain. He could easily have died in the explosion, and he suffered from PTSD. What was truly painful about the whole thing for him, however, was the loss of his old sergeant's son—the proxy son of the proxy dad. He was overcome with shame and guilt. He couldn't look his old sergeant in the eye. He couldn't stop thinking about what he could have done differently or what someone in his place could have done instead. The fact that there was nothing anyone could have done was no comfort.

Randy's story is just one among many I heard in which a type of nurturing, responsible, parental love frames the tragedy of soldiers' lives cut short by war—soldiers with families, soldiers with new wives, soldiers with babies on the way, or soldiers who were young and inexperienced but good and loyal, and who needed to be taken care of. These soldiers showed up in stories again and again as they got shot or blown up by mortars, rockets, or IEDs, as if their love-infused innocence was some sort of attractor for violence. Dime railed against this exact thing, talking about the younger guys in his unit who had died.

> Fucking nineteen years old, getting their asses blown the fuck up. They haven't even felt the warm embrace of a real woman and a real relationship, getting their asses blown up and never will know that shit. Sorry, that sucks. In my eyes, that blows. Never being able to have kids.

And then there is the other end of things—the soldiers whose death was made more poignant by their care for others in life. Dime's first sergeant got killed bringing hot chow out to the observation post where they had been stuck for weeks.

> He came to the mess hall, loaded up a bunch of hot chow for us, cause we hadn't eaten anything in forever, and was coming out with us, and got fucking killed, blown up by an IED. The only thing that kept him together long enough to put him in a

Blackhawk was his IBA [body armor], and he died on the way back to the aid station. He didn't make it. Bringing hot chow to us so we could eat. That's what kind of guy he was. [*He begins to weep.*] This was probably the most gung ho—he probably had a bigger dick than anybody you ever knew. I'm not shitting you. I mean, this man would stand in front of a bullet for you.

These men's condition vis-à-vis love—one stopped short in its realization, and one tragically undone by his heedless gift of it—is what gives meaning to their deaths. Paternalistic care, sexualized heroic prowess, youthful premasculine innocence, and the reproduction of the line collide with violence and are cemented by the white heat of explosives into a gestalt of idealized masculine love.

Dee told me about a convoy mission where they had to stop suddenly in some neighborhood of Talil. She was in the Humvee's turret, watching the perimeter along with everyone else while they waited for the long line of vehicles to get unfucked. A car emerged from the alley directly opposite her; it was moving too fast. Maybe he hadn't seen them, or maybe he was a suicide bomber. The rules of engagement specify a particular escalation of force: a verbal warning (which may be hard to hear, let alone understand), a warning shot (ditto), a shot into the engine block (with a .50-caliber machine gun, which is enough to disable a car or truck), and as a last resort, shooting the driver. But with a fast-moving target at a distance of two hundred yards, there was no time for this whole procedure anyway. Dee fired a warning shot, and the car came on. She had to act; she shot the driver. The car came to a halt. They investigated it. There were no weapons or explosives inside, just a middle-aged Iraqi man in slacks and a dress shirt with a giant hole in his chest. She added this latter piece of information basically as an afterthought. The important thing was that this man's actions made him a threat, and that fact was ultimately the deeper truth of the situation. "That man got between a mother and her child," she said, "and that's the most dangerous place you can be." Dee's daughter, suddenly present on a dusty street in Talil, was less than a year old when Dee deployed. I tried to imagine this presence literally, an arrangement of figures into which the car intruded, placing the young girl in danger. In danger of what, though? Of herself being killed by a terrorist imaginatively linked to the Iraqi insurgency that her mother was fighting? Or of suddenly finding herself without a mother?

The child is perpetually invoked as soldiers talk about why they do what they do. They signed up to get their kids health insurance. They go to work everyday to make a living and put up with the bullshit for them. "I'm doing this for my family"—a wife and young daughter—one soldier said. "If they told me to blow up a hundred hospitals, I'd do it." Or, as another soldier explained, "It's for our kids, so they don't have to worry about terrorists coming over here." It's easy to see what a figure of total, unimpeachable innocence might be good for in a scenario where the baseline conditions are unthinkable, let alone the particular things one can be asked to do in the midst of those conditions. It's so crudely obvious that even to state it seems like a violation, but invoking the innocence and vulnerability of the child can justify anything. The child conjures the innocence of national intentions and the vulnerability of the nation, the biological futurity of the population, and the very continuation of life that should be allowed to live and that must be preserved against threat by a watchful, jumpy, unhesitating trigger finger. Intimacy, vulnerability, and the simultaneous valorization and extermination of life dwell side by side. Yet that is something we know already. In biopolitics, state violence is always about the preservation of innocent and vulnerable life, so the life of the child, in an abstract sense, is always at stake on the battlefield. Knowing this does not lessen the charge of love and the real work that it does to make a virtue of the unbearable or create the possibility of an entirely new wound.

So we must reckon with this particular power of love. Here love becomes sovereign—asserts its capacity to break and make rules—by collapsing the state's responsibility for life and death in war on to individuals who are intimately bound to one another. As the institution becomes infused with the burdens of kinship and the substance of intimacy, the shared responsibility for life in a war zone may not devolve to the state or the Army. Instead, it passes first to the collective—your lives are in each others' hands, as Randy said—and then to the individual, like Randy, alone with his impossible responsibility: "He can't die, I promised his dad." The autonomy of kinship leaves Randy cut off from other ways of framing this loss. The freedom of love unmoors him from those social and institutional frameworks that could mitigate loss, responsibility, and vulnerability. The consuming freedom of love becomes a consuming curse; Randy thinks about the kid every day.

The cruelest counterexample comes in the form of the children who *are* on the battlefield, following the soldiers around, calling for handouts of toys, candy, and bottled water. "Mister! Mister!"—the soldiers imitate their tiny, eager voices as they tell stories. The kids cluster around the Humvees as the vehicles roll through villages; they sometimes get too close and are run over. They also wave and smile at soldiers even though they might know that a bomb or an ambush lies around the corner. The children ride in the cars that are shot up when they do the wrong thing next to a convoy or at a checkpoint. One friend said of her husband, "It's about the kids over there, that's what he says. He's doing it for them, so that they can have something better." But the child who really is on the battlefield is more complicated than the one who is only imagined there. The child really on the battlefield cannot be protected at all costs and cannot be imagined innocent.

Too many things too horrible to contemplate stack up on top of one another: being away from one's own child, making that child suffer in your absence, feeling your child to be in danger, and then seeing other children suffering and in danger, wanting to alleviate those things at the same time as you are suspicious of those foreign kids, but maybe also being a cause of that danger yourself. Love swallows it all, cuts the horror, and helps you cope with it. Yet it also makes the horror what it is in the first place. In the war zone's state of exception, like with love, all things are made possible. Love lets us see, even if we don't want to, possibility stretching in many unfathomable directions all at once.

FRIENDSHIP AND THE EXCESSES OF ATTACHMENT

Army friends are different than other friends, the soldiers told me while we were sitting around the office one day. They're not like your friends from high school (high school, of course, because these guys are young; most were under twenty-three, although they seem older).

Regular friends are people who you like, who you can choose to be around. But if someone from home called you up in the middle of the night and needed help, well, depending on who it was, you might go, or you might tell them to call back in the morning. But someone from your unit, even some guy you hated? Anything, anytime, anywhere, you would drop everything and go to him without hesitation or question. It's different, they all agreed, each chiming in after the other to complete the undefinable definition of Army friendship. Just as the life-and-death stakes—your lives are in each others' hands—frame the experience of loss, the soldiers also mean that "there's a lot of intensity to relationships" in general, as a chaplain in a combat arms battalion remarked to me. These are "friendships that last for years." As Evan Wright says in his account of the Iraq invasion with a Marine Corps reconnaissance battalion (2004, 99), there was the palpable sense among the men that if any one of them died, he would be "surrounded by the very best friends he believed he would ever have."

This intensity gives rise to surprising scenes of loyalty and solidarity. One day I came into the Foundation office to find Dale sitting at the desk by himself, looking worn out. The night before, he explained, a friend from his unit had shown up at his barracks room covered in blood. "And I was worried about what happened, 'cause he's racist," Dale told me. His friend had gotten in a fight with another soldier, a much bigger guy, and ended up stabbing him. Dale brought him inside, talked to him, and took his knife away. Then he put zip cuffs on him and brought him to the military police, since it's better if you turn yourself in, he explained. I ended up knowing Dale for a while, but the day after I first met him, his closest friend from his unit came by the office. "This is Adam," he said by way of introduction. "In Iraq, he shot a guy in the stomach." They both laughed.

If this bond is so powerful that it can put even the relative value of life and risk of death into question, perhaps it is no wonder that people seemed to find something dangerous and disruptive in it. It can be too much and overrun everything else. It pushes at the boundary of what a friend is properly meant to be. The word friend suggests a degree of autonomy: you can choose a friend and also leave them behind. "Friends are relatives who can be ditched if necessary," Schneider (1980, 54) writes, just as "relatives are friends who are with you whether you like it or not." Friends are interstitial, occupying some space between family and coworker. That interstitiality is artificial to begin with, of course. But in the Army, the institution's kin-like compulsions to intimacy and dependence completely collapse the space in between, and it becomes all the more important that it be aggressively demarcated, philosophized, critiqued, and when it grows dysfunctional, policed.

The classic story is that of the soldier who comes back from deployment, ignores his family, and spends every night back at the barracks with guys from his unit. He can't come home. The Army attracts intense, risk-taking people anyway, the chaplain told me. They get used to the intensity of training and deployment, though, and back home suddenly there's no outlet. "They're bored 50 percent of the time." They want to turn to each other. "You have to remind them that their wife is their best friend." Soldiers who just stay with other soldiers might summon a rising friction of violent potential, might insulate themselves from the checks of domesticity and civilization that are meant to level them out when they get back from war. In the narratives about violent crimes committed by returned soldiers, those who can only hang out with other soldiers are the ones considered the most dangerous.[2]

It can go the other way, too, with the intense closeness growing awkward or uncomfortable. Some people don't like to be around other folks from their units after they get back. Lena, the media and public affairs soldier, told me,

> We were so tight. But everyone's past it now and they don't want to bring it up. The friendship is built on hardship. You've seen things that people in real life would never see. You can't get that back because you're not forced to depend on each other anymore. You bond over loss—the loss of everything.

So the bond isn't something that can be taken for granted. It is a place and time; it is a context, a duration, and a relation. But it is not some chunk of ontological concrete that just *is*. There is a paradox in insisting on these intense, lasting bonds as merely the product of circumstances, for while circumstances birth them, they remain powerful and messy to deal with long after the conditions of their origin have faded.

Sometimes friendship isn't there, and that is bad too. People don't want to see each other after they get back simply because they couldn't stand being together in the first place; even if they like each other all right, the company itself might be a source of bad memories. There are bad units, places where people don't look out for one another and the leaders won't stand up for you, where you have to watch your back, and people pass the buck and set each other up. Stewart was in a bad unit. When he got orders for Fort Hood, everyone told him not to worry, it was a fine place, as long as he didn't end up in this one unit. Yet that was where he was sent. "I've never seen anything so disorganized," Kristen, his girlfriend, told me; she had been married to a soldier before. "Nobody helps each other out. Nobody. . . . The military I remember . . . even if they didn't like each other and had different personalities, they were still each other's keeper, you know what I mean?" Stewart went to Iraq to drive heavy equipment transporters, overgrown flatbed tractor-trailers that haul sixty-five-ton tanks. But he was sent off in a rush, without the training he really needed. The whole time he was there, his platoon sergeant was sitting beside him in the truck or waiting for him back at base, ready to cuss him out for every little thing he did wrong.

> "Why the hell aren't you doing this? Why the hell aren't you doing that? What the hell is wrong with you? Are you a fuckin' dumbass? Are you retarded? Are you really retarded, is that the problem?" . . . sitting in the truck. . . . And that was basically his and I's relationship: he screamed at me, I took it, and everything was good and golden, basically. Except it wasn't. [*Stewart laughs.*] So basically the whole entire first deployment was spent with me getting yelled at for one thing or another, [and so] volunteering to do missions on the road, and . . . the two of 'em combined just don't make you happy. And when you're still getting attacked, you want to come back to your home base and be like, "I can relax now." And when you get a second to relax, your platoon sergeant starts yelling at you again. And I'm like holy crap, man. I just spent frikkin' two weeks wondering whether I was gonna die in five minutes or not.

The solidarity that is supposed to be underwritten, refined, and made necessary by the presence of death collapses, turns inside out and shoves the soldier closer to his own lonely mortality instead of drawing him back from it. Stewart's same bad NCO carelessly lost his own Kevlar helmet and then moments later stole an unattended one from a junior soldier right in front of Stewart; he threatened Stewart into silence about it. The Kevlar costs a soldier more than three hundred dollars to replace, plus restriction and extra duty penalties if you get written up for losing it. Stewart told me an Army joke: "There's only one thief in the Army. Everyone else is just trying to get their stuff back." I laughed, and he said, "It would be funny if it weren't so true." "And this guy is my leader," Stewart went on in sarcastic wonderment. "And I'm supposed to have faith in him." This is a terrible irony of the Army's cool, calculating meritocracy: that just one person in the wrong spot can make things totally impossible, like a brother who bullies you or a mother who ignores you.

Just as you might have to depend on cruel or indifferent others, you can love people without trusting them, and in the midst of all this forced intimacy, it's better to know the difference. Debbie, the Foundation director, lived forty minutes away from the base, but when things got busy or some soldier was in a really bad way, she sometimes would stay on the post for days straight, sleeping on the recliner in her office. Debbie's dedication and generosity were vulnerable to abuse, though. Anything that wasn't nailed down or locked up around the place would get stolen. Soldiers snuck in and took doors off the hinges to get into the storerooms full of donated toiletries and packaged foods. They took hams, frozen turkeys, and cases of M&Ms. They opened up the computers—bolted down—and stole the RAM and motherboards. They stole each other's pain meds out of unattended backpacks and blouses. Debbie put up cameras, but soldiers figured out that with the lights off, the cameras' motion detectors wouldn't activate. "I don't even bring my purse in there," she told me. "I always say, you love them, but you don't know them." Love appears as the opposite of power/knowledge, of what you can know and what you can do. Love means that you don't know. It functions as a warning that your knowledge may be faulty or incomplete. Love is something to be guarded against. That is its constitutive magic too: it can be itself and its opposite.

When people invoke love, they name a potentially perilous ethics of attachment. Care, friendship, and solidarity appear as the most normal and natural of ties. And yet paradoxically, they are always in danger of becoming or being about something else; if they become themselves too strongly, they also become something unseemly. And once one begins to think that way, there are threats everywhere, and the safe places are not what they once were either.

DURATION AND DEFACEMENT

Against the background of possible violent death, love mediates the worth of life, the waste of waiting, and the ability to "live" life or not during periods of burden, stress, and constraining attachment to other people and things. On an early morning run, my friend's phone rang. It was her husband, calling from Iraq, just a few weeks out from returning. It was 7:30 or 8:00 a.m. for us, and so early evening for him. I went on ahead, out of earshot, while they chatted for a couple of minutes. They were just catching up, she said, talking about mundane things: his parents had been in town visiting, and their son was getting close to graduation. That's what these correspondences are like for most folks—catching up, checking in, paying bills and getting cars repaired, managing kids and pets, and other details of daily life. "You can only do, 'Oh my God, I miss you so much!' for so long."

The war and the Army churn inexorably onward with little concern for the temporality of personal crisis. Not long before he deployed, Kristen had caught Stewart in some manner of infidelity, which he declined to describe to me—"I was being an idiot," he said sheepishly—and they were on the brink of breaking up. The war and Army, however, were indifferent to the urgency of this turn of events. Stewart and Kristen found themselves having to negotiate when and even whether to talk about these things. Should they let them fester, or go through the pain of addressing them in costly, agonizing phone calls? Kristen had to take it on.

> [I was] just gonna leave him. And everybody's like, "Well, wait 'til he gets back." And I'm like, "Why?" I mean I understand the

whole   don't-make-things-worse-for-him-while-he's-there,   but
on the other hand, well, why lead him on the whole time he's
there? So we talked a lot about that stuff at first. And that was
difficult, because how do you repair a relationship when you're
not even together? And he kept saying, "Well, you know, I'm trying to do my best, and whenever I get back we'll handle it." And
I'm like, "Well, you're not getting back for a year, and what am
I supposed to do in the meantime? You know, I'm pretty much
hating you right now!" [*They both laugh.*]

She was both enraged at and terrified for him. "Things you want to
say, do you really want to say them?" she wondered. Barthes (1979)
depicts the pain of a lover who waits by a phone that never rings,
but there is that other terrible uncertainty of lovers hanging on the
line, exhausted and afraid, with nothing to say to each other and only
silence or the rush of breath between them. On the telephone, just
like everywhere else, love is not a transcendent thing but rather a
changeable ebb seeping through the grit of circumstance. It demands
strategy and practical decisions.

There is another kind of waiting, another side to the constant
and lengthy deferral of desire: the issue of fidelity. The lover sitting by the phone can't *not* wait, and yet how long can you wait for
another person? How long can your body wait for them? At what
point does waiting frustrate desire instead of constituting it? What
happens when desire finds an outlet that ends the waiting? There is
screwing around on both sides of the world, in these twin realms of
stress, loneliness, and steeply disproportionate gender ratios. People
describe the Army town as a sort of stage for self-perpetuating dra-
mas of sneaking around and testing boundaries, often in broad day-
light. Cheating couples canoodle in corners at parties. A truck from
across town shows up in front of a neighbor's house the day after
her husband deploys. The young wives—and even some of the older
ones—head out to the clubs the instant their soldiers leave town.
Or so everyone said and was eager to tell me. I had no way of mea-
suring the real frequency of these things, but the myth of them hangs
thick and heady in the air. "This town makes people into whores,"
Dale pronounced one day. I must have seemed a little incredulous in

my response, because then everyone chimed in—all of them young soldiers with wives, girlfriends, or boyfriends: "It totally does!" Opinion was unanimous. That's why he didn't bring his wife here, Dale said. He trusted her, but he didn't want her to be around it, so she stayed in New Mexico.

Suspicion itself is a major cause of strain.

> Chad takes me fishing. He hasn't been in weeks and he is feeling really stressed out. His wife, who lives in Tennessee, is being a pain in his ass. He loves her deeply, but the distance is a massive strain on them. She has medical problems, and her ex-husband gets on her case on a daily basis about caring for their kids. But then she gets on Chad's case. She accuses him of being unfaithful, and it is hard to tell by his reaction to what extent he is hurt by this versus simply resentful of its untruthfulness (so he says, and I believe), but in either case it definitely gets to him, angers him. "She says, 'Where were you? I bet you were out screwing around!' And I say, 'Well, I may as well if you're just gonna accuse me of it anyway!'" His earnest sentences are scattered amid long pauses. "You have to understand the history . . . and the psychology . . . of the wolf. . . . Wolves mate for life!" Which one of them is the wolf, or is it both of them, I ask. "I am!"

Everyone talked about all the cheating and divorces, bearing out what the sergeant's wife said to me at the manifest: "a lot of couples won't make it." People quoted extreme percentages to me: 60, 70, and 80 percent divorce rates for deployed soldiers, with the point not the number so much as that there were so many, that there were too many, that something was wrong. A friend based in Baghdad at the height of the worst fighting in 2006 said, "The JAG lawyers are like, 'We can't even keep up.' . . . [The] first sergeants would be like, 'Every day I have a soldier coming to me [about a divorce].' That's 365 days plus an additional 3 months that you have. That's a lot of divorces." Lots of soldiers cheat when they're deployed, too, despite the scarcity of both privacy and prospects, Jessica told me. "There's story after story." "Many" or even "most" soldiers do, or "maybe even a majority"; "they will find anywhere."

There are indeed many stories to match these proportions, not just isolated incidents. I heard a lot of them, mostly secondhand, circulating as a kind of salacious and disconcerting folklore. Jessica's friend divorced her soldier husband of twelve years because she discovered he was having an online relationship with another woman while he was deployed. Another friend of hers stumbled on the affair when she happened across pictures of the other woman on the soldier's Myspace page; she emailed a link to it to the wife, who happened to open it as her fifteen-year-old daughter was looking over her shoulder. Jessica said her husband, Cal, told her about how guys in his unit asked one another if they had "picked someone out yet" to be with in Iraq. There was a deliberation to it. She said they preferred exclusive dalliances so that they didn't have to worry as much about picking up sexually transmitted infections.

Again, and again perversely, all things become possible. To retain love in the form of fidelity means, Lydia told me, that you have to "work," you have to "fight." Love means laboring under the burden of being able to be betrayed. In that light, it seemed as though the point of all this talk was not merely to get to the bottom of what might actually be going on in one case or another. Rather, it was to acknowledge the peculiar and contradictory thrall of attachments, and the ways that people recognized them. It was, to borrow a term from Michael Taussig (1999), *defacement*: a social exercise in revealing the unspoken but obvious contradictions of things, like love, that generally escape serious questioning. The threat of betrayal feeds on absence, temptation, distance, and impatience—all of which contradict the proximity, self-renunciation, and fidelity that make up love. But where would love be without these antagonists, and what would become of the pleasurable secrets of suppressed or unleashed desire, lust, and scandal without these restraints?

These strains and dilemmas demand responses, sometimes in the form of unorthodox experiments, as waiting, wanting bodies run up against the limits of patience and obligation. A friend told me about some acquaintances, also military—two soldiers and their wives, all of them friends. One of the men deployed, and his wife was terribly lonely. The other woman was actually the one to bring up the idea of "loaning" her own husband to their friend to have sex with her. It never materialized, as they couldn't settle on ground rules. The wife would be there, but was the guy allowed to use his hands? Could they kiss? Should he or shouldn't he come? Sometimes the presence of another body is enough, though. On some of the bigger FOBs in Iraq, they have weekly dances and lessons—salsa, country, and hip-hop. Dee, who was married with a kid, went every week: "That's how I got my jollies. And every week, afterward, I went back to my trailer—*alone!*"

Sex and sociality overrun one another exactly as one might expect, but can nevertheless take the people caught up in them by surprise. Erotic friction builds unexpectedly in shared spaces and experiences. Doug, a reservist who had been deployed to work as a lab tech at Fort Hood, ended up becoming a good friend. One of the first times we hung out, drinking beer and enjoying the amicable yet generically nonlocal atmosphere at Applebee's, he told me a story about an acquaintance from another base. They weren't particularly close, but the guy really opened up when he started telling Doug about his deployment to Iraq. "You wouldn't believe some of what goes on over there," he said. In a series of confessional narrations that seemed to Doug alternately reluctant and relieved, the guy described not only attached men and women hooking up but also men hooking up with one another. Doug asked his friend if he knew anyone who had done this, and the guy responded with the same anxious equivocation, holding back, although apparently desperate to get something out. As it turned out, the guy said he himself had, with the other soldier in his hooch. At first it was just an intense platonic relationship, but then it developed into a sexual one. The acquaintance explained how he had then broken up with his girlfriend when he returned to the United States and still saw the other man somewhat regularly, every three or four months. It was always a little awkward at first, and then back to usual: "Platonic and sexual, but not romantic," said Doug.

About a month after this conversation, Doug told me he was bisexual. He had just started dating a man in Austin and wanted to be able to tell me about it. He is from a conservative and religious family, and his first homosexual experience was with another soldier. "It happened because of the Army," he commented.

Not everything I heard about cheating was anxious wondering or scandalized gossip coming from the outside; I heard about it from the inside, too. Randy and his wife, Susan, are very much in love. She is a few years younger and takes care of their kids full time—two each from their previous marriages. They were both married to other people when they met and fell in love. This fact maybe makes them a typical case, or maybe means that they are an atypical one—an exception and at the same time an embodiment of a stereotype about Army relationships. They met online, and he seduced her. By their frank account, their affair was pretty wild and lustful, but it was also carefully managed. In yet another extension of the compulsory mandates of kinship, adultery is illegal under the Uniform Code of Military Justice, and while it is not often prosecuted, the potential threat of such a thing can become a weighty bargaining chip in divorce proceedings. Randy and Susan had both had their reasons for getting married the first time. Randy's mention that he and his ex-wife "did not get along" was perhaps the kindest, most moderated thing I ever heard him say about her; they seemed to hate each other. They had gotten married for the housing and health benefits for her and the kids and the extra separation pay if he deployed. "It was wrong," Randy said. At the time he met Susan, his wife and their kids were living in another state. Susan's ex was a soldier too. He had problems, did a lot of drugs, and couldn't hold a job. She pushed him to join the Army in the hope that he would straighten out, but he didn't, and she started pulling herself away from him.

So both Randy and Susan were breaking the rules, the normative practices of love. Though these norms may not have been right to begin with, they took the shape that marriage assumes for people everywhere sometimes, including for a lot of others at Fort Hood—a fleeting desire, a mercenary impulse, a survival tactic, or the need to take care of kids. In Randy and Susan's cases, the Army was a big part of that shape, enabling, constraining, motivating, and surrounding them. The Army offered Randy and his wife, as it does many others, a material incentive to marry where other incentives might not have existed. It offered Susan the possibility of disciplining her juvenile husband into a reasonable human being. The deployments and duty stations that break up families separated Randy and Susan from their respective spouses and put them together with one another. "A deployment gave me my wife," Randy remarked of Susan.

As we talked through all this together, Randy and Susan pointed out the other factors involved, the things that seem to make cheating and war go hand in hand. What other occupation is there, they asked, where couples are separated for such long periods of time? "Name a corporation that's like that," Randy said—entire cities of people with the same job living together, everyone attuned to each other's comings and goings, knowing exactly who is there and who isn't, and how long they'll be gone for. One can imagine the blocks full of lonely spouses (wives) in Killeen and other Army towns, and the massive camps of tense, horny soldiers (mostly men) in Baghdad, Talil, and Arifjan. These are spaces where intimacy is compulsory and loneliness is built in, where proximity means visibility and surveillance, but also makes certain kinds of behavior possible. Commenting on what they had witnessed around them as well as what they had done, Randy said, "It seems like it's rampant, but at the same time, again, all these people who live in this area have the same job. And that's to go do something, to go away. And when they go away, what's left? Well, there's sex." "It sucks to be alone," Susan said. "That's why it's seen more in the military as opposed to just anywhere else."

Seen more—a telling construction. Whether intentionally or not, with this phrase Susan leaves aside the question of whether there actually *is* more. It muddles the feelings, practices, and appearance of attachment, highlighting both the broken rule and the reason for its violation in a way that empties the rule of its arbitrary significance. What matters is the visible defacement—the charge that accompanies the revelation of something that is common knowledge and yet that people commonly know should remain hidden. First is the density, the panoptic fishbowl of military life that makes for the scandal of things being seen and then talked idly about. Then, second, is the image of soldiers that holds that it is both more shocking and more expected for them to behave badly—as Susan said, "people forget that they're human." Susan's words sidestep the red herring of what's "real," for that only distracts from the true power of stereotype. What matters is the visible violation of a rule.

It was the defacement that Randy and Susan seemed to regard as most pernicious—all the idle talk and gossip, the indiscretion not of actions but rather of words and unwelcome judgments. They shared this perspective in common with other couples who were merely witnesses to cheating and not participants: the problem is not just the cheating so much as the failure of people to mind their own business and let others handle things themselves. It is another wrinkle in the constitutive social drama of making sure you know and don't know the right things. The problem is not the behavior itself but the excess that arises around it, the tense and oscillating moral standoff between sexual propriety and personal privacy. Busybodies may say that sneaking around and cheating are unseemly, but Randy regarded the contamination of other domains, especially professional life, by this nosiness as the greater offense. Perhaps it makes the Army look bad, he acknowledged. This is a time of war, however, and war itself has helped create conditions in which people are "naturally" going to cheat. You can't go kicking people out just because they're messing around. And just because they are messing around doesn't mean that you can't trust them on the battlefield. These are different kinds of attachment, different ways to depend on people and be responsible. Sex is not as big of a deal, at least not on its own terms; it's not the same as work, as war. Failing to recognize that is what causes problems, or makes problems in one domain out of problems that should have stayed separate in another.

I asked Randy and Susan if they felt like they fit the image of cheating military couples. Susan responded,

> I think we're in that category, because technically everybody has a reason for what they've done. So we fit into the stereotype regardless of the reasons. We did it. I mean, you've either done it or you haven't, it doesn't matter what your reasons are. You are part of the stereotype. So yeah, we definitely fit in it.

With a sensitivity and perceptiveness perhaps honed by painful personal experience, Susan deftly reduced the stereotype of military infidelity from judgment to mere taxonomy: it is about what they did, not about their reasons. For both of them, the story they told *was* the stereotype, and it *was* real life: the marriage for money, the loveless and entrapping unions, the worthless husband, the loneliness and distance, and their own wild and incautious coming together. They liked the Army. Randy was devoted to his job. Susan was dedicated to supporting him in it. They had lived through and come out better from all this bad behavior and broken taboo. Was it right, what they did? They both asked this question rhetorically a few times in their telling. And they both offered a kind of agnostic's confession as the answer: "not really," "two wrongs don't make a right," "it's what happened." "I'm sorry," said Susan, "and I'm not sorry, and I don't regret it." How bad are they supposed to feel about it, after all? They ended up together. Having violated lesser norms in pursuit of this greater one, they found love and so could confess all the wrong they wanted. "I believe you should be happy," Randy said.

What is love in all this? It is not exactly wholesome and pure. Randy and Susan broke all the rules and hurt people; they even took some small joy in having duped their respective exes and bidding good riddance to them. And yet it was all in the name of the same ideal, the same connubial happiness that "cheating" goes against. Love brought them together out of situations where it was absent. They care for each other. They have never before felt the connection they feel with one another. It's too easy to say that this is simply either a fortuitous romantic connection or nothing but a violation of how things ought to be. It is love as something that is excessive, boundary breaking, and binding. Love becomes a gesture of sovereignty in the midst of an environment of overwhelming disciplinary constraint, a way of declaring an exception from all the other things you should be doing instead. The imprint of love means that you, to echo Schmitt's words, are the one who decides. It is a sovereignty that weaves in and out of static norms and changing desires, breaking one rule and affirming another in the name of something that is more important, and furnishing the agency to say which rules rank higher than others.

ROOM FOR MANEUVER

It makes sense that one can also bend love in the service of other things: other rules, money, opportunity, or survival. There is a whole genre of talk about how young women marry young soldiers to get their money—the house, paycheck, and power of attorney they get when the soldier is deployed, and most ghoulishly, the four hundred thousand dollars in Servicemen's Group Life Insurance (SGLI) payout if he is killed. It's another of those figurations where a stereotype

is animated as much by ideas about how things simply are as by notions of what is right or wrong. In this story, young men and women
are heedless, lustful, and bad with money, and in general do unwise,
desperate things to get by. They claw a wild, hard-partying form of
survival from the strictest and most unforgiving of institutions, the
one that can make you live and let you die in so many different ways.
To be attached to another in the midst of such "compromised conditions of possibility," no matter if that attachment is toxic, opportunistic, or spoiled, is to maintain continuity, to preserve a "sense of what
it means to go on living" (Berlant 2006, 21).

Lydia would counsel other wives about divorce when things got
rough, or when the women got too comfortable with the independence of having their husbands gone. She wanted them to think
about it first. There are practical concerns and emotional ones. It's
not enough to be bored, frustrated, or lonely. You have to not love
him anymore, and you have to be ready to take care of yourself if you
are going to make the move. The material and affective stakes twist
up around one another.

> I say, "Right now you're having a good time. But think about it.
> Take his money away. Take all the money. Can you live on your
> own, by yourself? Can you support yourself? If you can support
> yourself and you no longer love this man, then you divorce him
> *when he gets back*. You tell him, 'I don't love you. Reason number
> one: I don't love you.' But if you still have love for that person,
> you stick it out." Now if he beats you up, I'm gonna tell you to
> leave his ass. But if he doesn't touch you, he's decent to you, he
> just has little bullshit crap, and you can deal with it by talking
> or whatever, then OK. But if *no*, I'll tell you do it. I don't really
> believe in divorce, but I'll support them. . . . I don't want my girls
> to be abused or beat up or mistreated. But I will tell 'em, I'll say,
> "Right now you're OK because you've got this money coming
> in. If you don't have that, if you can support yourself . . . go get a
> job. Go get yourself a lawyer. You pay for your divorce. You pay
> for half of it at least. You do something. *Do* something. Be *ready*.
> Be ready to support, to be on your own, without taking money.
> 'Cause you don't know what you're gonna get. You've been
> married ten years? I'll tell you, you'll get half of his retirement—

when he retires. If he's got ten, you still got ten years before he starts paying."

For Lydia, the personal stakes are especially high, since these are the women who are married to her husband's soldiers. She looks out for him and tries to keep him apprised of things, but also polices her loyalties carefully.

> I have seen so many who have opted for divorce, who tell them [the soldiers] when they are there [in Iraq]. And we're suffering, my husband's suffering. "I'm miserable. This guy is wearing me out. He is depressed. He wants to kill himself. Did you not talk to his wife? Did you not tell her what is going on over here?" *I did, I did*! I tried. My duty is done. I did the best I could. She chose the divorce. I asked her, "Please," I remember begging her, "don't do it while he's out there. Just wait."

One of her husband's soldiers found out that his wife was getting a lawyer when he spotted it on their bank statement. "She's a loser!" Lydia exclaimed, annoyed at the woman's stupidity. "You have to think it out." Such sneaky little detective story details, the banal and practical matters of survival, are part of what you have to do with love. Meanwhile, Lydia knew already that the woman was hiring a lawyer, and noted, "What the ladies tell me is private. I don't tell him everything."

Love can get you into a situation—exactly these kinds of situations—but fail to get you out of it. One day at the Foundation I met a woman married to a soldier who had had a series of catastrophic strokes. He couldn't drive or do his old job. He couldn't be left alone at home. He had the emotions of a seven-year-old, she said, and threw temper tantrums. The Army, in the form of this soldier's WTU platoon sergeant, said he had to show up at formation every weekday morning. His wife had to help him get dressed and drive him there herself. He was impossible to deal with: impulsive, forgetful, angry, and unreasonable. The WTU wasn't taking care of him. This soldier's own parents, who lived in another state, were indifferent. So she spent all her energy on him and had nothing left for their kids. She was considering a divorce. This woman was not cruel or neglectful. She seemed impatient as she described the burden of caring for her husband, and when she cried it was because she was overwhelmed by the prospect of making it through an unending succession of days with him.

Sometimes that highly circumscribed space—the space of getting stuck in the first place—is all the room to maneuver that you can hope for. Theresa, who owned a small shop in town and whose current and former husbands were both ex-military, told me, "You can count on two hands the number of jobs in the community that pay more than ten or twelve dollars an hour. My daughter [who is nineteen and going to college] works at the video store. And some of the stuff she tells me, Ken, [about] these women she works with, [military wives,] they can't even do basic math!" Jeannine, the daughter, lives with Theresa and her husband because there is no way to make enough money for rent: "There is no way for our young women to live on their own here!" And as a result, they go and marry soldiers, and then have kids. One of Theresa's regular customers was married to a soldier and recently had a baby, but she wanted to have another child before he went to Iraq again "in case something happens to him." Theresa knows another woman who has five kids by five different fathers; she ended up marrying her sister's ex-husband—an awkward situation for them both—but he was willing to help care for the kids.

Theresa had gotten stuck herself, married years ago to the military man who was her daughter's father. She made a decision to stay with him until she knew that she could support her daughter on her own. "He did his thing, and I did mine, Ken. Those were my rules." There is an uncanny mimesis here, a parallel logic of marrying for survival, and the soldier jargon of "making a number" or "filling a slot"—that sense of being reduced from a person to a body that has to be kept alive, working and occupying a position but expecting little in the way of care or recognition. In such circumstances, certain ways of getting by "become possible, acceptable, even inevitable" (Povinelli 2006, 204). Love might be a word for all that you need, or it might be a word for all that you have available.

Cindy's husband is a Black Hawk helicopter pilot and was deployed when we meet; she has a law degree. She founded a military spouse advocacy organization that took up the cases of soldiers who had been denied treatment for PTSD or TBI. These soldiers had been discharged from the Army for supposed bad conduct when they refused to deploy or turned to drugs and booze, and Cindy's group provided legal assistance and media visibility. The organization is avowedly nonpartisan, but it is outspokenly critical of Army and government policies that it sees as harming soldiers and military families. Most military folks are at least a little uncomfortable with this level of politicization, so it's hard for Cindy to get other wives on board sometimes, and her husband has caught flack for it too. Nevertheless, every time she finds herself discussing some fresh horror of institutional neglect with other spouses, she reminds them, "That could be your husband!" Her voice, as she tells me about the organization, is tinged with a vigor that's a little bit angry and a little bit manic, and very eloquent.

> It's my cross to bear. And I don't get anything out of it [the organization; it has no funding]. It's like your inner compass, a voice that's nagging you, that won't leave you alone. Military spouses bridge the gap between civilians and the military. Civilians can feel justified in looking down on soldiers, but not on spouses. Everybody knows what it's like to love somebody. It's not political. We just want someone to take care of our husbands! We can speak when they can't.

Again, pain, care, empathy, indifference, and identification collide in this melodramatic claim on the indisputable reality of what everybody knows—to suffer, to be exposed, and to be harmed for someone is to love them.

The love of marital loyalty translates the unthinkable and unsayable in a way that stories from the battlefield cannot. A husband gone for months; a husband who becomes a different person when he returns, violent, withdrawn, or screaming in the night; a husband crippled by his job and then kicked to the curb by those he served; a husband on whose service your life and the lives of your kids depend, and who suddenly cannot serve, or is deemed unfit to do so for reasons that have nothing to do with him. For those outside the Army, those to whom Cindy's organization tries to speak, the Army wife's love both domesticates and relays outward the shock and awe of war, making it *more* real, *more* comprehensible.

The organization's email list carries stories of lives badly broken and redeemed only through litigation and congressional intervention (the latter because it is so hard to sue the Army). Sometimes Cindy has worked on these cases herself. At other times she can't do anything for these women right away. But the women who send in the stories want urgently to be heard, and their emails get sent on just as they are. "I promise a story no one will ever forget, the truth, the brazen, bold, uncurtailed truth of this widow [the writer] and my kids and what my husband suffered before he finally died and went home to rest at last."

Love yokes you to this precarious state. Perhaps it can also pull you through to the other side, and make the fear and danger of some other person's experience legible and sympathetic. There is peril, we know, in assuming anything can ever be understood so clearly. There is peril in putting the violence in one spot, on one person, and then deceiving ourselves into thinking we know and feel what happened. And likewise there is peril in recusing ourselves with the assurance that we cannot know. Is there a better way out of this double bind? For Cindy, it is the only strategy that makes sense: you begin with what everybody already knows, and you channel it into a language and affective vocabulary of critique. Love and the institutional orders that appear to antagonize it share a secret complicity when the former is called on to right the injustices of the latter and fill in the gaps. The survival maneuvers of love are often opaque and undramatic. The grandiose staging of sovereign violence can slip easily into incoherence as one approaches its center, that place where violence seems to be happening only for its own sake, and where the institution's instrumental indifference to the soldier's battered life and his dependents' survival seems nothing more than unfathomable cruelty. Still, that is the place that people are bound to by love.

5

War Economy

Clausewitz (1982, 119) is well known—and frequently misquoted— for his definition of war as a simple means to an end, merely "a mere continuation of policy by other means." Fighting solves practical and ideological disagreements and rivalries of control. But the complementary pole of Clausewitz's dialectical definition is the notion of war as "nothing but a duel on a larger scale." Ultimately, war is not reducible to either mere brute force or purely rational policy (Bassford 1994). Elaine Scarry (1987, 12), following from Clausewitz, describes war as fundamentally a contest of injuring, in which the carnage of the interior of war proceeds according to the logic of little more than brute force, and only takes the form of ideological and political value *outside* the space of battle.

The preceding chapters sketched some of the shape of war's interior: the bodies worn down, dreams invaded, selves built and altered, and relationships frayed and reforged all largely in the space of what Clausewitz would call the organized production of violence for its own sake. In this last chapter, though, I return to the idea that war is *about* something, that it is doing something and serving a purpose. The people who labor at and with war—soldiers, their families, civilian boosters, politicians, contractors, and foreign civilians—all live inside the space in which otherwise-gratuitous destruction is minted into coherent narrative. This narrative takes its perhaps most explicit form in ideas about the debt of gratitude that the soldier is owed for his service. That recognition is a complicated, unstable exercise.

It draws attention to the fact that war is neither "nothing but" one thing nor "merely" another, and within this uneasy structure abide many economies and sources of value.

This book began with Dime sitting in his apartment, alternately gushing words and grasping for them, spilling the blood and guts of his loss, but unsure of how to articulate its worth. Dime told me to tell people what happened to soldiers who had done what they could and what they were told so that others would not have to do it. "At least give 'em that much." But as for what he wanted, he insisted he wasn't asking for anything, and as if to drive the point home, his demand for recompense trailed off into nothing: "Just give us . . . ." The soldier remains stuck, vulnerable to all those who stand ready with unsolicited assertions of what his labor is worth. He is stuck in the middle of even larger questions about what value can be drawn from the death and destruction, what debt is owed on it afterward, and what the exchange rate is between politics, the material world, and the "pricelessness" of life.

"YOU WILL ALWAYS BE 100 PERCENT IN DEBT"

I go with Jimmy and his wife, Liz, along with some WTU soldiers from the Foundation and a couple of their spouses and kids, to a barbecue in Waco. It is an annual soldier and veteran tribute event thrown by a wealthy businessman, Mr. Rogan—a "magnate," the local paper calls him in an article about the event—on his ranch about forty miles from Fort Hood. We get there in a small convoy—Jimmy's truck, a government van (we receive a briefing on riding in a "military vehicle" beforehand—no food, no smoking, and drink only water), and another soldier and his kids in a car behind us.

Mr. Rogan greets us from the back of a horse as we pass through the gate to his ranch. He looks stern and vigorous, and is clad in a sort of gentleman rancher style in vest, boots, bandana, and cowboy hat. An assistant collects a liability form that we have all signed. The van bumps over a cattle guard and down a long driveway through a pasture where longhorn steers are grazing. The road is full of people, many with the clipped hair, broad shoulders, and purposeful gait of soldiers, walking the same direction from cars parked in the grass, and we drive slowly. Because the van contains a group of injured soldiers, I gather, we have been accorded the privilege of parking close in. A group of costumed women on horseback surrounds the vehicles and escorts us down the road. The riders wear matching, sequined blue and silver shirts and elaborate blue-, white-, and silver-fringed chaps; the horses are decorated with swaths of blue and silver glitter on their flanks. The women carry flags—United States, Texas, and the seals of the various armed forces. The Navy flag, with its blue eagle and anchor on a white background, is immediately outside my window. Down the drive are more and more people, many looking less like soldiers than like civilians—bigger, older (some elderly), and with longer hair. They are clapping and waving flags as we pass. I wonder if, as has been the case at other events like this that I have attended, there is someone preceding us with a sign reading "wounded warriors." The mood inside the van is flat, a little uneasy. All along the drive are huge signs that Mr. Rogan has put up with quotations and bible verses printed on them: "Chop your own wood, it will warm you twice" (Henry Ford); "He will lift you up like eagles" (Isaiah 40:31).

We pull up past a large house with broad overhanging eves, tan plaster walls, dozens of large, dark windows, and an elaborately landscaped yard and patio. We debark from our military vehicle and slather ourselves with sunscreen. Jimmy, the ranking NCO and thereby in charge and responsible for us, pairs everyone with "battle buddies." Most of the group, including Jimmy, is with their spouses or kids; he asks me to go with a volunteer WTU soldier from the Foundation, Hank, who is talkative but socially awkward, a good-natured, teetotaling Baptist, and a bit of an outcast. Hank and I seat ourselves in front of the stage that has been set up in a swath of pasture between the houses and some outbuildings. A couple of big tents where volunteers will serve us food stand opposite it. The stage is a gooseneck flatbed trailer, bright red and gleaming new, with two semitrailers as a backdrop—one bearing the logo of Mr. Rogan's construction company, and the other the photos of two local news anchors' faces against a background of blue sky and the Stars and Stripes. There is bunting draped over everything, and flags—American and Texan—hang everywhere around the stage, tents, and house by the dozens. The crowd of guests and volunteers seems generally to favor a wardrobe of red, white, and blue that mirrors the flag palette and motifs. An elderly lady wears an oversize T-shirt printed with the word "PROFANITY" inside an interdicting red circle and slash. An overweight teenager sports a T-shirt in the University of Texas's burnt orange that says "Don't mess with Dubya" in big, goofy type.

The crowd is a little thin. In addition to our small crew, there are a few dozen soldiers from a combat unit at Fort Hood, some sitting down in front of the stage, and others checking out the fishing pond and horse paddock that Mr. Rogan has opened up to his guests. After a few minutes, a shuttle bus deposits ten or fifteen elderly World War II and Korea veterans from the VA hospital in nearby Temple at the row of seats closest to the stage; a few of them are in wheelchairs. There are a lot of volunteers, boosters, and other civilian guests; they easily outnumber the soldiers. More soldiers are expected, or were; no one seems certain. It is faintly embarrassing. Mr. Rogan has clearly gone to considerable expense and effort with this event, but the idea that there might not be enough soldiers to thank, to fill the space in front of his stage and eat his food, makes us a little nervous.

Neither Jimmy nor Ben and Valerie—an NCO and his wife who had organized the other group of soldiers—seem sure who else is supposed to show up. There is in fact some bad history between them, and they give me separate and conflicting explanations of what the other was supposed to do, how many soldiers they promised to bring, and how they may have fallen short. Gathering soldiers and delivering them to parades, picnics, and dinners, getting them to show up *to be thanked*, is one of the curious responsibilities of volunteer soldier advocates. It is part of an exchange, and not only as the price for enjoying an afternoon of bands, speeches, free barbecue, and the fishpond on the ranch. The Foundation depends on being helped by people who want to help soldiers, and so it tries to fulfill that desire for those who give time, attention, money, baked goods, sheets and towels, toiletries, and holiday cards. But the aim is nothing so instrumental as hoping to get some kind of donation out of Mr. Rogan. It is more diffuse, having to do with maintaining the spirit of goodwill and giving that the Foundation cultivates and nourishes, mediates and redirects, among the various interested parties to which it is bound by various exchanges. Hence the sense of anxiety and bitterness between Jimmy and the others over how it is that something here might have fallen short.

The women on horseback have gathered off to one side of the stage. The emcee is a trim, middle-aged white man in a dress shirt, jeans, and boots, sharing the stage with several other similarly attired trim, middle-aged white men. He gives a short speech welcoming the soldiers. A ten-year-old Boy Scout takes the mic and leads a presentation of the colors. The Texan and American flags are marched up to the stage by groups of Junior Reserve Officers' Training Corps cadets, Boy Scouts, and Girl Scouts. The scouts wear their militaristic tan uniforms, but with sneakers. The Air Force kids wear camouflage pants, polished jungle boots, and logoed T-shirts; the Navy kids wear blue dress uniforms with shoulder braids and garrison caps. They march in lockstep to the boy's commands—"Color guard . . . advance! Color guard . . . halt!" Following an instruction that those in uniform should salute and those not in uniform should place their hand over their heart, we say the Pledge of Allegiance and sing the national anthem. A preacher gives a benediction, frequently mentioning Jesus and asking God's protection for the soldiers as they do "His" work. There is more than one invocation of John 15:13, love epitomized by dying for others. The more intensely evangelical atmosphere here contrasts with the comparatively reserved religiosity of official Army proceedings, which tend to be unapologetically Christian but are much more generic and inclusive in tone. The color guard is excused, but as it begins to march out, one of the kids collapses directly on to an elderly vet in the front row, overcome by dehydration or the spring sun rising to the center of the sky. An EMT scoops him up and carries him to an ambulance parked behind the stage, and the ceremony goes on.

When I look back on them later, my notes from the day are spotty. I'm feeling a little sickly and somewhat besieged by all the sentiment. But it's also simply the case that everyone is a little confused about what we are there for, what the appropriate way to respond is, and what's happening next—all this effort to thank soldiers, yet without all the soldiers. We sit and wait for another load of soldiers to arrive, to be excused for lunch, or for something else to happen; it is not exactly clear. There are more speakers. A couple are veterans—a World

War II vet from the Army's first all African American artillery battalion, and Dave Roever, a Navy veteran who was horribly burned by a white phosphorus grenade in Vietnam, and now is a minister and professional motivational speaker. But besides that there are no soldiers on the stage. This is something *for* soldiers, something directed at them. The speeches that follow—from one of the television anchors, a couple of other local businessmen, and a conservative activist who is the father of a soldier killed in Iraq—are relentlessly affirmative and utterly sincere. They blur together, and Hank and I wander off to get plates of barbecue. The speeches continue, and the air is thick with this feeling of the boosters and thankers, although not as any kind of rapturous *communitas*. The deep emotional investment in the soldiers floats about seeking its outlet, and that outlet proves to be an ambivalent, moving target. Grave intonations of sentiment come in wavering or cracking voices as the speakers find themselves overwhelmed by their own emotion, a disabling excess of affect that breaks the language leaving their mouths. It seemed to happen often when I saw civilians talking to soldiers, especially in groups and organized settings, and I have even felt twinges of it in myself, the way that feeling rises to the surface, maybe even ambushing you a bit, as you work to answer a vague imperative to say something meaningful and appropriate.

There is certainly nothing cynical or false about the hyperabundance of militaristic and patriotic sentiment, but there is just so much of it, a single chord being sounded again and again. Indeed, one of the guests is a man from Dallas who tours the state towing a working replica of the Liberty Bell on a trailer; guests at the picnic are invited to ring it, and it tolls solemnly and at odd intervals throughout the afternoon. One speaker is invited by the emcee to "tell us your feelings on what we're doing here today and on America." The television anchor, clad in a Stars and Stripes button-down, says to the crowd of soldiers, "I need to tell you personally how grateful I am," and segues from his brief speech of thanks to a rendition of Lee Greenwood's "God Bless the USA" and a medley of other patriotic songs. Another speaker asserts that "if you're an American, you will always be 100 percent in debt" to soldiers who have served in war; it is not clear whether this is directed toward the soldiers in the audience, the civilians, or both.

One hundred percent—a quantity both hyperbolic and actuarially exact. That is some serious indebtedness, and I wonder what is to be done with it. Who else might we be indebted to and maybe welshing on? The Iraqi and Afghan civilians who have been hurt or killed, or who have fled their homes or had their lives upended? Those who go sick and hungry in the United States while the war soaks up billions of dollars? Who else's exposure, pain, immiseration, and death has helped earn whatever it is that the war is for? What else is owed on all this, by what measures, and in exchange for what, exactly?

THE GIFT OF DEATH

Political violence, Alan Klima (2002) suggests, is always tinged with an ambivalent spirit of giving, haunted by the restless ghosts of those who had to die for the present order of things to come into being.[1] Marcel Mauss (2000), in his essay on the gift, describes it not as an isolated object passed between subjects but instead as a gesture that initiates cycles of obligation, reciprocity, and debt. The "spirit" of the gift travels along with the actual thing given, and accumulates with and flows from the givers and receivers in their subsequent transactions. According to the Melanesian shaman whose words Mauss borrows, "no price is set" on the thing given. If you give the thing received to a third person, and then receive another object and attendant spirit in exchange, you become indebted not only to this new donor but also to the original one as well. The failure to hold up your end of the unspoken deal can result in "serious harm, . . . even death" (Mauss 2000, 11). The gift in this sense is a practice of social relations—relations of mutuality and dependence that are reaffirmed with every exchange and counterexchange, that defy rational, capitalist value, and that ultimately carry mortal stakes. The entire thing unfolds on the presumption that what has gone around will come around, even if by an as yet unforeseen avenue. The routes that the gift's value travels are much more circuitous and diffuse than the clean, impatient one to one of the marketplace, and this, combined with the absence of a price, makes the gift a dramatically noncapitalist and nonrational mode of transaction, an irrationality exemplified in soldiering's mortal altruism. Let us think of soldiers' work—the violence that they produce and are exposed to—as a gift, given to the state and population on whose behalf they labor—given, that is, to us.

This gift of death—exposure to death and the wreaking of death on others—is the thing that defines war, and defines the soldier's exceptional condition as agent, instrument, and object of legitimate violence. It is the sovereign, mutable, fungible quantity minted out of the raw matter of injured bodies, and transformed by fetish and fiat into the things that war is "about," things like territory, security, and ideology (Scarry 1987). But as it binds otherwise-incommensurable experiences together, especially when those incommensurables carry life-and-death stakes, the gift also bespeaks openness and uncertainty that surpass the mathematical finitude of 100 percent and the simple intentionality of "I need to thank you." Gifts always "contain within them" the possibility that their value and spirit will be misrecognized or mishandled; "the obligation to reciprocate . . . may fail to be observed," releasing destructive forces (Mauss 2000, 10). In its danger, ambiguity, relationality, and demand for participation, the gift gives a name to the problem of value and indebtedness that war presents. Like love, the gift both resolves and exacerbates the problem of worth and motive by injecting pricelessness into a worldly economy.

Soldiers are not free agents or self-interested actors. Soldierly identity derives from unbreakable loyalty, unquestioning obedience, and the virtuous asceticism that adheres to service and sacrifice; it derives, paradoxically, from the "voluntary" renunciation of individual autonomy. Soldiers cannot act as free agents, and indeed this subjection to authority is what makes their otherwise-unthinkable actions possible. Just as soldiers are not free, the gift that they give is not freely given. That this contradiction is so especially intense at the heart of the ultimate gift—the death that makes possible law, freedom, security, reason, right, and prosperity as we know them—says something of the unfree nature of all gifts, and the violence and coercion that lurk beneath so many things that appear to be free. Just as love is both a negation of the self and the realization of its fondest desires, the soldier's giving is at once the ultimate gesture of will and an act that is truly "selfless" by virtue of its enactor's ambiguous selfhood.

The other end of gift exchange is equally unfree and uninnocent. The power to give is the power to obligate, to place others in your debt. Indeed, as Jacques Derrida (1992) observes, there is no such thing as giving without anticipation of return. And as Mauss famously demonstrates in his account of the potlatch—the ritual giving away or destruction of valuable things—extravagant expenditure is a way of asserting dominance. Even in putatively modern times and spaces, Mauss says (2000, 65), "The unreciprocated gift still makes the person who has accepted it inferior, particularly when it has been accepted with no thought of returning it." A gift of sufficient magnitude can bury a rival giver, or it can subordinate a recipient if there is no way to pay it back; worth is proved by squandering something precious. And what could be more precious than the expenditure of safety, sanity, and life itself by going to war?

Some people, like the volunteers and boosters at the picnic, go out of their way to place themselves in debt (see Wool 2009). For many people—those in the United States and elsewhere who object to war, and those in Iraq who must live in it or die from it—the gift of war violence and its attendant death is unsolicited as well as unwanted. But while we may not have asked for this gift and may even have objected strongly to it, it cannot be refused. At least on our end of things, it is arguably the case that we have accepted the gift already merely by inhabiting a social order that is upheld by violence, by the dying of those who have gone before both here and in foreign elsewheres. On the other end of the exchange, soldiers confront a range of expressions of gratitude that they often don't know what to do with: the fetishization of the soldier in public culture, the volunteers who greet planeloads of returning soldiers with waving flags and baked goods, and the individual forms of thanks that people in uniform encounter while going about their business out in the civilian world. Such salutations continue today even as attention to the war fades. They are tinged as much with pity, guilt, and fascination as with gratitude.[2] Soldiers' responses to these things, while never ungracious, are generally ambivalent, for it is gestures like these that far from erasing the debt, help call the debt into being.

The emotionally overloaded thanking of soldiers, at 100 percent indebtedness, turns into a kind of abasement. It is a short leap to the sacred from here, to the idea of a sacrifice of life that cannot be paid back. And because it cannot be paid back, as Friedrich Nietzsche (1956) suggests in his discussion in *The Genealogy of Morals* of Christ's crucifixion, the sacrifice gives rise to a new order of things based on guilt and perpetual obligation. This kind of sacred debt provokes crisis. It runs counter to the capitalist notion that all quantities are fungible, alienable, and exchangeable—that there is a fair price for everything. It runs counter to the technocratic cost-benefit analysis of military decision making. And it runs counter to the modern, secular imperative that military force be subordinated to civilian political will and rationality. It is not merely that the debt is too great ever to be paid back but also that rationality simply cannot take full account of the sacred, even if it can present it as a mathematical absolute.

The traffic of value and obligation that actively produces the debt as permanently, a priori unpayable is set up by the way that soldiers and civilians are figured as opposite kinds or categories. Media imagery, conventional wisdom, and public and political discourse all support this notion. As Catherine Lutz (2001, 228–29) observes, the soldier is figured as "emotionally disciplined, vigorous, and hardworking. By definition, then, the civilian is weak, cowardly, self-centered, materialistic, and wealthy. The civilian is soft, lacking experience with both the physical discipline that hardens muscles and with the hard facts of death and evil that the soldier faces down." While civilians are "free" to do as they please, the soldier pursues a transcendent, higher purpose (whether fighting for freedom and democracy, or simply doing his duty). He is made righteous by threat and injury, and stands stoically in the face of trauma. Soldiers themselves reproduce versions of this binary. Despite sharing many of the same tastes, values, politics, and aspirations to the good life as nonmilitary Americans, soldiers would often tell me that they didn't know what "civilians" felt or believed because they weren't civilians themselves; some even said that they had never been civilians.

The relation between soldiers and civilians is not just simple opposition or categorical difference but an *exception*. The military is frequently figured from both within and without as an institution apart from the nation as a whole, existing to protect the public yet exceeding it in discipline, virtue, and moral authority (Lutz 2001; Brodie 2000; Ricks 1997). Soldiers are presumed to enjoy a sort of "supercitizenship," Lutz writes (2001, 236), as military rhetoric, especially in the form of recruitment advertising, motivates civilians to "value soldiers . . . in exchange for not being asked to kill and die." By default, all nonmilitary citizens are thus "subcitizens," a hierarchy of value that contradicts the very idea of military power as an instrument of democratic will (ibid., 237). Soldiers are excluded from the category of "regular" citizen at the same time as they exemplify it to an extreme by their mortal exposure on behalf of the nation. This exceptionalism finds its apotheosis in a poem called "It Is the Soldier," originally authored in 1970 by Charles Province, an Army veteran, but widely quoted and reproduced in military communities and promilitary public discourse.

> It is the Soldier, not the minister
> Who has given us freedom of religion.
> It is the Soldier, not the reporter
> Who has given us freedom of the press.
> It is the Soldier, not the poet
> Who has given us freedom of speech.
> It is the Soldier, not the campus organizer
> Who has given us freedom to protest.
> It is the Soldier, not the lawyer
> Who has given us the right to a fair trial.
> It is the Soldier, not the politician
> Who has given us the right to vote.
> It is the Soldier who salutes the flag,
> Who serves beneath the flag,
> And whose coffin is draped by the flag,
> Who allows the protester to burn the flag.[3]

Line by line, the soldier gives one precious thing after another. It is difficult to imagine a more plainspoken articulation of the notion that legitimized violence precedes and underwrites rights and freedoms rather than coming after them as an unfortunate last resort. And the soldier appears as both author and victim of this relationship.

The idea that soldiers do, produce, give, or give up something by practicing violence in the name of right and reason goes by familiar labels. The labor of making war is often called "service"—service to the public and the nation. It is a description applied to only a few other kinds of work, including teaching, medicine, and public safety, and one that suggests a relationship of commitment and subordination as opposed to the measurable transaction of wage labor. In this sense, service also bears the implicitly debased tinge of "servitude" and "service sector"—coincidentally or not, the type of civilian economy that dominates Killeen and many other military towns. Most of us believe that one does not go into service for the money but instead for loftier motives, and that in any case the money is not something that can balance out what is asked for in return; this is what lends soldiering its "weak if noble cultural reputation" (Lutz 2001, 231). Nevertheless, valorizing those who serve because they give more than they take means not having to think about what is not being given to them, not least the measurable, cold, hard, unsentimental cash that might really make a difference.

A soldier's death in war, or risk of death, is a "sacrifice." The civilians in whose name war is waged are nominally expected to sacrifice as well, but only in the Protestant sense of forbearance and abstention—or in self-torture over their failure to give anything up. The sacrifice of physical and psychic integrity, and of life itself, has the aura of sacred spectacle. The Army might be simply a job and livelihood, and skillful tactical soldiering might be nothing more than the reasoned use of a living body toward some practical end, but sacrifice—making holy through renunciation and destruction—is an excessive, violent consumption of life. It is antiutilitarian. Like service, sacrifice is an exercise in displacement and surrogacy—doing something for or in place of another. Sacrifice ups the ante even higher than service does, and entails yet another kind of balance sheet—one laden with unpayable debts. Soldiers die not merely so that we live but also so that life ordered by law and reason is even possible.

The problems here are several, although they all stem from the fact that we face a debt whose form and content are obscure. On the debtors' side, there is the insistence on thanking and the impossibility of repayment. On the side of the creditors—the soldiers—there is the burden of graciously accepting this repayment and conforming to the expectations of the indebted, even when it is not consonant with soldiers' own notion of what they are owed. The thing given is said to be priceless, and yet it is intractably bound up with more profane constructions of political and material value. It is said and felt to dwell between persons, and yet it cannot be spoken from one to another without invoking a vast sweep of enabling, intermediating structures.

THE BURDEN OF GRATITUDE

There is a lot of ambivalence on gratitude's receiving end. Soldiers are constantly thanked for their service, but for some, as Stewart told me when I asked him about it, "We don't really wanna talk about it." People saying thanks becomes a certain kind of unwelcome attention after a while. Stewart's wicked humor and theatrical expressions of exasperation cut some of the apparent bitterness. Kristen and I laughed along with him as he talked.

> On your first deployment, you know, you come back, and the Dallas Cowboy cheerleaders and this group and that group are there, and you're like, "Check it out! This is freakin' awesome!" All the fanfare, this, that, and the other, and you're like, "That's right, 'cause I freakin' rock!" [*We all laugh.*] It's all great and fine, you know, it's just fabulous. But after the second time, it's just like, "Yeah, whatever. Quit bothering me. Leave me alone!" And then, after the third time, you're just like [*in a weak, pained voice*], "Oh God, why do you even care? Just shut up and leave me the fuck alone!" But in the back of our minds, we do understand that it's just people showing their appreciation. We understand and we're grateful. But people don't understand that, we understand that you're grateful. You don't have to keep telling us.

The thanking becomes excessive. It gets out of hand. Stewart invoked the allegory of a gift as he struggled to explain his frustration to our continued laughter.

> Well, it's frustrating when it gets to be too much. If you give me a birthday present, and I say, "Thanks! Oh my God, oh my

God! Just . . . thanks! I appreciate it so much!" And then I keep just going on and on and on about it. [*We laugh.*] And then every time I see you the next day, [I say,] "You know man, I just really loved that birthday present! Holy crap, this is great! Wow! Oh my God!" And you're like, "OK, cool, we're friends. I appreciate your appreciation." And you think that's gonna be it. And then you see the guy the next day. [*In increasingly exaggerated tone*:] "Man, oh my God, that frickin' birthday present just rocks! Oh my God!" [*We laugh some more.*] After a while, it's just . . . it gets . . . it's too much, you know? You're overwhelming me.

You know, I know I'm not the only one that thinks this. . . . My best friend, we've talked about this. And he's like, "You know, I've gotten to a point where I just don't wanna be recognized as military. Because people are just gonna deluge you with compliments." It gets to be too much. You know, I appreciate the appreciation, but the appreciation is getting to be too much appreciating. [*Laughter.*] You know what I'm saying?

For Stewart, the soldier has given a gift, and seeks only that point at which the cycle of obligation can be recognized and the necessary gestures concluded. Instead what happens is a perverse sort of inflation. Stewart says that the soldier derives less value from the thanks after each trip to war and each successive expression of gratitude. But at the same time, the appreciation "appreciates," as it were, to the point of being too much. Indeed, in Stewart's narrative, it accumulates interest and gains some oppressive kind of value over time, building from a point of appropriately balanced acknowledgment to something that becomes cloying, then intrusive, and then burdensome.

We can consider the soldier's service in war as an originary gift, but what happens next is less clear; it is a muddled exercise in the impossibility of a countergift. Having been given something that seems impossible to repay, civilians struggle simply to say thanks. Like the speakers at the picnic, their voices choke and crack with stridency and insistence, their language literally broken and insufficient in the face of the thing they are trying to say. In Stewart's telling, it is as if this sense of insufficiency prompts a compulsion to repeat and compound, and with each iteration there is a fresh realization of the inadequacy of the previous one. Every time you say thank you to a soldier more interest has accumulated, the debt is even bigger than you realized, and you try to pay more, and it never works. You are overwhelmed, and at the same time, as Stewart says, "You're overwhelming me." We might like to think that enough thanks can somehow be dumped into the gap of obligation that lies between the civilian and soldier—some sort of emotional substrate that will fill in this chasm and make it passable. But instead it just draws attention to the gap. It pushes the soldier further away, prompting his retreat into a space of concealment and solitude. *You're overwhelming me.*

After all, the soldiers insist over and over, they are merely doing their job. Soldiers aren't out for glory, Jimmy told me the day after we returned from a tribute at the Houston rodeo to injured soldiers who had been invited from several different Texas military installations. Though the volunteers and civilian audience at the rodeo were all too eager to cast the soldiers in attendance as sacrificial victims, Jimmy made the complete opposite assertion: what he had done was not a sacrifice at all. I had sat next to them in the arena as an announcer's voice directed the crowd's gaze and spotlights swept down the vertiginous slope of the upper-deck bleachers to where our group was. Jimmy, Dale, Hank, and a few others all rose to the sound of applause, unsmiling and not quite comfortable under all that attention. As we talked about it the next day, Jimmy echoed Stewart: you don't know how to respond when people make a big deal of things. You want to say "thank you" and then "leave us alone." Jimmy was especially upset because he, as the ranking NCO from our Fort Hood group, had been invited to have his picture taken with the country music stars who performed at the culmination of the rodeo finals under a hail of red, white, and blue confetti. Hank was a much bigger fan, and Jimmy had wanted him to go instead. Hank has cancer; "He's dying," Jimmy said to me angrily. But all that the band seemed to care about was a photo op. No questions, no requests for autographs. And, said Jimmy, they didn't want any visibly wounded soldiers in the picture. The showy extravagance of sentiment overwhelms what ought to be a simple recognition of duty, and the soldier is left with the disappointment that people insist on showing appreciation on their own instrumental terms—yet another misfire of gratitude.

Kristen, Stewart's girlfriend, said people are "misguided" about how they throw their gratitude at soldiers.

> People always say, "Thanks for my freedom," and I'm like how does Iraq have any damn thing to do with your freedom of speech or whatever? And maybe in the long run it would, *if* we were preventing the problems . . . which ends up with that whole political crap about why are we in a war and whatever. But because it's misguided. You know, "thank you" is a bandwagon thing. [With some people, like the volunteers who come by the Foundation,] that seems to be motivated from the right place, regardless of what they're doing, why they're doing it, whatever the hell. All they're doing is recognizing, "Hey, you've been through a hard time here, we're gonna give you [something]." At the same time, the whole "Thanks for our freedom"—what the hell are you talking about?

As Zoë Wool (2011, 161) writes of the visibly injured soldiers at Walter Reed Army Medical Center who are frequently visited by volunteers and reporters, the experience of being "nominated" as a hero or sacrificial victim "is profoundly troubling." By saying thank you, the civilian tells one of the familiar and highly circumscribed stories flagged at the beginning of this book, converting deeply personal loss and pain into historical progress—steps on the way toward a victory or loss, a national story, or a political point. It's not just about the way it posits a wrong connection between one thing and another, like "How does Iraq have any damn thing to do with your freedom?" Presumably gratitude that is "motivated from the right place"—that is sincere and not theater—does not insist on bending the soldier's experience to some shape that is pleasing to civilian concerns. Stewart and Kristen distrust the frenzy of images and discourses that surrounds war and the soldier, and that compels civilians to thank unthinkingly, without "meaning it," thereby undermining the integrity of the exchange.[4] The tension over what the soldier's gift "has to do with" links directly to the problem of its value: what it's worth depends on what it was given for. Playing deliberately with the "weak nobility" of soldierly labor, Jimmy told me at one point, "I don't wanna die for this country. I don't wanna die for you. I mean, I will if I have to, but I don't want to." He paused. Then, with a smirk and a shift in tone that addressed the larger audience that my presence with notebook and tape recorder signified, he added, "That, and I need a raise!"

The soldier's status as an avatar of death or broken life adds another dimension to the cycle of thanks, to the binding together and mutual alienation of the giver and receiver of the gift, the giver and receiver of thanks. For Stewart, it was the way this desire to say thank you was mingled with a morbid curiosity. People want to know what you saw and what you did. It's not an obvious connection, but for Stewart the acknowledgment of the gift came to be tinged with an attraction to that violence, something prurient or voyeuristic.

> They're like, "Thanks for doing what you do! Yeah! Hooah!" and all this bullshit. And then they're like, "What's the worst thing you've ever done or you've ever seen?" . . .
>
> What the problem might be with it is, with all the appreciation, the appreciation leads to a conversation. You know, truthfully, I hadn't thought about that. The appreciation leads to a conversation, and then you get the ultimate question: "The worst thing ya seen?" "I don't wanna talk about it." And people don't accept that. They're like, "Aw, come on man, tell me something!" Most people don't get pushy like that, but you know . . . but that's it. The older vets are just subtly appreciative. They don't ask you that question, 'cause you know, they're like, "We love you guys, and we appreciate all that you're doing." And then they cut it off at that point, hand you a cookie—USO or whatever. . . . I mean, I know I can speak for all soldiers when I say, we appreciate that. 'Cause they show their appreciation, they talk to us a little bit, and then they go back home. As opposed to . . . Joe Somebody, because you're having dinner somewhere, finds out you're military and is like, "Aw man, thanks, thanks. What's the worst thing you've ever seen?" . . . I'm eating dinner here, guy. I don't wanna talk about it.

The vets, who know death, know how to moderate their appreciation. Is it not death that is ultimately so overwhelming in these encounters?

Stewart and Kristen were good friends with Dime, who had just gone to visit his family in California.

> *Kristen*: When I took him to the airport, he had his uniform on. I was like, "Why are you wearing your uniform? You hate that thing!" And he was like, "I always fly in uniform because everybody's nicer to you!"

> *Stewart*: And yet he said he's coming back in civilian clothes, like, "I don't even wanna be associated with the military on the way back. It just draws too much damn attention."

> *Kristen*: Something happen on the way there?

> *Stewart*: No, the way there he got bumped up to first class, everybody was buying him drinks, and it was all great. And if I'm lying may I be struck down. He said, "And then some guy asked me, 'What's it like over there?'" And there it goes, there's the question. "What's it like over there?" "What's the worst thing you ever seen?" Dime had to cut him off. He just politely said, "I don't wanna talk about it." 'Cause the guy would've eventually [asked], "What's the worst thing you ever seen?"

> *Kristen*: And unfortunately for Dime, the worst thing he's ever seen is his best friend get blown up.

Do you want to know that this happened to someone? Do you want to thank them for it? I knew this story from talking to Dime, and it appears in chapter 2, so now you know it too. It wasn't offered in response to my thanks, or a demand to know the worst thing he had seen or done. In fact, he began reciting it almost without preamble the moment I turned on the tape recorder. But it was one of the more horrific things I'd heard—gory, violent, heartbreaking, and hideously profane.

Indeed, what are people thanking you for? Thank you draws attention to the ill-defined content of the gift. It tries to make sacred the simple virtue of doing one's job or the irredeemable trauma of seeing a best friend dismembered before your eyes. Though "most people" aren't that pushy, even approaching the gift is upsetting. Thanks is not merely misdirected (because people misunderstand the gift); it becomes a provocation to reveal the nature of the gift, the vague and terrifying burden it continues to impose on both the giver and recipient, the tension and taboo that abide between soldier and civilian. The thanks and then the question ask the soldier to share what he has done with himself, and thus to relive and reveal what he might prefer to forget and withhold. In this way, saying thank you and knowing what to say in response become dilemmas of memory, of deciding what to resuscitate by remembering and what to let go by forgetting.

If thanks draws attention to the chasm that lies between soldier and civilian, trying to pave it over even as it widens it, then taboo—broken wide open and seething with the power of spilled blood—is what lies in that chasm. The civilian tries to step blithely over the carnage, as if it is not there, as if is not the thing that it is, or the civilian draws attention to it in a way that is unseemly—the unearned thrill of forbidden knowledge. Either way, the soldier retreats even more determinedly to the far side. Expressions of gratitude prolong the exchange when the giver would rather just let it go, forget about it, or at least not share it with that person at that moment.

At the scene of thanks, the double binds of giving and receiving multiply, and then spiral off toward some horizon that marks the impossibility of resolution. The soldier often wants to be thanked less and paid more. The soldier, as the one who has given, finds a burden of countergift placed on him in the form of the civilian's extravagant, interest-accruing gratitude. The soldier wants to be recognized and does not want the nature of the gift to be misunderstood, but he, and we, lack both the power and the language to define what the gift means; we lack a vocabulary of recognition or acknowledgment that would not reduce the soldier's experience. Instead, we are stuck with a series of inadequate clichés that, when spoken as thanks, leave the soldier feeling recognized for the wrong thing and preferring not to address the right thing. The causes, results, and reasons of war that lie outside its conduct—"our freedom"—are too abstract and bloodless to serve as an adequate basis for recognition, while the particularities of the labor of war—"the worst thing you ever saw"—are far too personal.

The soldier and civilian come by their relative position through a vast apparatus of power to which both are attached. It is this apparatus as much as anything else that has produced the debt, but paradoxically it is also the thing obscured when the debt is personalized in direct encounters between soldiers and civilians, in *I need to tell you personally*. Bringing the whole war down to *I*, *you*, and *personally* collapses the frame, shape, and scale of the debt and localizes the responsibility to thank. Death and debt move person to person without the intervening mass of the institution to dampen their force. At the same time, the force of war is just far too big a burden for any two people to shoulder on their own, even with a lot of speeches, songs, prayers, and free barbecue to back them up. And so both parties to the scene of gratitude struggle with all the unnamed excesses that surround the simple effort to say thanks, the effort to condense all of what war means and has done into a momentary face-to-face encounter.

At the picnic and in every military-civilian scene of appreciation, the soldier and civilian stand outside of war—in time, place, and experience—and pay a bloodless but deeply felt tribute to the violence of its interior. The thanks originates with the civilian's conception of war as a meaningful political endeavor—nothing but a continuation of politics—yet it draws attention to the soldier's direct experience of violence, moving into that space at the center of war where violence has no explicit meaning outside the immediacy of the contest. The soldier is either being thanked for war's political outcomes, which are alien to his actual labor, or for that labor of violence, which is alien to the politicized humanity that he is meant to be defending. The transaction of war takes on increasingly excessive and contradictory forms the closer you get to its interior, the place where the soldier labors, the place where violence appears to be transpiring for its own sake. As Dime said to me at one point, "If I had to go and explain myself to everybody about the shit that *I* fuckin' did, my God, I should be in jail right now! But no, I was under orders to do what I did." Means become divorced from ends, the soldier's labor resembles a crime, and war looks as though it is being waged not as a contest over values, land, or ideology, but according to the gratuitous logic of vengeance and satisfaction that governs the duel, where the only aim is to hurt and kill.

At the picnic, the prayers, speeches, saturation of patriotic symbols, and gestures of generosity all place these soldiers, in a quite
literal fashion, at the intersection of sacred, material, and political
value. But contrary to the at once ennobling and abasing insistence
on 100 percent indebtedness, the soldier's sacred labor on behalf of
the nation can never be separated out from the wage that he receives
for that labor or the unfeeling instrumentalization of his body by
the state. On the field of battle, the soldier is allowed to engage in
all sorts of acts that would otherwise be illegal, as Dime points out,
and likewise while deployed is subject to levels of indifferent physical danger that he would not otherwise be expected to endure. War
has no framework of judgment or evaluation tacked on. In soldiers'
talk, this space was thick with lived intensity, but in its subjective
immediacy, it was divorced from all those things that make a coherent story of war: politics, symbolic elaboration, or even ego—all of
which hover at its periphery as the recording angels that will later
translate things into an intelligible narrative. Dime said:

> A lot of people think we go over there to satisfy the whole testos-
> terone, male, go-over-there-and-be-a-warrior. That leaves about
> the first five minutes after you get your boots on the ground and
> you realize, "Holy shit, I'm actually here!" . . . That whole war-
> rior mentality, right out the window! [*Laughs.*] And you're like,
> "Holy shit, I'm actually here doing this, what in the hell did I
> just get myself into?" I mean you wanna serve your country with
> honor and distinction, but self-preservation kinda takes a little
> bit more precedence over that, and you're kinda like, "Wow, OK,
> um, shit, I'm carrying a weapon, and I'm walking around, and
> there's people actually trying to kill me now. Because of the flag
> that I'm wearing on my right shoulder." And it's very real. It's a
> very real feeling.

The civilian peers over the edge of this zone of killing and dying,
and is witness to it in various circumscribed ways. But in saying thank
you to the soldier and extending a hand in gratitude, the civilian is
also reaching across the border of this zone, and dragging with him
misapplied rules and values that do not make sense once they are
extended into the space of exception. As Dime explains, where the

civilian sees selfless fortitude and brave deeds, the soldier may ago-
nize over loss, or wonder over terror and crime. The soldier is not
exactly comfortable within this zone, but he knows it, and it offers a
logic that corresponds to his experience. When the civilian imposes
the standard, sacred, elevated values for life and death on this zone,
the soldier grows uneasy and then resentful, for he has, with no small
effort, learned to value these things in different, even alien ways.

DEAD-END COMMODITIES

One day at the Foundation, a couple of civilian workers from the
engineering building next door came in with a box they had pulled
out of a dumpster down the road. It was full of medals in small, blue
cardboard cartons. There were easily a hundred of them in the box.
They were mostly Global War on Terrorism (GWOT) Service Medals: a bronze medallion with an American eagle, shield, arrows, and
ivy in front of a sort of minimalist globe graphic, and the name of
the award in blunt, unlovely type around the edge, all hanging from
a blue ribbon striped in red, gold, and white. As Army medals go, the
GWOT (the soldiers say it "gee-wot") is pretty generic, an "automatic decoration": it recognizes service "participating in or in support of" any "War on Terror" operation, which includes just about
anyone who spent any time in the military since September 11, 2001.
You get one even if you haven't deployed abroad; for that you get the
Global War on Terrorism Expeditionary Medal (the GWOTEM) as
well. And there are other automatic decorations too.

Why there would be a box of them just chucked in a dumpster
was a mystery to me, but it didn't faze Jimmy, Dale, or any of the
other soldiers hanging around that day. Probably someone was just
cleaning out an office—a unit that was moving or deploying—and
dumping stuff that wasn't worth the trouble to keep. But the soldiers
decided to save the medals in case a returning unit might need them.
I was so intrigued by this find that I retrieved my camera from my
car and took a couple of washed-out, blurry photos, although only
after Jimmy shuffled the boxes around a bit so that the bar codes and

Figure 6 A box of discarded Global War on Terrorism Service Medals, required but unre-
       markable

product numbers on the boxes weren't showing. Dale chuckled as I
took the pictures. "You gotta write about all this wasteful shit that
they do," he said with the excitement of a muckraking coconspirator.

It wasn't the waste exactly that struck me, even though the full
medals cost about ten bucks apiece if you have to buy them yourself,
and if you multiplied that by the dozens of them in this box, it wasn't
exactly a pittance that was sitting there in the dumpster. To me it
was more the uncanniness of the things. First, there was the fact that
this was in some ways the most unremarkable of all medals, a nominally special recognition that was depleted of its specialness by being
bestowed on everyone; its combination of commonness and dignified pretension would seem to insult both giver and receiver. Then
there was the utter strangeness of seeing so rare a thing as a medal
reduced to a banal commodity and packed up wholesale in a box,
then reduced further to mere junk with a heave into the dumpster,
and then maybe reduced yet again by having been rescued. Would
you want a medal salvaged from the trash? More important, would it

make any difference? Think of a medal, any medal, as a materialized symbol that bespeaks a certain constellation of giving, receiving, and recognition: the work and service given, the medal and spirit of recognition given in return, some affirmation of solidarity, and the value and meaning of things achieved in the process. Without the gestures communicating things—a signed order, a ceremony, a handshake, a salute, a uniform for it to be pinned on, or whatever—the medals looked rather shameful and half dressed there in the box.

Dale laughed knowingly at the waste. But what about the expenditure involved in simply putting the things to their intended purpose in this bizarrely redundant exercise of distinguished service in which no one is distinct? What about all the certificates of achievement and appreciation and the plaques that decorate so many soldiers' walls or clutter their desk drawers, as they decorated the walls and cluttered the desk drawers of the Foundation office? What about the "challenge coins," individual, custom-printed brass and enamel medallions that officers and senior NCOs give out as awards and tokens of recognition? (A friend once told me that he had about seventy-five coins from his eight years in the Reserves, "and only one of them means anything to me.") These fetishes are born out of a curiously intense bureaucratic magic: it is dense with symbols and so obsessed with them that it makes them materially real things, objects that are so real that their symbolic meaning evaporates and they became clutter, like a too-big jar of change forgotten on a shelf. No one hands you this medal; there is no award ceremony. It just goes in your record that you have earned the GWOT. And in fact the medals themselves—the full kit with brass pendant, like those sitting there in the box—are a little pointless. All you need is the little rectangular ribbon with the same colored stripes that costs a buck or two, and the pinned bars that you also buy at the PX to slide it on to in the correct configuration with whatever other ribbons you have earned. When you have dress inspection, that moment when your ceremonial self-presentation is judged for its correctness in reflecting back the recognition being bestowed on it and illustrating your career biography on your chest, that ribbon better be there, the blue, red, yellow, and white stripes in the "fruit salad" of brightly colored blocks and stripes, the readable career biography hanging on your chest.

Getting a medal means another niggling bit of responsibility. Maybe the soldier loses one in his desk drawer and has to buy another. He has to be accountable for it and make sure it is displayed correctly. Danny told me, "Your E-6 never says to you, 'This is the GWOT. Think about what it means, because one day not everyone will be wearing one, and you'll be able to say to your grandkids that this medal was for serving in the Global War on Terror.' They say, 'You wear it because I said so.' And," he added, "I've been guilty of it too. We don't think about it." And so this nominal token of reward, thanks, and recognition is not a gift, and is barely even an attenuated sign of blood and valor; it is something trivial to be responsible for. It is a pain in the ass.

As long as I was there, the GWOTs just sat on a shelf in the storeroom next to boxes of candy and canisters of powdered iced tea. The Foundation functioned on donations, so perhaps it is not surprising that it was full of similarly dead-ended commodities. The forms these donations took were eclectic and sometimes odd. Hanging on the wall—between framed photos, plaques, and certificates of appreciation—were oversize copies of thousand-dollar checks from corporate and nonprofit donors. There were a couple of big-screen televisions—gifts from wealthy supporters. There were two-dozen computers that came directly from Michael Dell. And there were cases and cases of soda, bottled water, Girl Scout cookies, Doritos, and canned soup along with a freezer full of hamburgers and hot dogs—surplus dropped off by grocery distributors.

Even the food had a motley quality. The nonperishable miscellanea stacked in the pantry and the baked goods brought, left, and picked over, their remnants sitting out on the lounge tables for days, crumbs and oil subsiding into layers of wax paper and foil. One day, under a desk, Valerie found cookies that she had left there before Ben's previous deployment, months ago. The cookies were vacuum packed and still good.

But then there was the other stuff, cast-offs stockpiled against some future need and highly sentimentalized tokens of thanks without a specific destination that ended up sitting around collecting dust. The storerooms were entropic and claustrophobic: linoleum floor and wood-veneer walls, neither of which you could see, and stuff piled to the cork-tile ceiling in precarious arrays that booby-trapped and barricaded the things you were trying to reach. As part of my loosely directed volunteer labor, I spent a lot of time with these things—moving stacks of them around, consolidating piles of clutter, and sorting and taking stock, often in the company of a couple of young soldier volunteers assigned to the task who would forage vigorously through drawers and boxes, and label everything with arcane Army supply codes.

In the storerooms there were literally hundreds of stuffed bears, like the ones that the volunteers gave out at the manifests. Some were elaborate, with mass and shape, body and limbs sewn into a sort of upright, seated position, and button eyes and stitched-on mouth. Others were simply two pieces of fabric stitched back to back and stuffed. Their faces were printed on in a bright and clownish silk screen, with long-lashed eyes and a tongue sticking from a too-wide smile; the patterned fabric they were made from was less pleasant to touch, duller, and more obscure. A pamphlet I found in the office described how the bears were prayed over as they were assembled by hand by groups of volunteers. Seen singly and in context, the bears were somewhere between sweet and kitschy. But in their massed hundreds in the storeroom, they became something else altogether. They were packed into fifty-gallon-size cardboard and plastic drums, or stuffed in big industrial trash bags, and heaved out of the way in the highest, farthest corners. You would climb up to look for something and find these creatures hemorrhaging from the split bottom of a cardboard box or pressing their faces toward you from behind milky plastic. It was not really clear whom the bears were intended for—whether soldiers, soldiers' kids, or Iraqi kids. They had come in these massive loads from church and corporate volunteers. Sometimes Jimmy would drive considerable distances to pick a fresh shipment of them—not because they were needed, but because they could not be turned down.

Stashed here and there in the more disorderly corners of the office and the storage sheds outside were care packages from the churches and community groups of small Texas towns. The boxes themselves were decorated on the outside with collages of American flags, photos of soldiers on foreign desert city streets, and little handwritten signs saying "For the Troops!" Some of them were full of hygiene kits—toiletries, tissues, baby wipes, sunscreen, stationery, and cross-word puzzles, along with religious pamphlets that had to be removed from each one before we could pass them on. Others contained more obscure items. In one box, for example, there were small bits of red, white, and blue fabric folded in plastic-wrapped packages. Hansen, a soldier who had gone foraging in the boxes with me, thought these were lap blankets or maybe pillow shams. Each was packed with a typed note to the recipient naming the group it was from and re-minding the soldier that this same group had also sent them stuffed bears, cookies, and various other things. Many gifts came decorated with these little bits of explanatory flair. On Memorial Day, a group of volunteers dropped off a basket of individually wrapped Rice Krispie treats; attached to each was a miniature American flag pinned to an ink-jet image of a C130 cargo hold full of flag-draped caskets and captioned "Never Forget!" "Yeah, these are real nice, we'll just give these to the soldiers," sneered Tony, sweeping them off a table in the lounge and stashing them out of sight in an empty desk drawer. Many of the volunteers were Vietnam and Korean War vets; all of them were warm, dedicated, and sincere. But does a twenty-year-old soldier need to be reminded not to forget that he may come back from Iraq in a box? Or rather, who is reminding whom of what with a gift like this? Who is it really for?

It is unsettling to see these rather mysterious objects, invested al-most grandiosely with so much feeling, intention, and momentum, halted far short of their destination. They have left the swirling orbit of the gift; gravity has pulled them to earth and drawn a blanket of dust down over them. The little enclosed notes remain unread by the soldiers mean to see them, and perhaps they will always remain that way. Thus the storeroom houses a second stockpile, composed of the affirmative platitudes with which soldiers are barraged in the form of these many, many sincere but also mass-produced texts—care pack-age notes, pamphlets, banners covered in signatures, and valentines and Christmas cards from schoolkids. One could ask whether these things "mean" something to soldiers or not, whether they "agree" with their sentiments or not. But what provokes is the simple fact of their material presence, often in ignominious piles of stuff that get in the way or are ignored in a back corner—that are around, lingering as clutter in the corners of daily life.

WAR'S GENERAL ECONOMY

There are two related problems with pricing the priceless and paying back the noncompensable. The first is that despite any insistence that one scale of value cannot be translated into another, everything is connected to everything else, and unlike kinds—life and nation, love and money—must be exchanged for one another. Georges Bataille (1988) calls this first problem, the inevitable mingling of different kinds of worth, "general economy." The second problem is that in this mingling, there is always something left over, an extra quantity that cannot be balanced out. Bataille dubs this accounting remainder the "accursed share."

As part of the mingling of value, the destruction and waste of war is also a source of wealth and livelihood. Being a soldier is a job, and wages, bonuses, training, security, health insurance, college funding, loans, and housing are all things that attract the people who become soldiers. This is not to deny that many of these people are not also motivated by patriotism, ideology, a desire to serve, camaraderie, or professional pride—or by the search for thrills and adventure. All these things mattered to the people I met in different proportions, weighted mixtures of priority and motivation. But I didn't meet anyone who had only a single reason, whether material, ideological, or emotional, for joining the Army, or who derived just a single source of satisfaction from it. All of which is just to say that money, worldly value, is inescapably in the mix; it's never the whole story, but it's never absent either.

Though we may expend a lot of energy reminding one another of the fact, we generally take for granted that for good or ill, the established exchange of things, labors, and forces in which we live is protected, sometimes preemptively, by the exercise of violence. And we know that such violence is also good for business, again whether for good or ill. Think of Franklin Roosevelt sweeping the nation out of depression on a tide of righteous, homebuilt bombs and rivets; or the security and logistics contractors chummy with the very folks who decide when and how to invade our ostensive enemies; or the very idea of going to war in the first place to protect oil, that dark

and slippery substance that keeps the wheels of production and consumption turning so smoothly.

Just about everyone I met at Fort Hood subscribed to some version of this story. The cynical asserted that the war would continue
indefinitely, or at least as long as possible, because there was so much
money to be made by contractors and weapons makers. Everyone
acknowledged, unbidden and in various ways, that oil figured into
things, although they varied on whether America's concern for oil
was hypocritical looting, rational self-interest, or responsible custo-
dianship of this valuable resource that the whole world depended
on. Stewart told me that the war should be named "Operation Iraqi
Liberation—O.I.L.," instead of Operation Iraqi Freedom. Bullard
asked me one day why, in 2008, after five years of fighting, gas was
still so damn expensive. We consulted Wikipedia briefly, and I rambled
about OPEC, regional instability, and petroleum futures. "Whatever,"
he said. "I just wanna be able to drive my truck." Dime, ranting at one
point about the Army's failure to take care of his combat injuries, interrupted himself and said, "Sorry if I'm getting angry, but you know, it's
a little sensitive subject there." Leaning in close to the microphone of
my tape recorder, he yelled theatrically, "Hope you enjoy the gas!" We
both laughed, and he apologized again: "Sorry man, sorry."

So while soldiers themselves get paid for war, the real wealth
it produces seems vague and abstract. It takes the form of greater
prosperity to be collectively enjoyed, or it is someone else's wealth,
siphoned off the hard work of many to be enjoyed only by a few. It
makes sense, then, that as with all the talk of service, sacrifice, and
debt, we talk about the economies that surround war in terms of
cost. Wars may be profitable, but more important they are expensive.
Wars cost money just as they cost lives, and in general economy, these
things can be treated side by side. It is said that wars cost blood, as
in "blood and treasure" and "no blood for oil." Both expressions reduce to cliché the otherwise-unseemly notion that blood is somehow
fungible in crass material terms, but they also offer an instructive
contrast. Blood and treasure suggests that the two expended quantities, while they exist on the same plane, are not reducible to one
another. No blood for oil is arguably disingenuous in its righteous-
ness, for it seeks to preserve some distinction between the things

that we buy with money and the things that we pay for in human lives; it presumes that oil can somehow be gotten without spilling blood. Both expressions, however, link supposedly priceless blood—signifying both vitality and death—to the profaneness and finitude of worldlier costs. In practice it is impossible to disentangle the gift of death, the soldier's sacrifice, from the pursuit of filthy lucre—hence the significance of symbolically distinguishing the sacred and profane with the rhetorical juxtaposition of blood with oil. Everything that we might want to say about the intersecting and interwoven systems of exchange and expenditure—the economies—that surround war calls attention to the traffic between the profaneness of politics and wage labor and the sacredness of selfless expenditure, the pricing of the priceless.

Even as we tell one another that blood and lives are priceless, the costs of war are measured with actuarial precision—body counts are issued and published daily (leaving aside the question of whose bodies are counted); tallies are made of friendly and enemy casualties; strategic gains and losses are noted; timetables and troop levels are set; and governmental appropriations are measured in the hundreds of billions. Projecting the cost of today's soldiers' medical care and retirement benefits into the future, economist Joseph Stiglitz (2008) famously estimated the total cost of the wars in Afghanistan and Iraq at three trillion dollars, which was about the size of the entire US federal budget for 2008.

Discourses of war's cost circulate broadly in public culture, but for the soldiers and military families who inhabit and work at Fort Hood, the tension that this language points to is also a condition of everyday life. The base is responsible for literally billions of dollars of outlay annually, and a significant portion of that goes directly into the local economy of Killeen and the surrounding area, where business is driven by the urgent pace of continuous deployments and continuing war and by the more stately movement of the federal government's Base Realignment and Closure process. In accordance with the Army's dedication to the rationalization of violence, there are very real formulas for figuring the monetary worth of priceless quantities like life and limb, such as the SGLI death benefit of four hundred thousand dollars (plus a hundred thousand dollars for death in a war zone), or the fifty thousand dollars that a missing arm or leg is worth under SGLI, or the 30, 40, or 80 percent disability pension one might receive from the Army and the VA for a ruined leg, a wrecked vertebrae, or a TBI. There are plenty of less spectacular tallies that also accrue to military service as well. These range from the extra monthly pay for hazard, hardship, separation from family during deployment, or being stop-lossed, to the sales tax you don't pay when you shop at the base commissary and PX, and the "service charge" you pay instead, to the housing and medical benefits that sometimes cover what you need, and sometimes don't. These are the wages of war in a very real, practical sense.

The numbers are tricky, though. They are not deceptive, exactly, for in a way they simply lay things bare with a candor that red, white, and blue bunting and outpourings of sentimental gratitude tend to elide. The numbers state definitively the allotments of value—the salaries, the bills and car installments, the disability payments, the federal budget outlays, the gas prices—with which everyone will have to be content. But the numbers are also haunted by the ghosts of the incommensurable or immeasurable values that they are meant to stand in for, and even by the way that they can differ so vastly among themselves, multiplying and dividing unthinkably vast sums and tiny, unremarkable quantities into one another. This produces a vertiginous sense of scale, of where and in what context a quantity appears generous or scarce, dear or cheap. Any amount of money can matter, and any amount can go up in smoke in an eyeblink, desperately clung to or nervously spent with abandon. When soldiers talk about staying in the Army "for the money" or people gripe that the war is "about money," sometimes money means the same thing, and sometimes it means different things, depending on what form it's in—pocket change, a payday loan, an Army paycheck, a no-bid contract, or a Department of Defense budget line.

Let's give the numbers their due, though:

> The wars in Iraq and Afghanistan are projected to cost $3 trillion.
>
> The amount of cash unaccounted for by the Coalition Provisional Authority, shipped directly from the Federal Reserve Bank in New York to the Green Zone in Baghdad on shrink-wrapped cargo pallets, is $9 billion.

A week of US occupation costs $2 billion.

An Apache attack helicopter costs $16 million.

A loaded and armored Humvee costs $185,000.

With the tick of a pen, a twenty-year-old junior enlisted Abrams Tank System Maintainer (Military Occupational Specialty 91-A) can order a workup that costs tens of thousands of dollars.

A year driving trucks in Iraq for a private contractor like KBR in 2008 would get you about $100,000.

A new 2009 Dodge Challenger is $40,000, and one day in the lounge a soldier who, as a private, and in contrast to the KBR truck driver, makes a little over $21,000 a year, asked me if I thought it was worth the price.

An enlistment bonus is $20,000, before taxes; a reenlistment bonus might be almost that high, and a medical severance could be around the same amount.

A bedroom set is $1,700.

A sleeve tattoo is $1,000.

A two-bedroom apartment in Killeen is $490 a month plus utilities.

An Xbox 360 is $300.

Cable costs $80 a month.

Your neighbor sells you a washer and dryer for $50 apiece.

A complete SGLI policy with a $400,000 death benefit costs $27 per month.

Gas money is the $20 you hand to a friend and might not get back.

The hourly wage at Walmart in Killeen or Copperas Cove is $8. You can make more money in Georgetown or Austin, but this means driving forty, fifty, or sixty miles when gas is near $4 a gallon; the cost of my own frequent drives back and forth was about 12¢ per mile.

A pack of Merits is $6.

If you can handle the pain, you can sell some of your Percocet tablets for $5 each.

Buffalo wings at Applebee's are $4.99.

A beer at Joker's or the American Legion is $2.25.

A single 5.56-millimeter round for an M4 rifle costs 25¢.

Then there is another set of numbers—that most sacred of numbers, the currency that opposes and parallels money: the body count, which is to say the US military body count. Soldiers are both cynical and sentimental about this number; their rhetoric poses the relatively small toll against the massive personal grief of individual losses. Of civilians, they say, "They're pitching a bitch over three thousand dead—that's nothing!" A year of deaths in Iraq was a bad week's worth in Vietnam, as more than one soldier argued. On the other hand, civilians couldn't possibly understand the grief of the various individual losses that most soldiers and those close to them suffered. There were a lot of funerals. How many people did they know who had died? Four, six, ten, twenty, or more.

Confusion over costs arises not just from overlaid and overlapping systems of value—sacred, political, and economic—but also from the abundance of middlemen and mediating institutions that help to create and define scale (Tsing 2005). Beyond the simple opposition between service or sacrifice and paid work, and beyond the traffic across war's inside and outside, extends a long series of obligatory or debt relations that are useful for explaining war at one moment or another, any of which can be richly imagined from the perspective of either or both of the involved parties. You could make a map of all the different entities: soldiers, spouses, NCOs, commanders, the Army, the VA, the Department of Defense, the government, the American public, insurgents, al-Qaeda, Iraqi civilians, military contractors, oil companies, reporters, war movies, and the world at large. Draw arrows in the right directions to show assertions of debt and obligation (e.g., the Iraqi people to the US state and public, or the VA to the hurt soldier), real or expected expressions of thanks (in the other direction), actual material compensation (wages, insurance payouts, baked goods, or sacks of rice and concrete mix), relations of extreme obligation (to exceptional and caring leaders, hurt comrades, kids, or the dead), places where things broke down (bad leaders or unfaithful spouses), and relations where people took without giving (clueless civilians, contractors, or occupiers). There are myriad ways of tracing these lines and ranking sets of obligations, and each constellation offers a different image of the gift of war. It would be a mistake to create a hierarchy of these different circuits, or reduce one to another. At some point the arrows become inadequate, and they betray only a ricocheting and boomeranging of debt, misrecognition, unpayable burden, and unpardonable theft without beginning or end.

Framing these costs and payments within a general economy is instructive, because people at Fort Hood often prefer not to talk about politics in the way that invoking war and economy in the same sentence tends to conjure. But they do talk about the war and their part in it in a language of worth, effort, and compensation heavily freighted with political claims. Like Stewart and Kristen, they express a deeply felt and frequently ambivalent problem of recognition: how their labors and losses are perceived by others, especially the civilian others who make up most of the public, the country, and the institutions, both intimate and remote, that are responsible for giving monetary and symbolic value to the work of war. In this general economy, soldiers tell a narrative that is in many ways a more bitter and complete version of the one that the guilty-minded civilian public sphere tells itself already: that only a tiny fraction of the country is acquainted with the costs of the war; that civilians are ignorant of or indifferent to these costs, or overly hung up on body counts and price tags; that no "payment" is being demanded of the people whose "freedom" is being protected; and that those who bear the most hardship are chronically misrecognized as baby killers, hateful thrill seekers, and dupes. As much as soldiers' lives and livelihoods—the securing of basic necessities and pleasures—depend directly on material compensation for their labor, there is clearly something more at stake as well, circulating through the general economy in a way that piggybacks on wages and benefits, but is hardly reducible to them.

You can see this quantity in the campaign for recognition waged on car bumpers and tailgates in Killeen: bumper stickers proclaim "Busting Mine, Defending Yours!" "Home of the Free . . . Because of the Brave," and "If you don't stand behind our soldiers, feel free to stand in front of them!" Ribbons in yellow, camouflage, and red, white, and blue urge "support" and prayers for the troops, and even display the portraits and birth and death dates of soldiers who have been killed. Heart-shaped decals testify to the sacrifice borne by lovers and families with declarations like "I Love My Soldier" and "Half My Heart Is in Iraq." The upright red-and-white rectangles of service banners hang in living room windows; each blue star on them represents a family member in harm's way, and each gold star stands for one who died.

The town is thick with flags and banners blessing and thanking the soldiers. And then there are the memorials—monuments in the old downtown, Conder Park, and the entryways of the community center and high schools. Just south of town, there is a massive new veterans' cemetery, which in addition to hundreds of graves has its own OIF/OEF memorial, with thumbnail portraits of the fallen etched on massive black granite slabs. There are memorials all over the base; each unit has its own. There are memorials that soldiers make for themselves and each other, in the form of photo slide shows set to patriotic songs or melancholic alt-metal, or tattoos of the names of dead friends next to the inked outlines of teardrops or shell casings. All these things cluster densely in Killeen, as they do in all military communities, and their abundance there contrasts with their relative absence just about everywhere else. They are remembrances directed inward rather than appeals to the outside world. What does it mean that these material markers of giving are concentrated in sites where they are reminders chiefly to those who have given and sacrificed? Do they become tokens of resentment, signs that one's own suffering is ignored by powerful, indifferent others? All the while, other items of exchange, like the gallons of gas that everyone agrees are somehow on the line, are rendered completely anonymous and stripped of any imprint of sacrifice. War transpires in a world in which everything has its price, even when we prefer to think it is not fungible.

DEALS WITH THE DEVIL

I met a plumber a few weeks after I moved into my apartment near the base. My ancient water heater caught on fire, and he came to replace it. He talked about the construction booming all around Fort Hood. There were builders making bank throwing up rows and rows of identical spec houses and fourplexes all over rezoned ranch land. The plumber's amiable tone turned scornful as he talked about it. It's wrong to make a buck off war. It's blood money. He mentioned the Blackwater contract security guards who, in 2004, were ambushed and killed in Fallujah, and their burned bodies then hung from a bridge. They never should have been in Iraq, he said. I pointed out that they had signed contracts that took away all their rights, that they were killed in part because know-nothing bosses ordered them on a needlessly dangerous mission, and the dead men's families were now suing the company (Eviatar 2007). No matter, he responded; they sold their souls when they signed the contract. Maybe that's what's wrong with the country. "I agree with bin Laden that America is corrupt. I've talked to my preacher about it. Bush has horns, man!"

I was too nervous—too wary of appearing to split hairs when the condition of our and everybody else's souls was at stake—to point out to my new acquaintance what seemed like a much bigger and messier complicity. Weren't we all here because of war, one way or the other? Was there even any question of turning down blood money or not ending up with some of it in your pocket? The other tenant of the house I lived in was a soldier who was paying rent for a place to sleep by the base hours away from his wife and their home, so that both he and she could keep their jobs. I was there because a research fellowship was paying my rent while I talked to soldiers about what violence had done to their lives. The plumber himself had been in the Army, he told me.

But this is the distinction that people make between wage labor and service: contractors lack the nobility of a higher purpose and lower wage. Fair enough. Perhaps if you are going to kill someone, it should be for a reason other than money. And yet there is the lingering question of what it means to do something for money or not, the perhaps peculiarly American preoccupation with intentionality, sincerity, and purity of motivation, with meaning what you say and doing what you do for the right reasons. This is what service and sacrifice are all about. Are soldiers' motivations really that straightforward, though? Are they fighting only for ideals? Are they doing it for money? No matter how fervent their patriotism and devotion to duty, soldiers expect to get paid. Doing hard and dangerous work for a wage to support a family is generally regarded as a noble thing, after all. So then what is blood money and what is not?

Of course there are distinctions at work—distinctions having to do with motivations and the amount of money one gets paid, and distinctions that sort the weak nobility of soldiers' service from the material motivations of the mercenaries. Still, the distinctions don't necessarily hold up under inspection, not least because the mercenaries are apparently necessary to the mission. At the height of the war, there were almost as many US-employed contractors in Iraq as there were US military servicemembers. As many as thirty thousand of them were security—the hired guns—but most were doing laundry, serving food, building roads, and all those other things that the military did more of on its own in the days before the all-volunteer force. Contracting wages for Americans are often two or three times those for doing the same job as a civilian in the United States, or for doing it as a soldier in Iraq. Investigative journalist T. Christian Miller reports that many contractors cite patriotism and a desire to contribute to the war effort as part of their motivation for signing up (cited in Gross 2010). Yet how much should these motivations matter? Miller has written extensively on how civilian workers wounded in Iraq had simply needed a job, any job. Many of them are former military (Miller 2009a; Gross 2010). Geographically, they are concentrated in military states, especially North Carolina and Texas, home to Fort Bragg, Fort Hood, and numerous other installations that regularly cycle out large numbers of newly separated ex-soldiers in need of work (Miller 2009b).

Then there are all the things that contractors don't get. They do not enjoy such tangible benefits as insurance, housing, and the Army's long-term job security. They are privately insured at astronomical rates—war zone insurance costs about a hundred thousand dollars per employee and is ultimately borne by taxpayers anyway—but they don't get the benefit of the military's sustained, integrated medical care, or its sensitivity to and knowledge of battlefield conditions and injuries (Miller 2009a; Gross 2010). Contractors, like soldiers, put themselves out there. They are exposed, endangered, and far from home. But because they are paid more money, they are not seen as being owed anything for the particular gift of death that they bear.

The point of all this is not to sort out what the right reasons are; it is to reveal the constitutive power of distinctions even as they constantly break down or are contradicted. Distinctions are essential to rendering value out of war. People grasp for them to distill sense and reason from the macrolevel shit storm of callous, lethal power relations from which all are trying to find shelter. The immeasurable gift of death and the divine aura of service and sacrifice run up against the sovereign rationality of money and its profane capacity to travel anywhere, account for anything, and bend people to any purpose. Indeed, money travels the world to draw people to war zones and make middlemen rich off their labor.[5] Money is a curse; too little of it is a grave injustice, but too much of it is cause for suspicion. And in a city where so many people have the same boss and the same salaries, it's easy to make claims about who has too little or too much. Each way of resolving the equation, of putting a name to the right and wrong reasons for a thing, comes up with a different remainder, a different notion of what is wrong, excessive, or in need of further balancing out.

Many people, both nonmilitary and those soldiers who find themselves considering other options, resent the way that everything in this community revolves around the Army. It has less to do with how this makes war the source of wealth, and thus livelihood and even life itself, and more to do with the simple arrogance of monopoly. People resent the contract companies' cavalier treatment of livelihood—renewing and rehiring every six or twelve months with no benefits, no vacation, and no promise of long-term stability. Sign up to make blood money and maybe get shot, maybe come home from Iraq early and lose all your money, or maybe come to work on Fort Hood one morning and find out that you and your fifty coworkers are no longer needed. The relentless demand of service is replaced by the merciless absolutes of the contract and the precarity of living with little obligation—owing little and, more important, being owed little. And yet it is just a job.

The security contractors in Iraq have a spooky, spectral presence that mimics the fleeting contract job and the ghostliness of the rules they are bound by and exempted from. They are the bodyguards for US Department of State and other nonmilitary personnel, protecting people, convoys, and infrastructure. They look like soldiers, but not quite—decked out in jumpsuits or civilian clothes, "high-speed"

gear and armor, and different kinds of weapons, and they have neither nametags nor badges. They move on their own and show up out
of nowhere, running missions that the soldiers don't know about.
They're around on many of the FOBs, living there and eating in the
DFACs. Often they are just a banal presence; sometimes they're an
irritation. But sometimes they approach soldiers and try to recruit
them. Sometimes they seem to know things about the soldiers. They
address them by name, already know what job they do and where
they're from, and mention that some obscure third party had said
to look for them—friendly, casual, and smiling all the while. Like a
ghost Army moving in the shadow of the real military, they are sometimes nothing but normal, and at other times reach out to invite you
to the other side. They shift from category to category: engineers,
drivers, interrogators, or security; entrepreneurs, opportunistic hired
guns, bandits, or thugs; torturers, assassins, or other deadlier, unac-
countable agents of the darkest of military tasks. Their ghostliness is
that of the suspended rule that says there is no such thing as a private
Army, that says killing must be in the name of the nation and not just
for a paycheck.

REWARD AND EXPENDITURE

One of the figures of the soldier that gained in visibility as the war
dragged on is that of the debtor. This figure, familiar from public
discourse on soldiers, also circulates with incredible and intimate
vigor among soldiers themselves and within the communities where
they live. The young soldier—twenty-one years old, maybe—comes
back from Iraq with fifteen months of salary and combat pay, more
money than he has even seen in his life, even though he gets paid
comparatively little for a job that demands so much. We like to say
that the money is "burning a hole in his pocket," as if it is possessed
of a dangerous, radiant, and self-consuming energy. And this makes
sense. For though the very word economy suggests thrift and moderation, Bataille reminds us that exchange also depends on expenditure. The soldier buys a new truck and a set of rims for it. Maybe

he buys a new television too, and presents for his wife, girlfriend, or parents. Before you know it, he has outspent himself. He gets in over his head with the payments. He goes deep into debt and begins to borrow money. Then he gives back the truck, and has to move out of the new house and sell back the furniture, so that he can eat and pay his bills. He can't get out of hock, and as his contract nears its end, he reenlists to get the bonus. Then he goes back to Iraq.

Soldiers are a captive market for various semipredatory retail enterprises that congregate in military towns, such as pawnshops, used car dealers, storefront lenders, credit cards, and other enterprises that seem to exist for the very purpose of destructive spending. The digital zipper sign at the pawnshop at the intersection of Hood Road and Route 190 in the center of Killeen flashes,

WE LOVE OUR SOLDIERS!!!

GREAT DEALS!!!

BEST PRICES FOR YOUR STUFF!!!

WE LOVE TO LOAN MONEY!!!

WE LOAN MORE AND SELL FOR LESS!!!

Soldiers represent a guaranteed steady paycheck and have a built-in collection authority: if the soldier falls behind, all the creditor has to do is call his commander; the soldier's NCO can harangue him more aggressively than any civilian boss and even arrange for the debt to be garnished from his paycheck. This is because an indebted soldier is a security risk, vulnerable to exploitation; your debts can wreck your security clearance, and thereby your career.

That soldiers spend and indebt themselves in these excessive cycles is an article of faith as well as a feature of everyday experience among soldiers and those who live with them. One day as I was talking with Theresa, she launched into a (for her typical) rant against consumerist excess—"Things are just things! A job is there to support you, not to enslave you!"—and the extreme irresponsibility of free-spending soldiers. Why did she think they did it? "It's because they want to reward themselves," she told me. They've been to war, they deserve to have nice things, to have what they want. But what does rewarding oneself do to the right and proper exchange of gifts and the repayment of debts? In a gift economy—or even in a regime of service that "rewards" work well done—the spirit of the gift needs to arrive from elsewhere, from an other, and then be passed on. Keeping it to oneself—either by refusing to make good on a debt or by taking for oneself what one feels has been earned—can mean "serious harm, even death." Perhaps this is one reason that the dysfunctionally profligate soldier—the PFC paying for a Mustang, set of rims, television, and bedroom set on installment plans—provokes such anxiety.

One need not have been to war already for this to happen. You come into the Army knowing that that is where you are headed eventually; exposure to death is there, but in the near future rather than in the present or recent past. Whichever way, this knowledge enhances the volatility of the wads of cash you may suddenly find in your hands, whether it's your accumulated paychecks or a bonus for enlistment or reenlistment. Vincent, a lean, hyperactive tanker still waiting for his first deployment after being sidetracked into the WTU with a broken leg from a car crash, told me a story about an acquaintance from armor training who had squandered the bonus he got for coming in. After paying off a couple things, he had eight thousand dollars left, and he spent it like crazy—on new clothes, a truck, and tattoos that he grew tired of a few months later. He would invite friends out for dinner night after night. "It's cool," he would say, over and over, "I've got eight thousand dollars." He kept saying it even as he was spending it all, trying to have and consume it at the same time. The money was gone in a couple weeks.

The Protestant ethic says to expect reward only as payment for hard work, discipline, and abstemiousness. But the credit card companies and payday loan stores invert this logic. "Reward yourself," they invite. And pay later of course. The neat structural categories become jumbled up; war reward and consumer reward, war debt and consumer debt, all become confused. One quantity is depleted to pay off a perceived imbalance in the other. And the whole phenomenon takes on the quality of a thing in itself, recognizable, familiar, and related in a rueful as well as cautionary tone. A contradiction, an exception, but a normal one—one we know when we see it. In settings of abundance, the mechanisms for the expenditure of excess become objectified as ends in themselves, Bataille asserts. Is it not possible to think of easy but ultimately expensive credit in this way? It balances out one incommensurable debt at the expense of creating another one, and not via a primordial and humane web of interdependence but rather in a way that isolates and alienates individuals, loading them down with unpayable debts and then cutting them loose. The binding ties of obligation and exchange do not draw people closer together but instead enchain them to forces far beyond their control. There is no way of passing debt on; the debtor implodes.

The soldiers are doing for themselves rather than asking for things from someone else, but the process is destructive. It is a kind of madness. All the madness and dysfunctions of the gift seem wrapped up in this expenditure. The gift *"gets carried away with itself,"* as Derrida (1992, 46) puts it, and the soldier too is carried away in the tornado of being giver, receiver, and even gift itself all at once. The demonstrative and binding power of giving that Mauss describes includes "destroying so as not to appear to desire repayment" (ibid.). In this mad and socially unmoored potlatch, the self is given over to a spiral of extravagance. Some potlatches were potent enough to raise the dead (Mauss 2000). But such expenditure can also be understood as part of the extended life-in-death interlude inhabited by the soldier back from war, marked by his need for stimulation, gratification, and expenditure. It's there in the folklore that I described at the very beginning: soldiers buy motorcycles and sports cars in which they go hurtling down the highways to burn off the excess buzz of war, and sometimes these things kill them.

THE NATURE OF THE DEBT

When we, as a society, make war, what do we do to ourselves by insisting on our indebtedness in the ways we do? Why does the situation seem to entail a crisis of indebtedness at the same time as it obscures other responsibilities and obligations? This is the dilemma that is invoked when people say, as then-president George W. Bush did on Memorial Day 2008, that "we can never repay the debt" that we owe to soldiers present and past for their willingness to give their lives for their—our—country. But to insist that we cannot repay a debt is, essentially, to default on it, to abdicate responsibility.

In its unknowability, this debt is like the so-called toxic assets that were at the center of the financial crisis: no one is sure what it is worth or what price to attach to it, and great harm could result from misjudging its value. And all the while we insist on asking—cynically, guiltily, and in confusion—what the taxpayer can expect to get out of the whole enterprise anyway. This is hardly the neat, nostalgic structure of solidarity that Mauss exposes in the gift. Unable to give back, we in whose name war is waged are left with an accursed share only haphazardly accounted for by other dimensions of the economy. But by picking at that excess, we can try for a deconstructive retelling of the familiar story of who owes what to whom in war, and we can bring some of this messy complicity to light. As Klima (2002, 25) observes, in the ethnography of violence, "what matters is not how much death you have seen but how you handle it, and what you are willing to do with that accursed portion."

The nature of the debt remains unclear. We cannot even say what it includes. Does it include the 4,404 US military fatalities in Iraq? The hundreds of billions it is expected to cost to care properly for the wounded? What about the hundreds of thousands of Iraqi dead? And those 2.2 million forced to flee their country, and the additional tens of thousands displaced internally? What about the young veterans who are unemployed at rates far exceeding their civilian counterparts? What about the stressed-out and busted-up families, the tears and bad dreams, the car accidents, and the low-wage, unskilled economies that surround military bases?

This chapter is an argument against treating war as too straightforward a transaction. It is also an argument against treating this debt as something that needs to be closed or resolved, in favor of learning to live with the differences it engenders, the questions of responsibility it insists on keeping open, and the accursed share that it will not permit to dissolve. Instead of a nostalgic appeal to the primitive spirit of the gift and its affirmative solidarity, why not an acceptance of its abiding impossibility? This entire book is an argument for recognition—for collective social responsibility for violence done in the name of preserving the sociality that we inhabit. The logic of the gift tells us that this responsibility will never expire, so why not let it take the form of an open question?

Postscript

So-called Resiliency

At about 1:30 in the afternoon on Thursday, November 5, 2009, Major Nidal Malik Hasan, an Army psychiatrist, walked into the Soldier Readiness Processing Center at the west end of Fort Hood, drew a 5.7-millimeter FN Five-Seven handgun purchased from Guns Galore on Hood Street in Killeen, and began shooting. He fired more than a hundred rounds in the space of ten minutes, killing thirteen people and injuring twenty-nine, before being incapacitated by shots fired by two police officers. Paralyzed from the chest down, Hasan was taken to Brooke Army Medical Center in San Antonio. As of this writing, he awaits trial on thirteen counts of premeditated murder and thirty-two counts of attempted murder, and may face a court martial as well.

The Readiness Center is a large open space, with cubicles and desks lining all four walls, dozens or hundreds of soldiers waiting in line or sitting on bleachers or in rows of folding chairs, and a couple-dozen military and civilian staff members occupied at their posts. On a busy day, like the day of the shooting, there are people from one end of the room to the other, and nothing but desks and plywood partitions to offer cover from bullets. There were no security guards, military police, or metal detectors, either. In fact, only a few places at Fort Hood—the hospital, visitors' center, and gates—have that sort of visible security. And while soldiers can own personal weapons, they're not allowed to walk around armed. As many were quick to remark, it was supremely ironic that a roomful of soldiers about to deploy to a combat zone would present such an easy target.

Directly after the shooting, more information about Hasan emerged. Statements from the military and anecdotes from his former colleagues depicted a mediocre soldier who received poor performance reviews. He alienated his fellows by preaching aggressively against the wars in Iraq and Afghanistan. He seemed fixated on what he saw as the contradiction between his Muslim identity and the fact that he was weeks away from deploying to Afghanistan and would soon be making war in a Muslim country against fellow Muslims. Later accounts portrayed him as a fundamentalist who had been radicalized by online Islamist sermons and message boards, membership at the same Virginia mosque that one of the 9/11 hijackers had attended, and correspondence with radical Yemeni American cleric Anwar al-Awlaki, who later praised Hasan for the shooting and who himself was killed in Yemen by a US Predator drone strike in September 2011. Hasan was reported to have shouted "*Allahu Akbar!*" as he opened fire at the Readiness Center.

Statements from Hasan's family members, on the other hand, asserted that the conflict Hasan felt between his professional and religious identities and his objections to the wars had manifested as an acute personal crisis. He had been trying for years to find a way of legally leaving the military and repaying the Army for his medical school training, but to no avail. He had faced ethnic and religious discrimination at Fort Hood as well as his former post, Walter Reed Army Medical Center, in Washington, DC. The possibility that Hasan was traumatized to the point of violent action by his impending deployment or the stresses of his counseling work at Walter Reed was raised as a justification by some commentators, and dismissed as absurd by others. The discourse on Hasan focused, as it continues to today, on whether his actions could be explained by his religion, his recruitment as a terrorist agent, his objection to the wars in Afghanistan and Iraq, his own mental imbalance, or secondary trauma from years of treating returning soldiers.

Before all of this came to light, though, in the first hours after the shooting, the base was locked down, and practically the only images of the event, posted on the Web site of the *Austin American-Statesman*, showed traffic stacked up for miles outside the closed gates. In one otherwise-unremarkable photo, a woman stood leaning on her car, stopped in the middle of one of these snarls, with the evening sky darkening behind her. She was in her late twenties, dressed in shorts and a T-shirt, her hair pulled back in a ponytail. According to the caption, her husband was a junior enlisted soldier deployed in Iraq. She said of the shooting, "I expected it someday. I'm not shocked. We're not invincible, and our soldiers need help without stigma." This unsentimental and unsensational pronouncement, offered up before all the oversignifying details of Hasan's biography or even his identity were known, said far more about the state of things at Fort Hood than any other bit of noninformation or premature speculation possibly could. While everyone scrambled to account for the horror, this woman apparently did not feel obliged to express shock. Of course many people were shocked; acquaintances I spoke to afterward were sad, angry, and deeply unnerved to see a massacre unfold in their home. But this is a place where the pace of everyday life, rolling along at the relentlessly efficient clip of organized state violence, simply does not yield to the melodramatic temporality of tragedy.

In a way, this woman's cool assessment links back to the narrative that begins this book: the story of Dime. Both locate violence, stress, and harm as much with the soldier and the military institution as with the freakish, the foreign, and the enemy. Both insist that some accursed share remains lurking right out there in public and ready to erupt—a quantity that is conveniently banished from the figure of alienated, fanatic violence that Hasan has come to represent. And both are poised on the knife's edge that separates the pernicious stereotypes of the soldier as a vulnerable victim from the soldier as dangerous maniac and "crazy vet." These two stereotypes hover around Hasan, but Dime and the woman waiting at the gate explain violence with a both/and rather than a false telos: soldiers need to be recognized and helped without being pathologized, and violence can be evidence that this need is not being met without being a pathologizing indictment of individual soldiers.

Almost a year later, Fort Hood was suddenly in the news again. In the space of one week in late September 2010, four Fort Hood soldiers committed suicide—one of them after shooting his wife in the head. The deaths brought the total number of suicides at the base for the year up to fourteen, tying the previous year's record with three months left to go. The military and media had been monitoring the rise in military suicides since 2004, and during my fieldwork the average of about one suicide a month at Fort Hood circulated as a relatively well-known fact. This rate does not include soldiers who have separated from the Army, although according to VA figures there are an alarming eighteen suicides per day among the twenty-five million military veterans in the United States (Maze 2010). While the suicide rate is historically lower among soldiers than among civilians, the upswing that these Fort Hood deaths were part of began as early as 2004, and the military suicide rate surpassed the civilian one starting in 2008. During 2008–10, suicide killed more US servicemembers than did combat (Howell and Wool 2011; Maze 2010).

Two months earlier and with much fanfare, the Army had already documented this trend in a report titled *Health Promotion, Risk Reduction, Suicide Prevention.* The report maintains a tone of alarm and emergency: "No one could have foreseen the impact of nine years of war on our leaders and soldiers." The strain of prolonged and repeated deployments, lax enforcement of substance abuse regulations, a command climate inattentive to soldiers' mental well-being, and a lack of behavioral health resources are "pushing some units, Soldiers and Families to the brink" (Department of the Army 2010, 1). The report is frank in its assessment of the consequences of this precarious state for the Army: "What was once considered a private affair or a family matter now threatens the Army's readiness" (ibid.). From this perspective, suicide is a public health problem and a threat to the organizational body. So the report's emphasis falls not on the policies and doctrines that demand such long and frequent deployments in the first place but rather on the "stressors" that devolve from these things to afflict individual soldiers, and the deleterious "risk-seeking behaviors" to which they might be compelled as a result—drinking, drugs, fighting, and so on (ibid.). A slew of behavioral health initiatives and institutional reforms were announced in response, including expanded mental health screenings, the addition of more counseling staff, and limiting psychoactive and opiate prescriptions. But ultimately the imperative that appears to be the main driver of soldiers' self-harm—the relentless operational tempo of indefinite war—turns out to be the very thing that must be protected from the fallout of increasing suicides.

Fallout is the operative term. Suicide is a highly visible scandal for the Army. It doesn't signal neglect as powerfully as a dilapidated hospital ward or a veteran panhandling on a street corner. Yet it epitomizes the "crazy vet" stereotype, wedding vulnerable victimhood seamlessly with the potential for violence. Indeed, some fantasy of the suicidal soldier is arguably the logical resolution to civilian anxieties about how soldiers live with the unthinkable things we imagine them to have experienced; it attests that they cannot live with these things. Among soldiers I knew, the suicide rate, like the casualty or divorce rate, was one of those weighty, sobering, and sometimes (even for soldiers themselves) sensationalized facts that hung in the air, and was traded back and forth in conversation. But the notion of suicide just as often inspired cynicism. It showed up as a quixotic bureaucratic formulation, a threat—much like it appears in the July 2010 report—to be managed by the Army's coercive system of care and discipline.

Even in 2007–8, the fear of scrutiny and public anxieties about stressed-out soldiers seemed to have created an environment where the mere suggestion of suicide, even when spoken in exasperation or dark jest, triggered dramatic official responses. Dime, for instance, was assigned a temporary "battle buddy" to accompany him at all times after his WTU sergeant decided that it was not safe for him to be alone. Chris, Stewart, and Dale had all rhetorically invoked, or even joked about, suicide in moments of frustration or distress, and found themselves subject to what they regarded as punitive overreactions as a result. As suicide turns, in the report's words, from a "personal" problem to a "readiness" one, other concerns make it simultaneously an image problem and a language problem, in relation to which the tangible life-taking problem seems ever more remote (Department of the Army 2010, 1). How the thing looks to others and what you can say about it become the most important aspects of what it *is*. As with armor and medicine, special techniques swoop in to help protect the soldier from the dire conditions that he inhabits. In the process, however, they demand that he master his own reactions—his exhausted emotions and wiseass quips—all the more.

Over the course of 2009 and 2010, Fort Hood remained at the center of two wars that the civilian world was well acquainted with but had largely lost interest in. These extreme events—massacre and multiple suicide—attracted outside interest quite effectively, though. In the name of putting all this death in context, media accounts and public discourse inevitably staged it against the background of the strains of war and military life and the threat of foreign enemies. But as Berlant (2007, 760) suggests, it is a grave error to "to misrepresent the duration and scale of [a] situation by calling a *crisis* that which is a fact of life . . . in ordinary time." Dramatizing the shooting and suicides by dubbing them crises spawned by war risks making these extreme events the measure of what life at war is like. It sensationalizes that life while completely failing to attend to how heterogeneous, chronic, uneventful, and *ordinary* many of its challenges, satisfactions, and rhythms are. What that life does to and also for the people in it is so much less and so much more than sudden, violent death.

Crisis is a shallow rhetoric not only because it diverts attention from the ordinary but also because it is so easily personalized. It prompts an anguished *why?* Why, when pushed to the point of despair or extreme conflict, would a person respond with exterminating violence? The conventional narratives of the Hasan shooting and soldier suicides both inevitably turn inward in answer, probing the motivations and psyches of the individual perpetrators. In the hegemonic sway of individualism, blame, and victimhood—even in the hierarchy of the military—actors and structures are understood to be opposed rather than interwoven entities, and responsibility falls so much more readily on the former than the latter. Horrible as these events are, didn't they draw attention precisely because they lent themselves so well to the existential fetishism of why? That "why?" is a question we can insist on asking precisely because we know its answer is inaccessible, locked away inside a now-extinguished private life. The explanations for the shooting and suicides seized on feelings and moralizing essentialisms—hopelessness, loneliness, grief, anomie, hatred, madness, and evil—and stopped there, as if such things were simply birthed whole from within persons. And as if the feelings within us are not the stuff of what Butler (2009, 39) calls our "general predicament": our "unwilled proximity" to the social and material worlds outside ourselves that work in, on, and through us so thoroughly that we would not exist without them.

The answer to "why?" can assume the form of a paranoid quest for terrorist plots or the bureaucratic benevolence of "harm reduction." But the query draws a boundary between the expected and exceptional; it applies itself only to the latter, making it difficult to ask questions about the former. This is especially the case when it comes to violence, that most antisocial and most ordering force. The tale of the maniacal mass-murdering soldier and the anguished suicidal one are, like so many other stories of war, familiar. The stories we tell about war, as I suggested at the outset and have tried to demonstrate throughout, tend to confirm what we think we already know. They do this in large part by affirming that the violence of war is an exception rather than a condition produced only with massive organized effort, and to which soldiers and those close to them are subject as a matter of course, on purpose. The bright light shone on life at Fort Hood by the shooting and suicides cast some things into relief for brief moments, but with this glare came blindness to the fact that the ponderous burden of living with war has been building for years, and will remain for years more. It is no coincidence that these flares of spectacular violence should draw our gaze so close to the much slower, routine harms that sustain the order we are accustomed to, only to leave that latter, larger, and more ordinary violence once again obscured.

The shooting and suicides also prompted questions about how people were coping with and recovering from these traumas. After the shooting, one commentator after another observed that this community "had been through so much," "rallied in times of trial," and was "resilient." Resiliency also crops up frequently in the 2010 suicide report, and has become the watchword of the Army's new ambitious and expensive—and much-critiqued—forcewide behavioral health initiative.[1] It is not that these characterizations aren't true; people at Fort Hood are indisputably tough, determined, and resourceful. But at what point does celebrating and fetishizing the resiliency of those who are systematically subject to violence begin to stand in for a more complete examination of wider complicity and responsibility? The whole scheme of biopolitics hinges on the fact that humans are resilient. At Fort Hood, as in so many other places zoned for "slow death" (Berlant 2007), it could be asked, What choice does one have? Dime had to go to twenty funerals, the woman stuck at the gate after the shooting had to wait out her husband's return from combat as she wondered at the strained condition of the people around her, and everyone else had to go on remaining alive, all whether they were constitutionally "resilient" or not. Even as the casualty rates and deployment schedules spiked, reached a plateau, and tapered off, the grueling pace of life and death and their multifarious attendant feelings have continued.

Being subject to war's facts of life makes them normal, but it doesn't make them easier. And just because we can trick ourselves into seeing them as noble doesn't mean that we should accept them as good. We can, however, take up our own responsibility for these facts of life rather than safely insisting that they are too foreign for us to understand or assuming that we know them already. We may not be able to feel them for ourselves. But we can hold our gaze on them a little longer, and look with care.

Acknowledgments

Writing is a solitary labor, but this book comes from the care, so-licitude, and shared thoughts of legions. It would not exist with-out the people at and around Fort Hood who welcomed, enter-tained, engaged, befriended, questioned, and tolerated me during my time there, and who now populate this document. You gave me far more than I can express. You also gave me far more than could fit on these pages. Those of you whose stories did not appear in the book are very much here in spirit, and everything that you shared with me helped form my sense of the world that I try to depict here. I am truly saddened that I can only acknowledge you by the pseud-onyms that I used for you. Thank you to Debbie for opening the Foundation to my work, and to the many soldiers, volunteers, and others who shared their days with me there, including Jimmy, Pe-ters, Stewart, Kristen, Dime, Tony, Dale, Bullard, Childs, Dee, Hank, Juares, Frank, Kelly, Chad, Vincent, Fran, Ben, and Valerie. Thank you to Danielle and Gene, Ernie and family, Stan and family, Jes-sica and Cal, Lydia and Steve, Randy and Susan, Lena and Harry, Irene, Cheryl, Cindy, Theresa and Jeannine, Chris, Chip, and Danny. Thank you to the many vets and other wonderful folks I met through Disabled Veterans of America and the American Legion, along with the other advocates and volunteers who heard me out, shared with me, and trusted me, and the many others who I cannot name. I could ask for no higher compliment than that you find that what is written here does right by you, and no greater favor than that you will for-give any errors or missteps but not allow me to forget them.

I am deeply grateful to the funders of my research and writing. A National Science Foundation Graduate Research Fellowship funded the fieldwork for this project. My writing and revisions were supported by a Named Endowed University Continuing Fellowship from the University of Texas at Austin and a National Institute of Mental Health–sponsored traineeship at the Rutgers University Institute for Health, Health Care Policy, and Aging Research.

The Department of Anthropology and Program in Folklore and Public Culture at the University of Texas were my intellectual home for six years and the place where most of this work took shape. I owe much to my teachers at the University of Texas, especially my adviser, John Hartigan, and Katie Stewart (whose phrase "lived affects" informed the framing of this book), Ward Keeler, Ann Cvetkovich, and Kamran Ali. Thank you all for your discipline, provocation, and encouragement. Kamala Visweswaran and my colleagues in the 2008–9 dissertation-writing workshop gave me many attentive, generous readings of some of the earliest fragments of this work. I navigated the bureaucratic maze of university life only with the help of department staff members whose graciousness and keen sense of the absurd always made things more pleasant. Thank you especially to Chris Kini Cooke, Adrianna Dingman, Amy Hendrick, Elaine Hrissikopoulos, Heather Nathanson-Flowers, Anne Merrill, and Billy O'Leary. My friends in Austin were a constant source of joy and strength. For your solidarity, humor, emotional first aid, and intellectual comradeship, thank you to Alex Chavez, Can Aciksoz, Salima Alikhan, Claudia Campeanu, Dan Gilman, Jon Godwin, Santiago Guerra, Zeina Halabi, Ben Hodges, Diya Mehra, Adam Norwood, Marsha Riti, Hisyar Oszoy, Mubbashir Rizvi, Laura Rushing, Ruken Sengul, Kevin Sanson, Raja Swamy, Laura Turner, Halide Velioglu, and Tom Wald. Jenny Carlson, Nick Copeland, Terra Edwards, Maryam Kashani, Mathangi Krishnamurthy, Christine Labuski, and Jerry Lord all entertained more than their share of my worries, questions, and drafts. Dana DeLoca visited Fort Hood with me and took many photographs that in turn have been an invaluable visual archive; one of them appears in chapter 1. Emily Lynch merits special thanks for her near-constant company, endless incitements, and vision.

My time at Rutgers and the Institute for Health, Health Care Policy, and Aging Research brought many new friends and colleagues to whom I am indebted. Thanks to David Mechanic, Allan Horwitz, and Debby Carr for their interest, guidance, and the opportunity to come to the institute. Peg Polansky, Carol Boyer, Peter Guarnaccia, Jeff Longhofer, Joanne Hash-Converse, Sarah Hertzog, Dawne Mouzon, Jason Rodriguez, Azure Thompson, and Owen Whooley all made Rutgers a wonderful and stimulating place to be. Jerry Grob helped me track down the origin of "a normal response to abnormal circumstances." Tyson Smith, Ulla Berg, and Rocio Magaña did me the special favor of inviting me into their classrooms to share many of the ideas in this work with their brilliant students. Thanks also to Emily Martin, Rayna Rapp, and the New York University Science Studies and Ethnography Workshop for the opportunity to share my work with a truly great community of scholars. My colleagues in the Economies of Affect working group gave me the opportunity to think even further about the ideas that are so important to this book. Lauren Berlant's gracious and sensitive feedback was invaluable. The support, provocations, and friendship of Emily McDonald, Sandra Rozental, Jonathan Metzl, Dillon Mahoney, and Nell Quest made the work and the last two years of life in New Jersey and New York immeasurably richer.

I have benefited greatly from the relatively small community of anthropologists who study military life, and I am particularly fortunate to have Cathy Lutz, Seth Messinger, and Erin Finley as colleagues, all of whom have given me feedback on portions of this work in addition to helping build the field of which it now forms a part. Special thanks on this score are due to Zoë Wool for her uncanny ability to anticipate and clarify my thoughts while entertaining me in the process.

I am indebted to Fred Appel at Princeton University Press for his judicious editorial eye and the great care he has shown this project. Thanks also to Sarah David, Karen Carter, and Cindy Milstein, who shepherded my words along and made working with Princeton University Press a pleasure. Portions of chapter 2 appeared in slightly different form as an article in *Medical Anthropology Quarterly* 26, no. 1 (2012): 49–68.

I have leaned on many old friends near and far throughout the process of working on this book. Thank you to Yossi Berlow, Emilie Berlow, Andy Newman, Shaira Daya, Darren Flusche, Emily Anthony, Anne McPeak, Dan Buckley, Kristaps Paddock, Shira Siegel,

Sandy White, and Lily White. Thank you to my parents, Bruce and Patty MacLeish, along with Padraic and Shelby MacLeish, Bonnie, Howie, and Seth Pomerantz, the Fuller family (with whom I enjoyed some of my first forays into academia), the Zale family (especially Alec Zale for sharing his stories of Iraq), and all of the MacLeish and McCue clans. I treasure your love and your faith in me. Uncountable thanks to Rachael Pomerantz, who cast her lot with me long before this often-difficult undertaking got started, and who has been my light, home, and anchor throughout.

Appendix: Army Rank Structure

Like most militaries, including the other US service branches, the army has a two-tiered rank system consisting of enlisted and commissioned or officer ranks. The bulk of the army, about 85 percent, is composed of enlisted soldiers. Enlisted soldiers typically have task-specific responsibilities, and NCO oversee the direct hands-on leadership and supervision of soldiers. NCOs can be "in charge," but ultimate "command" leadership and administrative responsibility, from the platoon level upward, resides with commissioned officers. Some occupational specialties requiring advanced technical training—doctors, physicians' assistants, and pilots, among others—are also reserved for the officer ranks. NCOs can seek officer commissions, and many hold college or graduate degrees but elect not to pursue commission. Most officers enter the army with commissions, which is to say, without having served in the enlisted ranks.

While even the lowest-ranking commissioned officer—a second lieutenant—is technically the superior of the most senior sergeant major, in practice the two rank tiers function in a complex parallel relationship in which the respective role, responsibility, and legitimacy of different ranks varies from context to context within as well as among chains of command. In practice, NCOs, as the immediate supervisors of the enlisted ranks, have a far more active and regular presence than officers in the day-to-day lives of most soldiers. Because NCOs have themselves advanced through the enlisted ranks and have earned their seniority through years of experience rather than outside credentials, their authority possesses a degree of legitimacy not necessarily available to officers, especially junior ones.

Soldiers often address one another, and always address superiors, with the rank-appropriate title. For the various grades of sergeant, this address is frequently shortened to simply sergeant, although first sergeants and sergeants major are usually addressed by their full title. Typically, only commissioned officers are addressed as sir or ma'am; forgoing such honorifics from inferiors is a point of pride for many NCOs.

When referring to rank in the abstract or to a person of a particular rank, soldiers use rank titles interchangeably with the equivalent Department of Defense pay grade designations: for enlisted soldiers, E-1 to E-9, and for officers, O-1 to O-10. While I don't have any hard data on the subject, anecdotally it seemed that pay grades rather than rank names saw far wider use as terms of reference and self-description—such as, for instance, "some E-7" or "I made E-4 on my last tour." Pay grades are not used as terms of address.

Two tables describing enlisted and officer ranks along with their responsibilities appear on the following page.

Table 1 Enlisted ranks

Rank	Abbreviation	Pay grade	In charge of/duties
Private	PV1	E-1	
Private	PV2	E-2	
Private first class	PFC	E-3	
Specialist	SPC	E-4	Team or vehicle crew
Corporal	CPL	E-4	Team or vehicle crew
Sergeant	SGT	E-5	Team, vehicle crew, or fire team; squad second in command
Staff sergeant	SSG	E-6	Squad or platoon
Sergeant first class	SFC	E-7	Platoon
First sergeant ("top")	1SG	E-8	Company
Sergeant major	SGM	E-9	Battalion level and upward

Table 2 Commissioned ranks

Rank	Abbreviation	Pay grade	In command of/duties
Second lieutenant	2LT	O-1	Platoon
First lieutenant	1LT	O-2	Platoon; company command staff
Captain	CPT	O-3	Company; battalion command staff
Major	MAJ	O-4	Battalion executive or operations officer; brigade command staff
Lieutenant colonel	LTC	O-5	Battalion; brigade command staff
Colonel ("full-bird colonel")	COL	O-6	Battalion; brigade command staff
Brigadier general ("one star")	BG	O-7	Division
Major general ("two star")	MG	O-8	Division, corps
Lieutenant general ("three star")	LG	O-9	Force command
General ("four star")	GEN	O-10	Force command

Notes

PROLOGUE: "DON'T FUCKIN' LEAVE ANY OF THIS SHIT OUT"

1. In the Army, people refer just as often to uniformed services pay grades (followed in common across the service branches) as they do to rank. "E" stands for "enlisted," and "4" indicates enlisted rank (officer pay grades are O-1 through O-10). E-4 denotes a rank of specialist, or for a combat arms soldier like Dime, a corporal. For a chart outlining Army rank structure, including terminology and typical responsibilities, see the appendix.

2. The word improvised here sells short the considerable sophistication of many of these weapons. They were often constructed using scrap metal and old munitions, and hidden beneath rocks, trash, or even animal carcasses, but they also employed pressure plate, infrared, or radio triggers; they were cleverly camouflaged; and they were carefully arranged and sequenced to maximize surprise and damage. I treat the term IED the way it appeared in my informants' talk, as the generic and inclusive term for all roadside bombs, regardless of their construction.

3. All names in this book not quoted from news media sources are pseudonyms. Other identifying information has also been omitted or altered to protect participants' privacy and confidentiality.

4. ACUs are the standard all-purpose, digital-print camouflage uniforms used by the Army beginning in 2005.

5. Army Regulation 40-501, chapter 7, outlines a system of "Physical Profiling" for "classifying individuals according to functional abilities." A soldier's individual profile doesn't restrict or excuse him on its own but rather indicates to his commander what sorts of tasks he can and cannot perform. Soldiers suffering from the depressive symptoms of PTSD or TBI were often placed on what they called "no-weapon" profiles.

INTRODUCTION

1. This broad range reflects the variety of inclusion criteria and methods used to measure civilian death tolls (Roberts 2010). As of this writing, with the United States

in the midst of a full withdrawal from Iraq, 4,404 members of the US armed forces have been killed in Operation Iraqi Freedom. Approximately 16,000 members of the Iraqi security forces were killed over the course of the war, along with about 26,000 insurgent combatants. The estimated number of Iraqi civilian deaths varies widely. Figures from Iraq Body Count (http://www.iraqbodycount.org) and leaked US military documents range around 105,000, while a controversial but well-regarded study by the *Lancet* estimated that Iraqi civilian deaths from war-related violence had already reached 600,000 in 2006 (Burnham et al. 2006).

2. A military division is an organizational unit consisting of ten to twenty thousand combat and support soldiers; it is the largest-scale military unit capable of independent operation. A division is typically composed of four to six brigades, and is commanded by a general. As part of a doctrinal shift toward smaller and more flexible forces spearheaded by former US secretary of defense Donald Rumsfeld (2005), combat troops increasingly deploy on a brigade basis, and the organization within and between brigades is increasingly modularized (Moran 2007). While in my experience soldiers did not talk much in everyday conversation about such restructuring on the macro level, the more aggressive and rapid deployment schedules as well as exigencies of reflagging and reassignment that brigade restructuring facilitated unquestionably affected people's long-term experience of military life. Time between deployments, for example, could be cut short for subsidiary units that were reassigned from a brigade that had just returned to one that was getting ready to deploy.

The First Cavalry, the largest division in the Army, did not take part in the 2003 invasion of Iraq, but its brigades were deployed there for most of 2004, again beginning in the later part of 2006, and yet again in 2009–10. The cavalry's insignia—a shield with a diagonal bar and a horse's head silhouette—is a familiar sight in media images from Iraq. Fourth Infantry's brigades participated in the later part of the invasion, and carried out various security and combat operations across northern Iraq; its First Brigade was responsible for Saddam Hussein's capture in December 2003. The division's second twelve-month deployment began in January 2006, and consisted of security and Iraqi forces training in central and southern Iraq. From March 2008 to March 2009, much of the division was in central Iraq, while other brigades deployed elsewhere in Iraq and Afghanistan in 2009 and 2010. The Fourth Infantry has now completely relocated to Fort Carson, in Colorado, to be replaced at Fort Hood by the First Armored Division.

3. This deployment schedule is also a revealing indicator of the disproportionate burden borne by the Army—among the four service branches—in the war in Iraq. The Army is the largest of the service branches, with about 560,000 active duty personnel and another 500,000 Reserve and National Guard members. The Army supplies the main bulk of the personnel on the ground for the wars in Iraq and Afghanistan. And some units simply deploy more frequently. During my time at Fort Hood in 2008, for instance, the Ninety-Sixth Transportation Company, the Army's most deployed unit, left for its sixth tour in as many years.

4. This politics can be glossed generally as what Achille Mbembe (2003, 39) dubs *necropolitics*, "the subjugation of contemporary forms of life to the power of death." Its often-deterritorialized operation (Appadurai 1996) has been traced across a range of domains, beginning with analysis of the Nazi death camp by Hannah Arendt (1966), and taking its most influential contemporary form in taking its most influential contemporary form in Giorgio Agamben's *Homo Sacer* (1998), a synthesis of Arendt with the work of Michel Foucault, Carl Schmitt, and Walter Benjamin. Subsequent works in critical theory and anthropology have examined indefinite detention (Agamben 2005; Butler 2004), migration and deportation (De Genova 2002; Hansen and Stepputat 2005), humanitarian intervention (Fassin 2007; Pandolfi 2008; Fassin and Pandolfi 2010), police violence (Chappell 2006), and medicine and public health (Berlant 2007; Petryna 2002; Povinelli 2006).

5. In 1996 at the height of the US-led sanctions against the Hussein regime, for instance, Leslie Stahl of *60 Minutes* asked then-ambassador to the United Nations Madeleine Albright to respond to the fact that the sanctions had killed hundreds of thousands of Iraqi civilians, including half a million children. Albright answered, "We think the price is worth it."

6. Elaine Scarry (1987, 77) notes that in the abstraction of war, the "self-evident centrality of the act of injuring [is] itself steadily minimized."

7. Judith Butler (2004, 56) calls this position the "petty sovereign," a figure "reigning in the midst of bureaucratic Army institutions mobilized by aims or tactics of power they do not inaugurate or fully control."

8. Specifically, Agamben defines homo sacer as a human life that can be killed without either committing homicide or performing a sacrifice—that is, without the death having legal or sacred consequences. As examined in chapter 5, soldiers' deaths are indeed often celebrated as sacrifices, but the decisions that lead to those deaths have their basis in the unadorned calculus of rational, strategic violence.

9. All this is in keeping with Foucault's assertion that power is not something "possessed" or wielded by individual actors. Rather, "the individual is in fact a power-effect, and at the same time, to the extent that he is a power-effect, the individual is a relay: power passes through the individuals it has constituted" (Foucault 2003, 30).

10. The "obtrusive alterity against which the body finds itself can be, and often is, what animates responsiveness to that world" (Butler 2009, 39).

11. This is but one of the many ways the term has been put to work. In this conceptualization, affect is distinguished from emotion by its intersubjective quality, from psychoanalytic drives by its heterogeneity and the abundance of objects and actors it connects, and from discourse by its irreducibly embodied basis. Its chief claim is that the feelings provoked by capital, culture, structures of governance, and so on, are not peripheral but rather central to the experience of sociality—a stance synthesized in various measure from Foucauldian theories of self-management and conduct (Foucault 2003; Richard and Rudnyckyj 2009), feminist and queer critiques of biopolitics (Berlant 2006, 2007; Butler 1999, 2004, 2009; Cvetkovich

2003; Povinelli 2006; Sedgwick 2003), and a post-Marxian attention to the phenomenology of sensory and emotional experience (Benjamin 1969; Buck-Morss 1992; Seremetakis 1996; Stewart 2005, 2007; Taussig 2004). For a range of overviews of the uses of affect, see also Clough 2008; Mazzarella 2009; Thrift 2004.

12. Things do not always take the form of "visible and punctual events" (Cvetkovich 2003, 43), and as Elizabeth Povinelli (2006, 204) suggests, the model of event and decision does not explain much about power over life that is "slow, debilitating and blurred," rather than rapid and decisive.

13. See, among others, Caruth 1995; Fassin and Rechtman 2009; Leys 2000; Young 1995; Feldman 2004.

14. See, for instance, Finley 2011.

15. Women are also enlisted in higher proportions than this in the Army Reserves and National Guard—sectors of the Army that have in the last ten years been drawn on in unprecedented proportion for war-zone deployments.

16. Combat arms MOS are those dedicated to direct land combat, and include infantry, tankers, scouts, combat engineers, Special Forces, artillery soldiers, and combat aviators (although recent changes have admitted women to some positions in the latter two categories).

17. Anthropologist and filmmaker Meg McLagan's documentary *Lioness* (2008), for example, describes the use by Marine combat units of US women soldiers to "soften" search and checkpoint interactions with local Iraqi populations. See also Aranda 2008.

18. For firsthand accounts of military gender integration and the experiences of women soldiers, see, for example, Benedict 2010; Brodie 2000; Williams 2005.

19. In military exercises and war games, the protagonists are typically the "blue" team and the enemies are the "red" team.

20. See Aciksoz 2011; Belkin 2012; Ben-Ari 2001; Bickford 2011; Finley 2011; Higate 2003; Kilshaw 2010; Messinger 2010; Wool 2011.

21. The Development, Relief, and Education for Alien Minors or DREAM Act, which failed to win congressional approval in 2011, would grant provisional legal residency status to young undocumented immigrants who successfully complete certain amounts of high school or college education, or serve in the military. See, for example, Gleason 2007. Both symbolic and literal promises of inclusion are often extended in conditional and contradictory ways, however (see Garza 2011).

22. Private Danny Chen killed himself in a guard tower on a forward operating base (FOB) in Afghanistan in October 2011. His correspondence with family members depicted months of racially tinged abuse (A Soldier's Death 2011; Semple 2011). A Chinese American soldier named Harry Lew apparently killed himself under similar circumstances in Afghanistan in April 2011 (Goodman 2011).

23. Notions of space, geographic and experiential distance, and cultural otherness are crucial to the compartmentalization of violence in foreign and "dangerous" lands that are "zoned" for violence (Gupta and Ferguson 1992, 17). In a globalized world, war is always already a globalized phenomenon, and "the whole notion of

local wars, whether central or peripheral, is largely a fiction" (Nordstrom 1997, 4–5).

24. This approach and its concomitant "toolkit" approach to theorizing through description (Clifford 1983, 119) are arguably indigenous to ethnography itself. As George Marcus (1998, 18) writes, "The anthropologist really does have to find something out she doesn't already know, and she has to do it in terms that ethnography permits in its own developed form of empiricism."

CHAPTER 1: A SITE OF EXCEPTION

1. I heard many soldiers who had deployed express a sense of injustice and suspicion toward fellow soldiers who hadn't, though I met others who had repeatedly volunteered to go overseas and been tapped for domestic billets instead. At the end of 2007, about 37,000 of the Army's total Active Duty force of 522,000 had not deployed and were not scheduled to, and the Army was using elaborate software to mine its personnel databases in search of deployable soldiers (Baker 2007). Eighteen months later that number had shrunk to about 25,000 (Cavallaro 2008; Mitchell 2009), but for some the sense of an unfairly distributed burden persists (Finnegan 2011).

2. More revealing perhaps—and rarer—is the combat action badge, awarded, per Army Regulation 600-8-22, for direct engagement with the enemy. It's a small device of pressed black metal, with a laurel wreath encircling a grenade and bayonet, worn over the heart.

3. As Timothy Mitchell (1991) observes, the single most important feature of state power is its capacity to shape-shift, to create the effect of coherence while in practice defining and redefining its boundaries at will in pursuit of various ends. And the ways that it does this can often seem irrational, theatrical, or even magical (Taussig 1997).

CHAPTER 2: HEAT, WEIGHT, METAL, GORE, EXPOSURE

1. Benjamin (1969, 83–84) argues poetically that the introduction of modern artillery, air power, armored tanks, chemical weapons, and other novel dimensions of high-tech war fighting in World War I entailed a radical transformation of the experience of war: "Never has experience been contradicted more thoroughly than . . . bodily experience by mechanical warfare. . . . A generation that had gone to school on a horse-drawn streetcar now stood under the open sky in a countryside in which nothing remained unchanged but the clouds, and beneath these clouds, in a field of force of destructive torrents and explosions, was the tiny, fragile human body."

2. Seremetakis (1996, 20, 6) highlights both the baseline "embodied and pervasive material experience" of bodily life, and the way that such a life is bound by "involuntary implication in a sensory horizon" specific to its historical and material circumstances.

3. This is a claim made by Colonel (formerly Brigadier General) Janis Karpinksi, who asserted that some women soldiers died of dehydration as a result. Karpinski was in command of the US Army detention facility at Abu Ghraib in 2003–4 when the prisoner abuse scandal there broke, and was the highest-ranking officer to be charged in connection with the abuses. In statements at the Bush Crimes Commission Hearings, an activist tribunal, Karpinski claimed that "in fear of getting up in the hours of darkness to go out to the port-o-lets or the latrines, [they] were not drinking liquids after 3:00 or 4:00 in the afternoon. And in 120-degree heat or warmer, because there was no air-conditioning at most of the facilities, they were dying from dehydration in their sleep." Karpinski also stated that her commander, Lieutenant General Ricardo Sanchez, ordered that dehydration not be reported as the cause of these deaths (Cohn 2006; Goodman 2007). For a far-reaching survey of the challenges and threats faced by women servicemembers in the current conflicts, see Benedict 2010.

4. Meditating on Louis-Ferdinand Céline, Taussig (2004, 40) writes that "all that is wretched about the colonial experience . . . fuses with a swarming sense of heat to produce a strangely familiar bodily unconscious."

5. The resonance between this language and Buck-Morss's discussion of Benjamin and German writer and World War I veteran Ernst Jünger is striking. Jünger described technology as a "great mirror," writes Buck-Morss (1992, 32), offering an image of humanity that "is displaced, reflected onto a different plane, where one sees oneself as a physical body divorced from sensory vulnerability."

6. Many of the notorious Nazi medical experiments on concentration camp prisoners, for instance, were intended to figure out how best to protect military bodies from cold water, pressure extremes, and infectious disease (Agamben 1998). The United States, as well as various other governments, has intentionally exposed soldiers and prisoners to disease, radiation, toxic chemicals, and untested medications through World War II, the Vietnam War, and the Gulf War (Moreno 2000; Presidential Advisory Committee 1997; Uhl and Ensign 1980).

7. This is perhaps best exemplified in the latest edition of the Army's *Emergency War Surgery Handbook* (Nessen, Lounsbury, and Hetz 2008), which itself became controversial when the Army tried to withhold it from public access in the name of protecting the privacy of the US and Iraqi soldiers and civilians depicted in its incredibly graphic photographs.

8. For a thorough and critical portrait of fortification and convoying practices before the surge in Iraq, see Bissell 2006. Descriptions of convoying appear throughout many Iraq War memoirs and journalistic accounts (see, for example, Buzzell 2006; Fick 2006; Filkins 2009; Finkel 2009; Hedges and Al-Arian 2009; Mejía 2007; Williams 2005; Wright 2004).

9. The Hague Conventions and UN Convention on Certain Conventional Weapons (a 1980 annex to the Geneva Conventions) restrict the use of small-caliber expanding, separating, fragmenting, and incendiary rounds against personnel (along with various other weapons), but the United States is not a signatory to the Hague Conventions, and the Department of the Army routinely issues legal memorandums on its own interpretations of what these international conventions do and do not permit. See Alvermann and International Committee 2005, 1781–82.

10. The Abrams is equipped with Chobham armor, a ceramic-metal composite that on the Abrams includes a backing of depleted uranium, prized as much for its extreme density as for its hardness. The armor is not literally sixty-four inches thick, but rather on parts of the tank possesses stopping power of sixty-four inches of now-outdated steel armor, measured on a scale known as Rolled Homogeneous Armor Equivalent (RHAe). The armor's RHAe is lower against kinetic energy weapons like EFPs than other types of antitank munitions (Hunnicutt 1990).

11. On the politicization of corpses and the meaning of gory imagery, see Allen 2009; Caton 2006; Feldman 1994, 2004; Klima 2002; Verdery 1999.

12. Carolyn Nordstrom (1997, 156) describes how in the Mozambican civil war, "the grotesque . . . is a double-edged sword: it is used by military and paramilitary forces to effect terror and thus control; and it is used by the citizenry as a way of defeating the holds of terror."

13. Agamben (1998, 74) asserts that taboo itself is a sort of ethnological mystification that ignores the fundamentally political dimensions of life taking.

14. "The 'abject' designates that which has been expelled from the body, discharged as excrement, literally rendered 'Other.' . . . The boundary of the body as well as the distinction between internal and external is established through the ejection and transvaluation of something originally part of identity into a defiling otherness" (Butler 1999, 169–70).

CHAPTER 3: BEING STUCK AND OTHER PROBLEMS IN THE REPRODUCTION OF LIFE

1. Suicide, of course, is one of the original sociological problems, and Émile Durkheim (1952, 191) was particularly concerned to unravel what he saw as the "special aptitude" for suicide of the soldier, whose situation of intense social integration also raised the possibility of intense anomie. As Stewart's experience illustrates, this premise, which asks nothing of the social meaning of suicide (cf. Douglas 1967), has now taken the form of a sort of public health imperative carried out through surveillance and discipline. For further discussion, see the postscript.

2. WTUs are more formally know as Warrior Transition Battalions, but WTU was the term of common usage during my fieldwork, so I retain it here. Fort Hood's WTU was organized as a battalion and commanded by a colonel, and during my

research period, it increased in size from four to five companies and consisted of about eleven hundred soldiers.

3. In February 2007, the *Washington Post* published an account of the decaying facilities and substandard care at Walter Reed Army Medical Center in Washington, DC. The hospital's patients, many of who were soldiers seriously wounded in Iraq and Afghanistan, and their families described disinterested and incompetent staff along with dangerous and unsanitary buildings plagued by rats, roaches, and mold (Priest and Hull 2007).

4. Such language is essentially a colloquial description of an MTOE, the document that lists any Army unit's equipment and personnel requirements. (Pronounced "em-toe," it stands for modification table of organization and equipment.) The MTOE specifies the precise number and type of soldiers that a unit's commander and personnel officers are obliged to procure for it, just as it specifies the number of Humvees, bullets, and MREs it should have when it deploys.

5. This phrase does not actually appear in the *DSM*, but it is widely used in scholarly and therapeutic literature. Its apparent origin is in a post–World War II examination of combat stress by Roy Richard Grinker and John Paul Spiegel (1945, 440): "Anxiety is a signal of normal biological reaction to danger, becoming pathological only when experienced in excessive quantity, or for too long after an appropriate stimulus, or when persisting without adequate external provocation."

6. In *DSM-III*, the stressor is something "outside the range of usual human experience and . . . markedly distressing to almost anyone" (American Psychiatric Association 1980, 236). In *DSM-IV*, the stressor comes if the sufferer "experienced, witnessed, or was confronted with events that involved actual or threatened death or serious injury" to self or others, and responded with "intense fear, helplessness or horror" (American Psychiatric Association 1994, 424). The draft language of *DSM-V* retrains this language, but abandons the qualifier regarding emotional response.

7. Elizabeth Wilson (2004b, 26), writing on Peter Kramer's *Listening to Prozac*, elaborates just such a perspective, pointing out the existence of psychiatric symptoms that are "not amenable to the interpretive strategies of psychotherapeutic technique: they don't symbolize anything, nor do they originate in infantile or unconscious events."

8. This coconstitution of discursive categories and medical reality is the product of what Hacking (1995, 21) famously dubbed a "looping effect": "people classified in a certain way tend to grow or conform into the ways they are described; but they also evolve in their own ways, so that the classifications and descriptions have to be constantly revised."

9. The January 2011 issue of *American Psychologist* was entirely given over to articles by positive psychology founder Martin Seligman and a host of affiliated civilian and military researchers responsible for the Army's new Comprehensive Soldier Fitness program. See Casey 2011; Cornum, Matthews, and Seligman 2011; Tedeschi and McNally 2011.

10. As Allison Howell and Zoë Wool (2011) note, when "resiliency" programs are "figured as an alternative to 'reactive' responses, medical, psychological and psychiatric care come to be treated as a negative outcome: treatment is reduced to being 'reactive,' and only necessary when services personnel fail to be responsible for their own mental states."

CHAPTER 4: VICISSITUDES OF LOVE

1. http://old.armymwr.com/portal/family/.

2. See, for example, journalist Dave Phillips's account of a string of violent crimes committed by soldiers from a frequently deployed Fourth Infantry Division battalion at Fort Carson in Colorado. Wives, girlfriends, parents, or civilian friends described several of the perpetrators as having withdrawn dramatically, spending time only with one another (Phillips 2009a, 2009b).

CHAPTER 5: WAR ECONOMY

1. As Klima (2002, 81) writes, echoing Hegel, Benjamin, and Arendt, any image of progress relies on forgetting the dead: "Underneath the victorious new world lie the historically buried cadavers of those who had to be murdered in order that a clean and orderly monument of public imagery could be erected."

2. Various commentators have suggested that guilt over not serving, civilian alienation from military experience, and the casting of soldiers as damaged victims all continue to play significant roles in how soldiers are understood. See, for instance, Jaffe 2011; Samet 2011.

3. http://iwvpa.net/provincecm/.

4. Hervé Varenne (1987) has suggested that the American idiom of "meaning it" reflects a culturally distinct preoccupation with the capacity of language to adequately convey interior states. Stewart and the others seem to indicate that despite their effusiveness—or perhaps because of such excessive emotion—civilians' thanks is a failed linguistic performance, one that betrays ignorance of what sort of thanks is owed.

5. See, for instance, Sarah Stillman's account of "third-country" workers brought to Iraq by recruiters subcontracted by the US Department of Defense. Workers were frequently housed in cramped, dangerous conditions, denied food, and paid a fraction of the wages they had originally been promised (Stillman 2011).

POSTSCRIPT: SO-CALLED RESILIENCY

1. This program, dubbed Comprehensive Soldier Fitness, was developed through a partnership between Army personnel and a group of civilian research psychologists led by Martin Seligman, the founder of positive psychology (Casey 2011; Cornum, Matthews, and Seligman 2011; Tedeschi and McNally 2011). It was created outside the Army Medical Command, and its proponents are actively critical of medical approaches to posttraumatic stress. The program's critics assert that among other problems, its effectiveness remains essentially untested and unproven (Horgan 2011; Eidelson, Pilisuk, and Soldz 2011).

References

Aciksoz, Salih Can. 2011. Sacrificial Limbs of Sovereignty: Disabled Veterans, Disability, and Nationalist Politics in Turkey. PhD diss., University of Texas.

Agamben, Giorgio. 1998. *Homo Sacer: Sovereign Power and Bare Life.* Translated by Daniel Heller-Roazen. Stanford, CA: Stanford University Press.

———. 2005. *State of Exception.* Translated by Kevin Attell. Chicago: University of Chicago Press.

Allen, Lori. 2009. Martyr Bodies in the Media: Human Rights, Aesthetics, and the Politics of Immediation in the Palestinian Intifada. *American Ethnologist* 36 (1): 161–80.

Alvermann, Carolin, and International Committee of the Red Cross. 2005. *Customary International Humanitarian Law: Practice.* Cambridge: Cambridge University Press.

American Psychiatric Association. 1980. *Diagnostic and Statistical Manual of Mental Disorders, 3rd Edition.* Washington, DC: American Psychiatric Association.

———. 1994. *Diagnostic and Statistical Manual of Mental Disorders, 4th Edition.* Washington, DC: American Psychiatric Association.

Appadurai, Arjun. 1996. Sovereignty without Territoriality: Notes for a Postnational Geography. In *The Geography of Identity*, ed. Patricia Yaeger, 40–58. Ann Arbor: University of Michigan Press.

Aranda, Jessica. 2008. Lioness Program Trains, Maintains Female Search Team. *Operation New Dawn: Official Website of United States Forces—Iraq.* http://www.usf-iraq.com/?option=com_content&task=view&id=20372&Itemid=128 (accessed February 17, 2011).

Arendt, Hannah. 1966. *The Origins of Totalitarianism.* New York: Harvest.

Aretxaga, Begoña. 2004. Before the Law: The Narrative of the Unconscious in Basque Political Violence. In *Violence*, ed. Neil Whitehead, 3–24. Santa Fe: School of American Research.

Army Bans Privately Bought Body Armor. 2006. *New York Times*, April 1, International/Middle East sec. http://www.nytimes.com/2006/04/01/world/middleeast/01armor.html?scp=2&sq=body+armor&st=nyt (accessed March 31, 2011).

Asad, Talal. 1996. On Torture, or Cruel, Unusual, and Degrading Treatment. In *Social Suffering*, ed. Arthur Kleinman, Margaret Lock, and Veena Das, 285–308. Berkeley: University of California Press.

———. 2007. *On Suicide Bombing*. New York: Columbia University Press.

Baker, Fred W., III. 2007. Army to Tap Troops Not Yet Deployed. *ARMY.MIL*, December 21. http://www.army.mil/-news/2007/12/21/6717-army-to-tap-troops -not-yet-deployed/ (accessed April 5, 2011).

———. 2008. Sensors May Lead to Faster Treatment for Traumatic Brain Injuries. *American Forces Press Service*, January 14. http://www.defense.gov/news/news article.aspx?id=48660 (accessed June 10, 2010).

Bakhtin, Mikhail. 1968. *Rabelais and His World*. Cambridge, MA: MIT Press.

Banerjee, Neela, and John Kifner. 2004. Along with Prayers, Families Send Armor. *New York Times*, October 30, International/Middle East sec. http://www.n ytimes.com/2004/10/30/international/middleeast/30equip.html?scp=10&sq =body+armor&st=nyt (accessed March 30, 2011).

Barthes, Roland. 1979. *A Lover's Discourse: Fragments*. New York: Hill and Wang.

Bassford, Christopher. 1994. *Clausewitz in English: The Reception of Clausewitz in Britain and America, 1815–1945*. New York: Oxford University Press.

Bataille, Georges. 1988. *The Accursed Share: An Essay on General Economy*. New York: Zone Books.

Baudrillard, Jean. 1995. *The Gulf War Did Not Take Place*. Bloomington: Indiana University Press.

Belkin, Aaron. 2001. Breaking Rank: Military Homophobia and the Production of Queer Practices and Identities. *Georgetown Journal of Gender and the Law* 3:83–106.

———. 2012. *Bring Me Men: Military Masculinity and the Benign Facade of American Empire, 1898–2001*. New York: Columbia University Press.

Ben-Ari, Eyal. 2001. *Mastering Soldiers: Conflict, Emotions, and the Enemy in an Israeli Military Unit*. Oxford: Berghahn Books.

Benedict, Helen. 2007. The Private War of Women Soldiers. *Salon*, March 7. http://www.salon.com/news/feature/2007/03/07/women_in_military (accessed June 9, 2010).

———. 2010. *The Lonely Soldier: The Private War of Women Serving in Iraq*. New York: Beacon Press.

Benjamin, Walter. 1969. *Illuminations*. Edited by Hannah Arendt. Translated by Harry Zohn. New York: Schocken Books.

———. 1986. *Reflections: Essays, Aphorisms, Autobiographical Writing*. New York: Schocken Books.

Berlant, Lauren. 2006. Cruel Optimism. *differences* 17 (3): 20–36.

———. 2007. Slow Death (Sovereignty, Obesity, Lateral Agency). *Critical Inquiry* 33 (4): 754–80.

Berlant, Lauren, and Michael Warner. 2002. Sex in Public. In *Publics and Counter-publics*, ed. Michael Warner, 187–208. Cambridge: Zone Books.

Bickford, Andrew. 2008. Report from the Field: Skin-In Solutions—Militarizing Medicine and Militarizing Culture in the United States Military. *North American Dialogue* 11 (1): 5–8.

———. 2011. *Fallen Elites: The Military Other in Post-Unification Germany*. Palo Alto, CA: Stanford University Press.

Bissell, Tom. 2006. Improvised, Explosive, and Divisive: Searching in Vain for a Strategy in Iraq. *Harper's*, January, 41–54.

Bourdieu, Pierre. 1987. *Outline of a Theory of Practice*. Cambridge: Cambridge University Press.

Brodie, Laura Fairchild. 2000. *Breaking Out: VMI and the Coming of Women*. New York: Pantheon Books.

Brown, Wendy. 1995. *States of Injury*. Princeton, NJ: Princeton University Press.

Buck-Morss, Susan. 1992. Aesthetics and Anaesthetics: Walter Benjamin's Artwork Essay Reconsidered. *October* 62:3–41.

Burnham, Gilbert, Riyadh Lafta, Shannon Doocy, and Les Roberts. 2006. Mortality after the 2003 Invasion of Iraq: A Cross-sectional Cluster Sample Survey. *Lancet* 368, no. 9545 (October): 1421–28.

Butler, Judith. 1999. *Gender Trouble: Feminism and the Subversion of Identity*. New York: Routledge.

———. 2004. *Precarious Life: The Powers of Mourning and Violence*. London: Verso.

———. 2009. *Frames of War: When Is Life Grievable?* New York: Verso.

Buzzell, Colby. 2006. *My War: Killing Time in Iraq*. New York: Penguin.

Canaday, Margot. 2009. *The Straight State: Sexuality and Citizenship in Twentieth-Century America*. Princeton, NJ: Princeton University Press.

Cantrell, Bridgett, and Chuck Dean. 2005. *Downrange: To Iraq and Back*. Seattle: Wordsmith Publishing.

Caruth, Cathy, ed. 1995. *Trauma: Explorations in Memory*. Baltimore: Johns Hopkins University Press.

Casey, George W. 2011. Comprehensive Soldier Fitness: A Vision for Psychological Resilience in the U.S. Army. *American Psychologist* 66 (1): 1–3.

Caton, Steven C. 2006. Coetzee, Agamben, and the Passion of Abu Ghraib. *American Anthropologist* 108 (1): 114–23.

Cauchon, Dennis. 2010. Rising Pay, Benefits Drive Growth in Military Towns. *USA Today*, August 17. http://www.usatoday.com/news/military/2010-08-16 -military-towns_N.htm (accessed February 18, 2011).

Cavallaro, Gina. 2008. If You Haven't Deployed Yet, Stand By. *Army Times*, February 24. http://www.armytimes.com/news/2008/02/army_deploy_080225w/ (accessed April 4, 2011).

Chappell, Ben. 2006. Rehearsals of the Sovereign: States of Exception and Threat Governmentality. *Cultural Dynamics* 18 (3): 313–34.

Clausewitz, Carl von. 1982. *On War*. Translated by J. J. Graham. New York: Penguin Classics.

Clifford, James. 1983. On Ethnographic Authority. *Representations* 2:118–46.

Clough, Patricia. 2008. The Affective Turn: Political Economy, Biomedia, and Bodies. *Theory, Culture, and Society* 25 (1): 1–22.

Cohn, Marjorie. 2006. Military Hides Cause of Women Soldiers' Deaths. *Truthout*, January 30. http://www.truthout.org/article/military-hides-cause-women -soldiers-deaths (accessed June 9, 2010).

Cornum, Rhonda, Michael D. Matthews, and Martin E. P. Seligman. 2011. Comprehensive Soldier Fitness: Building Resilience in a Challenging Institutional Context. *American Psychologist* 66 (1): 4–9.

Coward, Noël. 2011. *The Noël Coward Reader*. Edited by Barry Day. New York: Random House.

Csordas, Thomas. 1993. Somatic Modes of Attention. *Cultural Anthropology* 8 (2): 135–56.

Cvetkovich, Ann. 2003. *An Archive of Feelings: Trauma, Sexuality, and Lesbian Public Cultures*. Durham, NC: Duke University Press.

Dawson, Debi. 2009. Helmet Sensors Providing Data That May Decrease Brain Injury. *ARMY.MIL*, September 1. http://www.army.mil/-news/2009/09/01/ 26829-helmet-sensors-providing-data-that-may-decrease-brain-injury/ (accessed June 10, 2010).

Deleuze, Gilles, and Félix Guattari. 1987. *A Thousand Plateaus: Capitalism and Schizophrenia*. Minneapolis: University of Minnesota Press.

Department of the Army. 2010. *Army Health Promotion/Risk Reduction/Suicide Prevention Report 2010*. Washington, DC: Department of the Army.

———. 2012. *Army 2020: Generating Health and Discipline in the Force Ahead of the Strategic Reset*. Washington, DC: Department of the Army.

Derrida, Jacques. 1992. *Given Time: I. Counterfeit Money*. Chicago: University of Chicago Press.

Douglas, Jack D. 1967. *The Social Meanings of Suicide*. Princeton, NJ: Princeton University Press.

Dumm, Thomas L. 1999. *A Politics of the Ordinary*. New York: New York University.

Durkheim, Émile. 1952. *Suicide: A Study in Sociology*. London: Psychology Press.

Eidelson, Roy, Marc Pilisuk, and Stephen Soldz. 2011. The Dark Side of "Comprehensive Soldier Fitness." *CounterPunch*, March 24. http://www.counterpunch .org/2011/03/24/the-dark-side-of-comprehensive-soldier-fitness/ (accessed January 6, 2012).

Elting, John Robert. 1984. *A Dictionary of Soldier Talk*. New York: Scribner Book Company.

Enloe, Cynthia H. 2000. *Maneuvers: The International Politics of Militarizing Women's Lives*. Berkeley: University of California Press.

Eviatar, Daphne. 2007. Contract with America: Hard Terms for the Soldier of Fortune. *Harper's*, October.

Fassin, Didier. 2007. Humanitarianism as a Politics of Life. *Public Culture* 19 (3): 499–520.

Fassin, Didier, and Mariella Pandolfi, eds. 2010. *Contemporary States of Emergency: The Politics of Military and Humanitarian Interventions*. Boston: Zone Books.

Fassin, Didier, and Richard Rechtman. 2009. *The Empire of Trauma: An Inquiry into the Condition of Victimhood*. Princeton, NJ: Princeton University Press.

Feldman, Allen. 1994. From Desert Storm to Rodney King via Ex-Yugoslavia: On Cultural Anaesthesia. In *The Senses Still: Perception and Memory as Material Culture in Modernity*, ed. C. Nadia Seremetakis, 87–108. Chicago: University of Chicago Press.

———. 2004. Memory Theatres, Virtual Witnessing, and the Trauma-Aesthetic. *Biography* 27 (1): 163–202.

Fick, Nathaniel C. 2006. *One Bullet Away: The Making of a Marine Officer*. New York: Houghton Mifflin Harcourt.

Filkins, Dexter. 2009. *The Forever War*. New York: Random House.

Finkel, David. 2009. *The Good Soldiers*. New York: Farrar, Straus and Giroux.

Finley, Erin P. 2011. *Fields of Combat: Understanding PTSD among Veterans of Iraq and Afghanistan*. Ithaca, NY: Cornell University Press.

Finnegan, Laura. 2011. Army's "Deployment Inequality" Still a Problem. *Yahoo! News*, February 1. http://news.yahoo.com/s/ac/20110201/cm_ac/7756291_armys_deployment_inequality_still_a_problem (accessed April 4, 2011).

Finnegan, William. 2008. The Last Tour: A Decorated Marine's War Within. *New Yorker*, September 29. http://www.newyorker.com/reporting/2008/09/29/080929fa_fact_finnegan (accessed December 12, 2011).

Fort Hood Public Affairs Office. 2009. Fort Hood Overview. August 19.

Foucault, Michel. 1979. *Discipline and Punish: The Birth of the Prison*. New York: Vintage Books.

———. 1988. *The History of Sexuality*. New York: Vintage Books.

———. 2003. *Society Must Be Defended: Lectures at the Collège De France, 1975–76*. New York: Picador.

Freud, Sigmund. 1989. *Civilization and Its Discontents*. New York: W. W. Norton.

Garza, Irene. 2011. A Mother's Love: Gold Star Mothers and the Sacrifices of Citizenship. Paper presented at the annual meeting of the American Studies Association, Baltimore, October 21.

Gawande, Atul. 2004. Casualties of War: Military Care for the Wounded from Iraq and Afghanistan. *New England Journal of Medicine* 351 (24): 2471–75.

De Genova, Nicholas P. 2002. Migrant "Illegality" and Deportability in Everyday Life. *Annual Review of Anthropology* 31 (1): 419–47.

Gilbertson, Ashley. 2007. *Whiskey Tango Foxtrot: A Photographer's Chronicle of the Iraq War*. Chicago: University of Chicago Press.

Glasser, Ronald. 2005. A War of Disabilities: Iraq's Hidden Costs Are Coming Home. *Harper's*, July, 59–62.

———. 2006. *Wounded: Vietnam/Iraq*. New York: George Braziller.

Gleason, Carmen L. 2007. Wounded Troops Become Citizens at Walter Reed Ceremony. *ARMY.MIL*, March 14. http://www.army.mil/article/2253/Wounded_Troops_Become_Citizens_at_Walter_Reed_Ceremony/ (accessed January 19, 2012).

Goodman, Amy. 2007. The Private War of Women Soldiers: Female Vet, Soldier Speak Out on Rising Sexual Assault within US Military. *Democracy Now!* March

8. http://www.democracynow.org/2007/3/8/the_private_war_of_women_ soldiers (accessed on June 9, 2011).

———. 2009. Rape in the Ranks: The Enemy Within. *Democracy Now!* October 27. http://www.democracynow.org/2009/10/27/filmmaker_pascale_bourgaux_on_ rape_in (accessed on June 9, 2011).

———. 2011. U.S. Troops Charged after Fellow GI, Hazing Victim Danny Chen Found Dead in Afghanistan. *Democracy Now!* December 23. http:// www.democracynow.org/2011/12/23/us_troops_charged_after_fellow_gi (accessed on June 9, 2011).

Grady, Denise. 2009. Autopsies of War Dead Reveal Ways to Save Others. *New York Times*, May 26, Health sec. http://www.nytimes.com/2009/05/26/ health/26autopsy.html?_r=1&hp (accessed May 26, 2009).

Grinker, Roy Richard, and John Paul Spiegel. 1945. *Men Under Stress*. Philadel- phia: Blackinson.

Gross, Terry. 2010. Wounded In Wars, Civilians Face Care Battle at Home. *Fresh Air*, National Public Radio, January 11. http://www.npr.org/templates/story/ story.php?storyId=122444062 (accessed April 13, 2010).

Gupta, Akhil, and James Ferguson. 1992. Beyond "Culture": Space, Identity, and the Politics of Difference. *Cultural Anthropology* 7 (1): 6–23.

Hacking, Ian. 1995. *Rewriting the Soul: Multiple Personality and the Sciences of Memory*. Princeton, NJ: Princeton University Press.

Halberstam, Judith. 1998. *Female Masculinity*. Durham, NC: Duke University Press.

Hansen, Thomas Blom, and Finn Stepputat, eds. 2005. *Sovereign Bodies: Citizens, Migrants, and States in the Postcolonial World*. Princeton, NJ: Princeton Univer- sity Press.

Haraway, Donna Jeanne. 1991. *Simians, Cyborgs, and Women: The Reinvention of Nature*. New York: Routledge.

Hartigan, John. 1999. *Racial Situations: Class Predicaments of Whiteness in Detroit*. Princeton, NJ: Princeton University Press.

Hawkins, John P. 2005. *Army of Hope, Army of Alienation: Culture and Contradiction in the American Army Communities of Cold War Germany*. 2nd ed. Tuscaloosa: University of Alabama Press.

Headquarters, Department of the Army. 2001. *FM 3-90—Tactics*. Washington, DC: Headquarters, Department of the Army.

Hedges, Chris, and Laila Al-Arian. 2009. *Collateral Damage: America's War against Iraqi Civilians*. New York: Nation Books.

Herzfeld, Michael. 1997. *Cultural Intimacy: Social Poetics in the Nation-State*. New York: Routledge.

Higate, Paul, ed. 2003. *Military Masculinities: Identity and the State*. New York: Praeger.

Horgan, John. 2011. Cross-check: Beware the Military-Psychological Complex; A $125-Million Program to Boost Soldiers' "Fitness" Raises Ethical Questions. *Scientific American*, April 18. http://www.scientificamerican.com/blog/post.

cfm?id=beware-the-military-psychological-c-2011-04-18 (accessed April 27, 2011).

Horwitz, Allan. 2012. *All We Have to Fear: Psychiatry's Transformation of Natural Anxieties into Mental Disorders*. New York: Oxford University Press.

Howell, Allison, and Zoë Wool. 2011. *The War Comes Home: The Toll of War and the Shifting Burden of Care*. Providence, RI: Watson Institute for International Studies. http://costsofwar.org/article/us-veterans-and-military-families (accessed December 12, 2011).

Huggins, Martha Knisely, Mika Haritos-Fatouros, and Philip G. Zimbardo. 2002. *Violence Workers: Police Torturers and Murderers Reconstruct Brazilian Atrocities*. Berkeley: University of California Press.

Hunnicutt, R. P. 1990. *Abrams: A History of the American Main Battle Tank*. Novato, CA: Presidio Press.

Hunter, Aina. 2010. PTSD Soldiers Misdiagnosed: Army Said They Had Personality Disorders. *CBS News*, August 16. http://www.cbsnews.com/8301 -504763_162-20013690-10391704.html (accessed December 12, 2011).

Institute of Medicine. 2007. *Treatment of PTSD: An Assessment of the Evidence*. Washington, DC: Institute of Medicine.

Isenberg, David. 2007. How the US Army's Being Worn Down in Iraq. *Asia Times Online*, February 7. http://www.atimes.com/atimes/Middle_East/IB07Ak01 .html (accessed November 27, 2011).

Jaffe, Greg. 2011. Troops Feel More Pity Than Respect. *Washington Post*, November 14, World sec. http://www.washingtonpost.com/world/national-security/ troops-feel-more-pity-than-respect/2011/10/25/gIQANPbYLN_story.html (accessed December 20, 2011).

Jain, Sarah S. Lochlann. 2006. *Injury: The Politics of Product Design and Safety Law in the United States*. Princeton, NJ: Princeton University Press.

Kennedy, Kelly. 2007. Critics: Army Holding Down Disability Ratings. *Army Times*, February 25. http://www.armytimes.com/news/2007/02/TNSmedhold money070222/ (accessed December 12, 2011).

Kilshaw, Susie. 2010. *Impotent Warriors: Perspectives on Gulf War Syndrome, Vulnerability, and Masculinity*. Oxford: Berghahn Books.

Klima, Alan. 2002. *The Funeral Casino: Meditation, Massacre, and Exchange with the Dead in Thailand*. Princeton, NJ: Princeton University Press.

Korb, Lawrence, Loren B. Thompson, and Caroline P. Wadhams. 2006. *Army Equipment after Iraq*. Washington, DC: Center for American Progress.

Kurzman, Steve. 2007. Hillbilly Armor and C-Legs: Technologies and Bodies at War. In *Bodies in the Making*, ed. Nancy Chen and Helene Moglen, 164–78. Santa Cruz, CA: North Atlantic Books.

Leys, Ruth. 2000. *Trauma: A Genealogy*. Chicago: University of Chicago Press.

Lutz, Catherine. 2001. *Homefront: A Military City and the American Twentieth Century*. Boston: Beacon Press.

———, ed. 2009. *The Bases of Empire: The Global Struggle against U.S. Military Posts*. New York: New York University Press.

Marcus, George E. 1998. *Ethnography through Thick and Thin*. Princeton, NJ: Princeton University Press.

Massumi, Brian. 2005. Fear (the Spectrum Said). *positions: east asia cultures critique* 13 (1): 31–48.

Mauss, Marcel. 2000. *The Gift: The Form and Reason for Exchange in Archaic Societies*. New York: W. W. Norton.

———. 2006. Techniques of the Body. In *Techniques, Technology, and Civilisation*, ed. Nathan Schlanger, 77–96. New York: Berghahn Books.

Maze, Rick. 2007. Filner Says PTSD Misdiagnoses Cheat Vets. *Army Times*, June 28. http://www.armytimes.com/news/2007/06/military_misdiagnosedvets_070628w/ (accessed December 12, 2011).

———. 2010. Eighteen Veterans Commit Suicide Each Day. *Army Times*, April 22. http://www.armytimes.com/news/2010/04/military_veterans_suicide_042210w/ (accessed January 17, 2012).

Mazzarella, William. 2009. Affect: What Is It Good For? In *Enchantments of Modernity: Empire, Nation, Globalization*, ed. Saurabh Dube, 291–309. New York: Routledge.

Mbembe, Achille. 2003. Necropolitics. Translated by Libby Meintjes. *Public Culture* 15 (1): 11–40.

McLagan, Meg, and Daria Sommers. 2008. *Lioness*. Room 11.

McNeil, Donald G. 2008. To Heal the Wounded. *New York Times*, August 5, Health sec. http://www.nytimes.com/2008/08/05/health/05surg.html?scp=1&sq=army%20surgery%20text&st=cse (accessed April 2, 2011).

Mejía, Camilo. 2007. *Road from Ar Ramadi: The Private Rebellion of Staff Sergeant Camilo Mejía*. New York: New Press.

Messinger, Seth. 2010. Getting Past the Accident. *Medical Anthropology Quarterly* 24 (3): 281–303.

Miller, T. Christian. 2009a. Contractors in Iraq Are Hidden Casualties of War. *Los Angeles Times*, October 6. http://www.propublica.org/feature/kbr-contractor-struggles-after-iraq-injuries-1006 (accessed April 13, 2010).

———. 2009b. Injuries and Deaths to Civilian Contractors in Iraq and Afghanistan by State. *Pro Publica*, June 19. http://www.propublica.org/special/map-injuries-and-deaths-to-civilian-contractors-by-state-614 (accessed April 10, 2010).

Mitchell, Bryan. 2009. Army Seeks "Deployment Equality." Military.com, May 19. http://www.military.com/news/article/army-seeks-deployment-equality.html (accessed April 4, 2011).

Mitchell, Timothy. 1991. The Limits of the State: Beyond Statist Approaches and Their Critics. *American Political Science Review* 85 (1): 77–96.

Moffeit, Miles, and Amy Herdy. 2004. Female GIs Report Rapes in Iraq War. *Denver Post*, January 25. http://www.denverpost.com/search/ci_0001913069 (accessed June 9, 2010).

Mol, Annemarie. 2002. *The Body Multiple: Ontology in Medical Practice*. Durham, NC: Duke University Press.

————. 2008. *The Logic of Care: Health and the Problem of Patient Choice*. New York: Routledge.

Moran, Michael. 2007. U.S. Army Force Restructuring, "Modularity," and Iraq. Council on Foreign Relations, October 26. http://www.cfr.org/iraq/us-army-force-restructuring-modularity-iraq/p14212 (accessed December 6, 2011).

Moreno, Jonathan. 2000. *Undue Risk: Secret State Experiments on Humans*. New York: Routledge.

Moskos, Charles C., and John Sibley Butler. 1997. *All That We Can Be: Black Leadership and Racial Integration the Army Way*. New York: Basic Books.

Moss, Michael. 2006. Pentagon Study Links Fatalities to Body Armor. *New York Times*, January 7, Washington sec.

Mosse, George L. 1996. *The Image of Man: The Creation of Modern Masculinity*. New York: Oxford University Press.

National Institute of Mental Health. 2008. *Virtual Reality, Psychotherapy, Show Promise in Treating PTSD Symptoms; Civilian Access to Care Remains a Concern*. Rockville, MD: National Institute of Mental Health.

Nessen, Shawn Christian, Dave Edmond Lounsbury, and Stephen P. Hetz. 2008. *War Surgery in Afghanistan and Iraq: A Series of Cases, 2003–2007*. Washington, DC: Borden Institute, Walter Reed Army Medical Center, Department of the Army.

Nietzsche, Friedrich Wilhelm. 1956. *The Birth of Tragedy and the Genealogy of Morals*. Translated by Francis Golffing. New York: Anchor Books.

Nordstrom, Carolyn. 1997. *A Different Kind of War Story*. Philadelphia: University of Pennsylvania Press.

Office of Army Demographics. 2010. *FY 10 Army Profile*. Washington, DC: Department of the Army.

Pandolfi, Mariella. 2008. Laboratory of Intervention: The Humanitarian Governance of the Postcommunist Balkan Territories. In *Postcolonial Disorders*, ed. Mary Jo DelVecchio Good, Sandra Hyde, Sarah Pinto, and Byron Good, 157–88. Berkeley: University of California Press.

Petryna, Adriana. 2002. *Life Exposed: Biological Citizens after Chernobyl*. Princeton, NJ: Princeton University Press.

Phillips, Dave. 2009a. Casualties of War, Part I: The Hell of War Comes Home. *Colorado Springs Gazette*, July 25. http://www.gazette.com/articles/iframe-59065-eastridge-audio.html (accessed July 4, 2010).

————. 2009b. Casualties of War, Part II: Warning Signs. *Colorado Springs Gazette*, July 28. http://www.gazette.com/articles/html-59091-http-gazette.html (accessed July 4, 2010).

Povinelli, Elizabeth A. 2006. *The Empire of Love: Toward a Theory of Intimacy, Genealogy, and Carnality*. Durham, NC: Duke University Press.

Presidential Advisory Committee on Gulf War Veterans' Illnesses. 1997. *Final Report*. Washington, DC: White House. http://www.gulflink.osd.mil/gwvi/ (accessed November 22, 2011).

Priest, Dana, and Anne Hull. 2007. Soldiers Face Neglect, Frustration at Army's Top Medical Facility. *Washington Post*, February 18. http://www.washingtonpost

.com/wp-dyn/content/article/2007/02/17/AR2007021701172.html (accessed June 9, 2010).

RAND Center for Military Health Policy Research. 2008. *Invisible Wounds: Mental and Cognitive Care Needs of America's Returning Veterans*. Arlington, VA: RAND Corporation.

Rhodes, Lorna. 2004. *Total Confinement: Madness and Reason in the Maximum Security Prison*. Berkeley: University of California Press.

Richard, Analiese, and Daromir Rudnyckyj. 2009. Economies of Affect. *Journal of the Royal Anthropological Institute* 15 (1): 57–77.

Ricks, Thomas E. 1997. *Making the Corps*. New York: Scribner.

Rieckhoff, Paul. 2006. *Chasing Ghosts: A Soldier's Fight for America from Baghdad to Washington*. New York: NAL Caliber.

Roberts, Adam. 2010. Lives and Statistics: Are 90% of War Victims Civilians? *Survival* 52 (3): 115–36.

Rosenberg, C. E. 2002. The Tyranny of Diagnosis: Specific Entities and Individual Experience. *Milbank Quarterly* 80 (2): 237–60.

Rumsfeld, Donald H. 2005. *2004 Annual Defense Report to the President and the Congress*. Washington, DC: US Department of Defense.

Samet, Elizabeth. 2011. On War, Guilt, and "Thank You for Your Service." *Bloomberg*, January 4. http://www.bloomberg.com/news/2011-08-02/war-guilt-and -thank-you-for-your-service-commentary-by-elizabeth-samet.html (accessed December 20, 2010).

Scarry, Elaine. 1987. *The Body in Pain: The Making and Unmaking of the World*. New York: Oxford University Press.

Scheper-Hughes, Nancy, and Margaret M. Lock. 1987. The Mindful Body: A Prolegomenon to Future Work in Medical Anthropology. *Medical Anthropology Quarterly* 1 (1), new series: 6–41.

Schmitt, Carl. 1985. *Political Theology: Four Chapters on the Concept of Sovereignty*. Cambridge, MA: MIT Press.

Schmitt, Eric. 2004. Troops' Queries Leave Rumsfeld on the Defensive. *New York Times*, December 9, International/Middle East sec. http://www.nytimes.com/ 2004/12/09/international/middleeast/09rumsfeld.html (accessed June 9, 2010).

Schneider, David Murray. 1980. *American Kinship: A Cultural Account*. 2nd ed. Chicago: University of Chicago Press.

Sedgwick, Eve Kosofsky. 2003. *Touching Feeling: Affect, Pedagogy, Performativity*. Durham, NC: Duke University Press.

Semple, Kirk. 2011. Eight Charged in Death of Fellow Soldier, U.S. Says. *New York Times*, US sec., December 21. http://www.nytimes.com/2011/12/22/us/8 -charged-in-death-of-fellow-soldier-us-army-says.html?scp=2&sq=danny%20 chen&st=cse (accessed January 18, 2010).

Seremetakis, C. Nadia. 1996. *The Senses Still: Perception and Memory as Material Culture in Modernity*. Chicago: University Of Chicago Press.

Serlin, David. 2003. Crippling Masculinity: Queerness and Disability in US Military Culture, 1800–1945. *GLQ: A Journal of Lesbian and Gay Studies* 9 (1–2): 149–79.

Singer, Peter W. 2003. *Corporate Warriors: The Rise of the Privatized Military Indus-
try*. Ithaca, NY: Cornell University Press.

———. 2009. *Wired for War: The Robotics Revolution and Conflict in the Twenty-First
Century*. New York: Penguin Press.

A Soldier's Death. 2011. *New York Times*, Opinion sec., December 22. http://www
.nytimes.com/2011/12/23/opinion/a-soldiers-death.html?scp=6&sq=danny%20
chen&st=cse (accessed December 23, 2011).

Stallybrass, Peter, and Allon White. 1986. *The Politics and Poetics of Transgression*.
Ithaca, NY: Cornell University Press.

Stewart, Kathleen. 1991. On the Politics of Cultural Theory: A Case for "Con-
taminated" Cultural Critique. *Social Research* 58 (2): 395–412.

———. 2005. Cultural Poesis: The Generativity of Emergent Things. In *Handbook of Qualitative Research*, ed. Norman Denzin and Yvonna Lincoln, 1027–42.
London: Sage.

———. 2007. *Ordinary Affects*. Durham, NC: Duke University Press.

Stiglitz, Joseph E. 2008. *The Three Trillion Dollar War: The True Cost of the Iraq
Conflict*. New York: W. W. Norton.

Stillman, Sarah. 2011. The Invisible Army. *New Yorker*, June 6. http://www.new
yorker.com/reporting/2011/06/06/110606fa_fact_stillman (accessed June 10,
2011).

Stone, Andrea, and Dave Moniz. 2005. Worn-out Army Equipment to Cost U.S.
USA Today, January 25. http://www.usatoday.com/news/washington/2005-01
-25-old-equipment_x.htm (accessed on November 28, 2011).

Swofford, Anthony. 2003. *Jarhead: A Marine's Chronicle of the Gulf War and Other
Battles*. New York: Scribner.

Taussig, Michael T. 1992. *The Nervous System*. New York: Routledge.

———. 1997. *The Magic of the State*. New York: Routledge.

———. 1999. *Defacement: Public Secrecy and the Labor of the Negative*. Stanford, CA:
Stanford University Press.

———. 2004. *My Cocaine Museum*. Chicago: University of Chicago Press.

Tedeschi, Richard G., and Richard J. McNally. 2011. Can We Facilitate Posttraumatic Growth in Combat Veterans?" *American Psychologist* 66 (1): 19–24.

Thrift, Nigel. 2004. Intensities of Feeling: Towards a Spatial Politics of Affect.
Geografiska Annaler. Series B, Human Geography 86 (1): 57–78.

Uhl, Michael, and Tod Ensign. 1980. *GI Guinea Pigs: How the Pentagon Exposed Our
Troops to Dangers More Deadly Than War—Agent Orange and Atomic Radiation*.
New York: Wideview Books.

Varenne, Herve. 1987. Talk and Real Talk: The Voices of Silence and the Voices of
Power in American Family Life. *Cultural Anthropology* 2 (3): 369–94.

Verdery, Katherine. 1999. *The Political Lives of Dead Bodies: Reburial and Postsocialist
Change*. New York: Columbia University Press.

Veterans Health Administration. 2005. *VHA Handbook 1172.1: Polytrauma Rehabili-
tation Procedures*. Washington, DC: Veterans Health Administration.

Virilio, Paul. 1989. *War and Cinema: The Logistics of Perception*. London: Verso.

Williams, Kayla. 2005. *Love My Rifle More Than You: Young and Female in the U.S. Army*. 1st ed. New York: W. W. Norton.

Wilson, Elizabeth A. 2004a. Gut Feminism. *differences* 15 (3): 66–94.

———. 2004b. *Psychosomatic: Feminism and the Neurological Body*. Durham, NC: Duke University Press.

Winterfilm Collective. 1972. *Winter Soldier*. Millennium Zero.

Wool, Zoë. 2009. Subjects of Sacrifice: The Im/possibilities of Everyday Life at Walter Reed Army Medical Center. Paper presented at the annual meeting of the American Anthropological Association, Philadelphia, December 3.

———. 2011. Emergent Ordinaries at Walter Reed Army Medical Center: An Ethnography of Extra/Ordinary Encounter. PhD diss., University of Toronto.

Wright, Evan. 2004. *Generation Kill: Devil Dogs, Iceman, Captain America, and the New Face of American War*. New York: G. P. Putnam's Sons.

Young, Allan. 1995. *The Harmony of Illusions: Inventing Post-traumatic Stress Disorder*. Princeton, NJ: Princeton University Press.

———. 2010. Traumatic Memory through the Lens of Social Neuroscience. Paper presented at the Institute for Health, Rutgers University, New Brunswick, NJ, October 21.

Index